*f***P**

Also by Mark Kriegel

Pistol: The Life of Pete Maravich

Namath: A Biography

Bless Me, Father (a novel)

Ray and Boom, 1994. Copyright Arlene Schulman

THE
GOOD SON

The Life of
Ray "Boom Boom" Mancini

Mark Kriegel

FREE PRESS

New York London Toronto Sydney New Delhi

Free Press
A Division of Simon & Schuster, Inc.
1230 Avenue of the Americas
New York, NY 10020

First Free Press hardcover edition September 2012

FREE PRESS and colophon are trademarks of Simon & Schuster, Inc.

For information about special discounts for bulk purchases,
please contact Simon & Schuster Special Sales at 1-866-506-1949
or business@simonandschuster.com.

The Simon & Schuster Speakers Bureau can bring authors to your live event.
For more information or to book an event, contact the Simon & Schuster Speakers Bureau
at 1-866-248-3049 or visit our website at www.simonspeakers.com.

DESIGNED BY ERICH HOBBING

Manufactured in the United States of America

1   3   5   7   9   10   8   6   4   2

Library of Congress Cataloging-in-Publication Data

Kriegel, Mark.
The good son : the life of Ray "Boom Boom" Mancini / Mark Kriegel.
p. cm.
1. Mancini, Ray, 1961– 2. Boxers (Sports)—United States—Biography. I. Title
GV1132.M26K75 2012
796.83092—dc23
[B]
2012001417

ISBN 978-0-7432-8635-0
ISBN 978-1-4516-7461-3 (ebook)

For my brother, Eric Bruce Kriegel

Contents

The Good Son

Prologue | Dementia

The longer it went, this stubborn accrual of brutalities, the more it thrilled—not just the millions watching at home—but his fellow celebrities at ringside. One could see Sinatra transfixed, his admiration palpable. Bill Cosby left his seat to volunteer advice in the champion's corner.

This was America's champion: symbolically potent, demographically perfect. And during this brief moment in American life the public observed little distinction between flesh and fable, between Boom Boom Mancini and Rocky Balboa.

Hey, people would ask, *when you gonna kick that Mr. T's ass?*

But against almost every expectation, this fight was even better than a movie. Each passing round became an homage to the champion's father, who had been a fighter himself. I never took a step back, *he told his son.*

The challenger, for his part, had no father to speak of, a source of great embarrassment back in his native Korea. But his manner of combat, the eagerness with which he endured abuse, seemed to gentle the condition of his birth, as if he'd descended from the Hwarang knights who famously admonished against retreat.

He was enchanted, *said an old friend.*

By now, both fighters were purplish and quilted with bruises. And as the champion went wearily to his corner, he wondered what the fuck Bill Cosby was doing there and why he was speaking in that Fat Albert voice. Was this a dream?

What's he got to do? *wondered the champion's corner man. Kill this kid?*

One of the television announcers had seen it before. And between rounds, he issued a muttering prophesy: Something bad's going to happen . . .

Almost three decades later, Ray Mancini mumbles a prayer as a waiter sets the plate before him. Red sauce, pink sauce, white sauce, or grilled. It matters not. Mancini's devotional rituals do not change.

The regulars at table twenty-four enjoy the whole bit, from mannerism to mantra, the way it ends with Ray pressing fingers to his lips. But, more than that, they envy his capacity to believe.

Fucking Ray'll believe anything, they say.

Present, as usual, are the hard-wired playwright, the much-loved television star, and the producer who made it big with cop shows. Il Forno Trattoria—"the joint," as they call it—is tucked into a strip mall on Ocean Park Boulevard in Santa Monica. "We all grew up in neighborhoods where a great premium was placed on being able to sit around and talk shit," explains the playwright. "So, instead of this Hollywood nonsense, guys talking about their diets, we remember."

Remember the fight? Remember the night?

And that fat detective from Brooklyn, remember him?

Louie Eppolito, an ex-cop with an epic comb-over, had proclaimed himself a screenwriter. Everybody at table twenty-four tried to warn Ray. The guy was no good, dirty, mobbed up. Mancini listened to all the advice, of course, then promptly bankrolled Eppolito's screenplay.

The resulting motion picture went straight to video while Eppolito got life plus one hundred years for moonlighting as a mafia hit man. Still, the most corrupt detective in the history of the NYPD had failed to corrupt Mancini, or diminish the ingenuous instinct that made Ray a national hero. Ray liked Louie. What's more, the guy had great stories.

"Ray *loves* the stories," says his ex-wife. "Don't you get it?"

He'll tell you his story is that of his father's. But, in fact, it's what he made of his father's story, an unwittingly theological construct he conceived as a child, while pondering sepia-toned glossies and brittle-brown clippings of a heroically battered boxer.

"I didn't win 'em all," said the father. "But I never took a step back."

Lenny Mancini had been the number-one contender in an abundantly talented lightweight division. However, his chance for a championship ended not with a title shot, but with fragments from an exploding mortar shell, keepsakes from the Wehrmacht he'd carry with him the rest of his life. That was November 10, 1944, just outside the French town of Metz. The Virgin Mary had appeared to him just days before, hovering over his trench.

A generation would pass before Lenny's youngest son would enter the national consciousness. Ray called himself "Boom Boom," too, just like the old man. But coming out of Youngstown, Ohio, in the early 1980s, he also represented those felled when the steel belt turned to rust. As refracted through the lens of television, Ray became The Last White Ethnic, even more valiant than violent, a redemptive fable produced by CBS Sports.

This teleplay, of course, made no mention of the older Mancini brother. With Ray on the cusp of fame, he was found with a .38-caliber slug an inch and a half behind the right ear. Nielsen families didn't want to hear that. "Boom Boom" was a family show, serialized for Saturday afternoons.

Ray won the lightweight title with a first round KO live from Vegas, the broadcast sponsored by Michelin ("the company that pioneered the radial"), Michelob ("smooth and mellow"), and the Norelco Rotatract rechargeable. That was 1982. He was only twenty-one, but already a modern allegory, as bankable as he was adored.

Warren Zevon wrote a song:

Hurry home early,
Hurry on home,
Boom Boom Mancini's fighting Bobby Chacon . . .

True story: Sinatra once sent Jilly Rizzo to Mancini's training camp to apologize.

"For what?" asked Ray.

"For not being here in person."

Yes, Sinatra was ringside when Mancini killed a man. If that's not exactly what happened, that's how it's remembered.

Duk Koo Kim hit the Korean exacta at birth: dirt poor and dark skinned. When Duk Koo was two, his father died. But the epic battle with Ray ennobled him. He'd become fierce for his fiancée, her belly already swollen with a son.

If only Kim had taken a step back, he might've lived to see that boy.

"Don't worry, Raymond," said his father. "It could've been you."

Could've been me?

It was like telling Ray to believe in ghosts.

Now Ray sits at table twenty-four, overlooking the strip mall's concrete veranda. It's likely he'll be joined by one of the regulars: the playwright David Mamet, the actor Ed O'Neill, or maybe Ray-Ray, now fifteen, the youngest of Mancini's three children.

He drives Ray-Ray to all his games—freshman football and AAU basketball—and makes sure the boy finishes his homework. Meanwhile, occasional patrons pull the waiter aside, asking for help in reconciling this dutiful dad with someone they think they remember.

"What was he *in*?" they ask.

"That's Ray 'Boom Boom' Mancini," says the waiter. "Lightweight champion of the world."

"He's the guy who killed the guy, right? The Korean?"

Soon, they'll make their way over to table twenty-four.

"I was a huge fan, champ."

"I remember Arguello."

"I remember Chacon."

"I remember your father. Huge fan."

Still, the most devout and deferential pilgrims belong to a phylum of the story-telling classes.

"The actors," says the waiter. "The guys who do make-believe, love the guys who do it for real."

"One loves being around fighters," says Mamet. "Everything in acting is subjective . . . But you knock a guy out, that's something different."

Something better: John Garfield as Charley Davis, Sylvester Stallone as Rocky Balboa, Robert De Niro as Jake LaMotta. There's no better role. But if actors want to play fighters, then fighters want to play fighters, too. They know Hollywood doesn't love them as much as the *idea* of them.

Isn't that the point, though? To fuck with the stories until that line between player and pugilist becomes hopelessly blurred?

No surprise that Stallone produced Ray's story as a movie of the week.

Or that Mickey Rourke asked him to work his corner.

By then, of course, Ray wanted to be John Garfield. Mickey had to settle for casting old man Lenny as—what else?—a mumbly cornerman.

That was the eighties. LaMotta would bump into Ray at banquet-style press lunches. "You see Vickie?" he'd ask. "I'm talking to you, Ray. You fucking my wife?"

It only sounded like lines from the script. He meant it.

Then again, maybe Jake didn't know the difference. It's better to play a fighter than to be one. An actor doesn't lose his stories. The concussed mind of a fighter, however, becomes a spooky place. Dementia is a supernatural disease; the stories become ghosts.

"How do you keep a jackass in suspense?" asks Bobby Chacon.

Beat.

"I'll tell you tomorrow," he says, slapping his knee.

Chacon loves his jokes, reciting each one as if it had a virgin punch line. But he's even more delighted to sing:

Hurry home early,
Hurry on home,
Boom Boom Mancini's fighting Bobby Chacon . . .

His eyes grow large and giddy, like a small child or an old drunk, happily reassured by a familiar melody. But his voice isn't a voice so much as a long, low moan. It takes a practiced ear to understand Bobby "Schoolboy" Chacon, as he speaks in the language of ghosts.

"Tell Boom Boom it was the girls," he says. "That's the only reason he beat me."

Chacon trained for Mancini in a trailer park near Reno. At least that's how he recalls it these days: the girls materializing at the foot of each trailer and hiking up their skirts.

Hi, Bobby . . .

"What could I do?" he asks.

What about me, Bobby?

"What was I supposed to do?"

I love you, Bobby.

"Tell Ray it was the girls."

Beat.

"How do you keep a jackass in suspense?"

Now, at table twenty-four, Ray inquires as to the condition of his erstwhile idol.

"He said the only reason you beat him was the girls."

"If I knew that, I would've sent more."

"How do you keep a jackass in suspense?"

"What?"

"He forgets. Keeps telling the same joke."

"Sure. Just like my father."

Chapter 1 | Lenny Mancino

Not long after his release from prison, Nick Mancino pulled aside his stocky ten-year-old son, Lenny:

"I have to go," he said.

"I'll go with you," said the boy.

"No," said Nick. "You have to stay here and take care of your mother."

Lenny cried all that day and through the night. He cried so much that by the next morning, he knew he'd never cry again.

Nicola Mancino, son of Leonardo Mancino, of the Sicilian fishing village of Bagheria, left his ancestral home in the summer of 1913 and arrived at Ellis Island aboard the SS *Palermo* on September 5. He was eighteen, and slightly built at five foot two. After assuring the immigration officer he could both read and write, Mancino, a surname that translates as "lefty" or "southpaw," was designated a "labourer" in the ship's manifest. With twenty-five dollars left, he was headed for the stretch of mill towns that pocked the land from western Pennsylvania to northeast Ohio.

Youngstown, Ohio, the city in which he would settle, was home to U.S. Steel's Ohio Works, Truscon Steel, and the Youngstown Sheet and Tube on the east side. Trumbull Steel, eventually absorbed by Republic Iron & Steel, was in nearby Warren. Not long after Mancino's arrival, the Mahoning Valley had become second only to Pittsburgh in the production of pig iron, those rectangular ingots liquefied in a furnace to make steel.

The by-products of such mass production included slag heaps and a permanent cloud of smoke and soot hovering about six thousand feet above the city. Pilots landing in Youngstown typically did so with dirty faces. There were also regular bouts of industrial violence. For example, shortly after 4 P.M., on January 7, 1916, a single revolver shot from a crowd of well-armed, though not sober, picketers elicited a volley of rifle fire from guards stationed at Sheet and Tube's Poland Avenue entrance.

"What followed," according to one account, "was sheer anarchy . . . the torch was put to building after building by a frenzied mob that poured gasoline on the fires to intensify the flames. Building fronts were battered in to provide draft to speed the blaze. . . . Not until 2,100 infantrymen and machine gunners were brought in toward morning was anything like order restored."

On December 12, 1917, at Our Lady of Mount Carmel Catholic Church, Nick took a wife. Annie Cannazzaro was American by birth, but her family also hailed from the village of Bagheria. Her mustachioed, broad-faced father, Beneditto, drove a horse-drawn cart bearing fruits and vegetables. She grew up with brothers named Michael, John, and Paul, and an older sister, Margaret, at 410 Lansing Avenue, on the east side, where children were bathed in a zinc basin in the kitchen. Annie was fifteen.

Though the groom is again described as a laborer in their marriage license application, Nick would soon discern new and more profitable opportunities. The Volstead Act was passed in 1919, the same year his son Lenny was born in the Cannazzaro home on Lansing Avenue. Better known as Prohibition, it would prove a windfall for men with the inclination and balls to violate it.

Youngstown's immigrant classes, most of them from southern and central Europe, didn't share the Anglo-Saxon concept of vice. They played the numbers, known locally as *the bug*. They played a dice game of Turkish origin called *barbut*. And they drank. In 1910, a city with a population of 79,066 had 324 grocery stores and 345 saloons. By 1930, ten thousand gallons of illegal beer were being brewed each day in Youngstown.

The typical mill worker did twelve-hour shifts, six days per week, at twenty cents per hour. Strikes were periodic occurrences, like changing seasons. Hence, it didn't take much for Nick to figure he'd do better as a bootlegger. Not only would the new family man have money in his pocket, he'd have respect.

Family photographs show a man unlike his Cannazzaro in-laws: no pork-pie hat, no rolled up sleeves, no work boots. Nick Mancino has the unmistakable air, by stance, demeanor, and attire, of a *padrone*. His suit is three pieces and well tailored. His tie is fastened by a stickpin. His hands are clasped behind his back, his gaze calm but unnaturally direct.

One can imagine what an outsized presence Nick Mancino was to his son. Even as an adult himself, Lenny would often remind his own children. "Grandpa Nick," he'd say, wagging his finger, "what a great man he was." On the east side, there was little stigma making a living from liquor or numbers. The only shame was in doing it dishonorably. Nick's progeny would take great pride in the fact that he never snitched.

There were two kinds of illicit activities in Youngstown: those committed under the aegis of mafia interests in Pittsburgh or Cleveland, each of those cities being approximately 75 miles away. Nick was affiliated with the Cleveland crew, which could count on him for months at a time of reliably discreet incarceration. If only his young bride had been so loyal.

In 1929, upon his last release, he'd learned that Annie, variously described as "a free-spirit," "kind of a flapper type," and "one of those women who liked to party," had become involved with another dapper man. His name was Valentine Pavone, better known as Slick, sometimes known as Slick Marino. Slick wore suits and ties and kept his hair parted and plastered back like one of the Dorsey brothers. For an aspiring patriarch like Nick, Annie's dalliance was an intolerable blow, the resulting complications and shame outweighing even the tearful supplications of his now-ten-year-old son who begged him to stay.

Lenny never spoke of the circumstances that led to his dad's departure, at least not to any of his pals at Gumbo's pool room or the Pearl Street Mission or the bare-ass beach, as it was called, down by Jackson Hollow. All they knew is every once in a while he'd go off to Buffalo to visit, as John Congemi, a friend of Lenny's, put it, "his real father."

"My father was basically a bootlegger in Youngstown and came to Buffalo to work in the same capacity, probably numbers, too," says Vincent Mancino, the first son of Nick's second marriage. "He used to always say the judges were his biggest customers. Anyway, once the country went back to drinking, he went into construction."

Neither the separation nor his father's new family did anything to diminish him in Lenny's eyes. If anything, the boy became more awestruck by the great man. "Lenny loved my father more than anything else," recalls his stepbrother.

Meanwhile, custody of Lenny was effectively awarded to a committee of Cannazzaros: mother, grandparents, aunts, and uncles, the most memorable of them then known on the east side as "Firpo." Paulie Cannazzaro's namesake was Luis Firpo, the Wild Bull of the Pampas. Famous for knocking Jack Dempsey through the ropes in their 1923 title bout at the Polo Grounds, the real Firpo was six foot two and a half. Uncle Paulie was about the same, another heavyweight, and caught rail at Truscon Steel, literally catching pieces of railroad track as they came off the line. If any man were naturally suited for such a vocation, it would be Firpo, whose nephews would recall his hands the size of baseball mitts. He could hold a gallon jug of wine upside down, his meaty fingers like clamps around the bottle's circumference.

As generous as he was gregarious, the bachelor Firpo would treat the Cannazzaro children to haircuts, ice-cream cones, and cherry sodas. In particularly rough times, he would show up in his Buick with a week's worth of groceries, declaring he had just hit the bug.

Yes, Firpo, known to sleep off a hard night in the pool room on Albert Street, was always amenable to a sporting proposition. Once the Depression arrived, he even volunteered his services as de facto street-corner matchmaker.

"My nephew will fight your boy," he'd say.

"They got a kick out of it," says Congemi, who recalls Firpo among the fraternity of older brothers who used to make the kids fight.

My boy against yours. How much?

"The boys weren't even mad at each other," says Congemi.

How much?

Sensing reluctance or poor odds, Firpo would hype the wager himself, raking his huge paw across Lenny's mouth.

Lenny could feel his face redden, as if it were on fire.

"Look," said Firpo. "The kid don't even cry."

In May 1932, Mayor Joseph Heffernan described Youngstown's plight in the *Atlantic Monthly*. "The Hungry City," as the piece was titled, cited the "hundreds of homeless men crowded into the municipal incinerator, where they found warmth even though they had to sleep on heaps of garbage." It closed with a mention of Charles Wayne, fifty-seven, father of ten and a hot mill worker at Republic Steel, who "stood on the Spring Common bridge this morning . . . took off his coat, folded it carefully, and had jumped into the swirling Mahoning River. . . ."

"We were about to lose our home," sobbed Mrs. Wayne.

By 1933, a third of Youngstown's workforce was unemployed. It is unknown whether Lenny figured in this tally, but at fourteen, his formal education had already come to an end. The family account would have him advancing as far as the fifth grade at Lincoln Park Elementary School. It wasn't unusual for a child of the Depression to be found hanging around on the streets of Youngstown. The United States Bureau of Education would issue a scathing report on the local school system, detailing a plague of inefficiency, mismanagement, poorly trained teachers, and substandard curricula.

Diversions were plenty for truants on the east side of Youngstown. Lenny spent most of his days helping his grandfather on the horse-drawn wagon, selling fruits, vegetables, milk, and probably a little bit of hooch. His idle hours might be spent watching the dice games and high rollers who came to the Albert Street pool room all the way from Newcastle, or to watch a fight (there was always a fight in Youngstown) at the Rayen-Wood Auditorium. He could raid the local farms for apples and pears or could hang out at the Royal Oaks, the diner on Lansing Avenue. Or he might play football for the Pioneers, a team organized by one of the many local missions.

But Lenny, who'd grow to a height charitably listed as five foot two, wasn't much good at football or baseball. His true talent had been discerned early on by Uncle Firpo. "He was so tough that nobody wanted to fight him," says Congemi, recalling an afternoon at the pool hall. "My brother Dukie comes in and says three colored guys were giving him a hard time by the Royal Oaks. Lenny says, 'Let's go.' He lays all three of those colored guys out."

More than seven decades later, Congemi contemplates his own fists, now gnarled with age, in wonder of Lenny's. "Man, he had clubs."

Unlike other Depression-era dropouts, he already had his destination clearly marked, a vocation, even a calling. Lenny Mancino began his amateur career as a flyweight, having to eat a bunch of bananas just to make the 108 pound minimum. "My mother would hand make my trunks," he'd say, recalling the diminutive stature that belied his natural ferocity. "I couldn't get a pair of ready-mades." By 1936, his physical virtues had become more apparent. Broad, stocky, vigorous, and durable, he earned some local repute as a featherweight in the Ohio Golden Gloves tournament.

Lenny could punch, especially to the body, but his skills were less impressive than his desire. Lenny's inclination—unnatural even by fighter's standards—was to literally push through pain and brutality, to always move forward.

Talent is honed by circumstance, of course. Deprivation breeds pugilists. In that respect, it was an advantage to come of age in the Hungry City. What's more, as every fighter must drink from a reservoir of untold rage, the Oedipal drama didn't hurt Lenny, either. By the mid-thirties, Slick fancied himself Youngstown's most dapper boxing trainer, insisting on coat and tie even in a fighter's corner. In fact, he was a beater who treated Annie as an opponent.

"Lenny's mother was nice looking," recalls Congemi. "Slick used to give her a hard time."

"An ex-pug with a short man's complex," says Lenny's cousin, Benny D'Amato. "One of the meanest men I ever met."

As Lenny himself would look back and say: "I should've killed the sonofabitch when I had the chance."

The summer of 1937 saw greater Youngstown become a battlefield in an industrial war, known as the Little Steel Strike. About thirty-two thousand workers went out against local producers like Republic and Youngstown Sheet and Tube, both of which had been hiring armed guards and stockpiling munitions in anticipation of the riot that finally broke out June 19. That's when police opened fire at a crowd of picketers outside Republic's Stop Five gate. Casualties included two dead strikers and twenty-three wounded. A month later, Ohio's governor called in the National Guard.

As Lenny's pal Red Delquadri would recall, the fix was in: "The National Guard was there in the street to keep the workers from going after the scabs. They were working for the company."

It would be another four years before the Roosevelt Administration could compel Little Steel to recognize the unions. Meanwhile, with no real work to be had, Lenny would find work under the auspices of another presidential initiative, the Civilian Conservation Corps, a public works program for unemployed, unmarried, and unskilled men between eighteen and twenty-six. For a standard wage of thirty dollars a month—twenty-five dollars of which was sent back to the enrollee's family—Lenny lied about his age and signed on in Shreve, Ohio.

The new conscript in Roosevelt's war on poverty was sixteen and barely one hundred pounds. After a year or so, he was transferred to Ely, Nevada, Indian Springs Camp, Company 2532, an outfit charged with the construction of cattle fences for the Department of the Interior's Division of Grazing. He worked mostly as a cook. Photographs taken at the camp show Lenny holding a shovel at the base of a mountain, or posing in the scrub with the bill of his cap turned up at a jaunty angle. In each, he smiles for the camera: a short, thick-set teenager on the verge of manhood.

"We used to call him bear," says George DeLost, another member of Company 2532 by way of Youngstown. "He was like a little bear."

But that grinning, cublike quality could disappear at the slightest sign of a threat, a confrontation, or unwanted authority. "He would fight anybody," says DeLost. "Like one night, we was at this place called the Copper Club in Ely, and they had one of those hillbilly bands there. They had a big bass drum, one of those you hit with your foot.

"Well, during the intermission some of us guys were monkeying around with it, and some big, tall hillbilly said something to Lenny. Like, 'get away from those instruments.' So Lenny puts his foot right through that big drum. Then all hell broke loose. We broke the joint up a little bit.

"I think it only cost us seven or eight dollars to fix the drum, put a new skin on it. But then they made an agreement we weren't allowed back into the Copper Club."

It wasn't an isolated example of Lenny's talent for raising hell. On July 26, 1938, the camp's superintendent wrote to his commanding officer:

"Numerous complaints have been received from our Foreman in regard to enrollee Leonard Mancino . . . It is also recommended that disciplinary measures be taken in regard to the disgusting language and names which he has used to Foreman Harry Oeters."

Might've been worse for the foreman if Lenny didn't have a place to channel his aggression. As it happened, there was a makeshift ring in the center of camp: bare planks with posts of pipe or wood in the corners, as DeLost recalls it. At six feet, about 190 pounds, DeLost had almost a foot and sixty pounds on Lenny, who was already fighting in local smokers in nearby mining towns under the name of Tony Manchucho.

Don't worry, Lenny would assure him, we'll just be going light.

"But every once in a while you'd sting him a little bit, and he'd lose his head," recalls DeLost. "Then you'd be going toe-to-toe."

That didn't last long. Soon, another enrollee would be trying to go a couple rounds with Lenny. Then another. And another. And so on.

"Soon as you ran out of gas, you took off the gloves and handed them to the next guy," says DeLost.

Hours would pass. Lenny stayed in the ring until he had finally exhausted his supply of sparring partners.

"Sometimes," says DeLost, "he'd go thirty rounds."

Without ever taking a step back.

Lenny would credit his twenty-seven months in the CCC for having endowed him with invaluable vocational experience. Later, he'd seem glorified, even sanctified, in telling the stories of those smokers to his own family. His progeny would envision him proudly, their patriarch as a ferociously stubby teenager whacking out those big cowboys in Nevada.

Lenny was probably home on furlough when he made his pro debut, September 21, 1937, in a four-rounder at Youngstown's Rayen-Wood Auditorium. The card was headlined by sensational featherweight contender Henry Armstrong, who knocked out Bobby Dean of Washington, DC, just sixty-two seconds after the opening bell. Frank B. Ward, ringside for the Youngstown *Vindicator*, noted that Armstrong's twenty-first consecutive knockout victory left Dean "writhing on the canvas, and as completely out as though he had been hit with a sledgehammer."

Armstrong's finale concluded a show that began four bouts earlier with Lenny, who'd been suddenly rechristened Mancini.

"Got a better ring to it," said the promoter, Al Zill, born Angelo Zielli, indicating that the subject was not up for discussion.

If Lenny's new name anticipated some success, then so did his opponent, Emil Tanner, another 128 pound local lad, already 1–5. "Mancini's execution is a little ragged, but he is busy and a hard worker and carried the fighting from start to finish," wrote

Ward. "Tanner appeared a little perplexed by the bruising tactics of his opponent, and during the four rounds landed but two solid punches."

Ward finished his ringside dispatch with a reminder that Youngstown—just a couple months removed from the Little Steel conflagration—remained immersed in the Depression. "The show was an artistic success, but a financial flop," he wrote.

Despite a healthy crowd estimated at two thousand five hundred, one of the best indoor turnouts of a year or more, the gate amounted to only one thousand six hundred dollars.

In other words, economic circumstances didn't bode well for a kid like Lenny Mancini. Hell, if the great Henry Armstrong had to make ends meet running a shoe-shine stand, then what was Lenny to do? Head back to the CCC, of course.

More than a year would pass before Lenny had another sanctioned bout, and he'd have to face a 141 pounder just to get it. That was Halloween night, 1938, at Rayen-Wood, when he outpointed Pat Murphy, a former Marine, in six rounds. But with fewer than 650 fans in attendance, the *Vindicator* noted that "Promoter Zill took a worse beating—financially, of course—than any fighter on last night's card."

With paydays so scarce, Lenny was better off as a cook in Ely. "I stay here, I'll starve," he'd begun to say. It would be almost four months before his next fight.

Again, he proved the star of a Rayen-Wood undercard, displaying an entertaining style one newspaperman called "short on stature, but long on stamina." He was also relentless to the body of his opponent, described as "a colored boy" from nearby Warren. From the *Vindicator*: "The Lenny Mancini–J.D. Williams six-rounder at 135 pounds was the best. The ex-amateurs tossed caution to the winds as they slugged it out with Mancini scoring a well deserved victory."

More fortuitous, at least for Lenny, was that evening's main event, a rematch between Newark's Johnny Duca and Billy Soose, who left his opponent "blinded by blood streaming from cuts above his eyes." A fine middleweight from nearby Farrell,

Pennsylvania, Soose was trained by the great Ray Arcel, who had already worked with champions like Frankie Genaro, Sixto Escobar, and Jackie "Kid" Berg. It was Arcel who heard Lenny's appeal.

Their conversation, as replicated in the Cleveland *Plain Dealer*, went like this: "I was pretty fair in the amachoors here," Lenny explained, "and I did all right in fights out in a CCC camp in Nevada, and I'd like to get a chance to go to New York and fight for the dough. Could you help a young fella, Mr. Arcel?"

"If you can get to New York," said Arcel, "I'll get you the right kind of manager. And if you've got the stuff, you'll get somewhere."

Twenty-two days later, Lenny made his New York debut. The venue was the Broadway Arena, 944 Halsey Street, Bushwick, Brooklyn. The opponent was Charley Varre, a promising lightweight with a record of 7–1. Again, Lenny won on points, though not before Varre broke his jaw.

"I'll be back in six months," he told his manager.

"Sure," said the manager. "Sure, you'll be back."

If the manager, one Frankie Jacobs, seemed less than sanguine about the prospects of Lenny's return, he wasn't alone. "The fight mob," that fraternal order of pugilistic cognoscenti, had seen this before: Kid arrives, Kid gets busted up, Kid goes home. There was nothing special about Youngstown Lenny. As one old hand remarked: "Nobody expected to see him again."

Chapter 2 | The Business

His jaw wired shut, Lenny convalesced at 410 Lansing Avenue. It was always easier for him at his grandparents' place. Besides, by now Slick and Annie had a baby girl of their own, so he spent the spring of 1939 taking his meals through a straw, sipping at his aunt's split pea soup, and plotting a return most oddsmakers would've deemed a prohibitive long shot.

Lenny was wearing overalls and a torn sweater the day he walked back into Stillman's Gym. "Just had to be a fighter, I guess," recalled one of the old-timers.

Stillman's was founded in Harlem as part of the Marshall Stillman Movement, an organization dedicated to ending the scourge of juvenile delinquency. The man in charge of its day-to-day operation, Lou Ingber, was an ill-tempered, pistol-packing former cop. He took the name Stillman because it was easier than answering questions from strangers and tourists.

At the time of Lenny's return later that summer, the gym was located next to Wing's Chinese laundry at 919 Eighth Avenue, between 54th and 55th streets, just a few blocks from Madison Square Garden. The sign outside read:

WORLD'S LEADING BOXERS.

TRAIN HERE DAILY

FROM 12 to 4pm ADMISSION 25¢

The gym was open every day, including Yom Kippur and Christmas. But Jesus Christ himself, it was said, could not get in without paying.

A narrow wooden staircase led up from the street and emptied into a large, loftlike space, the air foul and heavy with sweat, smoke, and liniment. Windows were kept shut on the orders of Stillman himself. The floors went unwashed for years at a time. And as the proprietor was loath to repaint, plaster chips would rain down at regular intervals on the fighters and their seconds.

"The golden age of prizefighting," Stillman once said, "was the age of bad food, bad air, bad sanitation, and no sunlight. I keep the place like this for the fighters' own good. If I clean it up they'll catch a cold from the cleanliness."

Even as the proprietor gloried in its squalor, Stillman's was also the unquestioned epicenter of New York's booming fight scene. "The capital of the world," said the *Brooklyn Eagle*'s Harold Conrad. Sparring sessions were conducted in two identical, adjacent rings, with uncovered ropes and posts of bare metal. On one side, fighters and trainers—with the wise Arcel already considered mandarin among men—would gather and await their turns. "The joint was so thick with fighters they used to knock each other down shadow boxing," Stillman would recall.

On the other side, a dozen or so rows of wooden folding chairs were positioned for the fedora-wearing spectator classes, among them managers, touts, newspapermen, gangsters who owned fighters in percentages deemed "pieces," and gamblers who understood it was easier to compromise the dignity of men than that of thoroughbreds. There were five busy pay phones near the entrance, and a snack bar offering hot dogs, soft drinks, and raw eggs for those in training. "Managers and matchmakers congregated at the rear of the gym," writes Ronald K. Fried in his book, *Corner Men*, "in an area which Stillman dubbed 'the Stock Exchange of Boxing.'"

Like crime and politics, boxing was a business of territories, all of them breeding prospective main eventers for Friday night fights at Madison Square Garden. In Manhattan, there was St. Nicholas Arena, at the corner of 66th and Columbus, which featured a regular Monday night card. The Bronx Coliseum was busy on Thursdays. In Queens, there were Sunnyside Gardens and Ridgewood Grove (one block from the Brooklyn border). Brooklyn had the Fort Hamilton Arena and the Broadway Arena, where men like Frankie Jacobs and veteran promoter Max Joss, both regulars at Stillman's stock exchange, wasted little time getting Lenny on their regular Tuesday night shows.

What Jacobs and Arcel—who'd collaborated profitably in handling Kid Berg, after his emigration from Jewish East London— had in mind for Lenny was certainly more nourishing than Aunt Margaret's pea soup. On a steady diet of beatable opponents, he racked up eight wins, seven by knockout, in little more than two months, from September 7 to November 14, 1939. The combined records of Paul Trinkle, Patsy Pesca, Solly Pearl, Johnny Cockfield, George Zeitz, Bobby Sylvester, Young Chappie, and Jimmy Lancaster were 98–146–42. Typically, after each fight, Lenny would head to the Western Union office.

September 16: HELLO MOM WON FIGHT BY KNOCKOUT IN THIRD ROUND TONIGHT

October 11: HELLO MA I FOUGHT AGAIN TONIGHT AND WON BY A KNOCKOUT IN THE FOURTH ROUND DON'T FORGET TO ANSWER MY LETTERS NEW ADDRESS 27 WEST 89 STREET

November 15: DEAR MOTHER WON BY KNOCKOUT IN SEVENTH ROUND I AM FEELING FINE YOUR LOVING SON

By now, still only twenty, the grade-school dropout had acquired some cachet. One New York paper declared him "one of the hits of the Fall season." He also had a new nickname, which he saw for the first time while ambling up Halsey Street and looking up at the Broadway Arena's marquee.

"Boom Boom" Mancini was Joss's idea. Soon, Lenny would be posing for men with Speed Graphic cameras: bare-knuckled and bowlegged in his new black trunks, each thigh embroidered with the word *Boom*. He'd straddle a Howitzer cannon for the publicity shots Joss and Jacobs would hand to the writers. *Boom Boom*. The name took. It was alliterative, catchy, and congruent with the style of a fighter the newspapers were now calling "the broad-shouldered little Italian."

Arcel—whose "severe and decisive" manner reminded A. J. Liebling of "a teacher in a Hebrew school"—never tried to remake Mancini in the style of a previous champion, his or anyone else's. "The trainers of that day knew every boxer was different," Arcel would recall. "No two were alike. What was food for one was poison for another."

You didn't tamper with a fighter's nature, especially a fighter like Boom Boom. Lenny never won on style points. His victories, like those approving bellows now coming his way from the cheap seats, were rooted in desire, his savage endurance, and his obstinate instinct to keep coming forward. He'd even earn acclaim on the occasion of his first pro loss, by decision to Johnny Rinaldi, December 5, 1939.

Lenny took the fight on short notice, after an uncommonly long three-week break, and a drunk that lasted almost as long. No problem, he figured. He'd sparred with Rinaldi in Stillman's. "I bounced him around like a rubber ball," Lenny would recall.

But after three profligate weeks, Rinaldi dropped him three times on left hooks in the opening round. Twice the referee counted to eight. After the third, he was saved by the bell. He went down for another eight count in the second. "But Boom Boom came back for more," noted the Brooklyn Eagle's Conrad. "He launched a brilliant rally and became stronger as the fight progressed."

A more breathless ringside correspondent wrote: "All fall Broadway Arena fans had been saying: 'Lenny Mancini is a good young fighter because he never loses.' Last night they said: 'The kid is a great little fighter'—and it was after a defeat!"

Though he resided in a rooming house on Manhattan's Upper West Side, the newspapers identified Boom Boom as a resident of Brownsville, a Brooklyn neighborhood known as a spawning ground for Jewish and Italian fighters and gangsters, most famously, the criminal consortium known as Murder Inc. Boom Boom quickly became a big local draw; few fighters were more adored at the Broadway Arena. And why not? What with the way Lenny fought, any of Brooklyn's tribes would be honored to claim him as a native son.

Photographs from 1939 and 1940 show a young man delighted with himself. His features are prominent, but still smooth and supple, his eyes mischievous and clear. The picture on his boxing license from the New York State Athletic Commission shows him with an almost impish smile, his shirt collar fashionably splayed over his jacket lapel. No more government issue brogans for Lenny Mancino. It was wing tips, pleated pants, and suspenders. He would strut about, in a playboy V-neck, or in his new suit from Berger's, a three-piece job, with Lenny proudly flashing its label and silk lining. He's arm in arm with Frankie J., in his manager's wood-paneled office, 1650 Broadway. And there he is as a broad-nosed Gatsby: hair slicked and parted, silk tie, with a striped dress shirt under his cardigan, and Max Joss's proud arm draped over his right shoulder. One imagines the twenty-year-old as an aspiring padrone himself, sending the photos to 136 North Fruit Street, Youngstown, Ohio: *"Look, Ma!"*

Technically, Lenny was still an understudy in Jacobs's stable, second to Bernie "Schoolboy" Friedkin, who really *was* from Brownsville. However, Friedkin's loss to Pat Foley, an Irishman from Boston, resulted in an impassioned request. Foley was already being mentioned as an opponent for the great Lou Ambers, a fighter who'd beaten two of Lenny's idols, Armstrong and Tony Canzoneri. Lenny wasn't even a full-fledged main eventer. Who was he to be asking for Foley?

"Joss gave the offer careful consideration," according to one account.

A week after outpointing the Schoolboy, Foley went off as a considerable favorite, 17–5, against Boom Boom in a feature bout at the Broadway. Mancini took six of the eight rounds and knocked down Foley with a right hand in the second. Though the arena's seating capacity was about four thousand five hundred, attendance was estimated between five thousand and five thousand five hundred.

At seven thirty-five the next morning, Lenny sent a telegram: DEAR MOM LETTING YOU KNOW THAT I JUST WON AN 8 ROUND DECISION AND FEELING THE SAME AS WHEN I ENTERED THE RING. YOUR LOVING SON.

Before long, Frankie Jacobs was telling the *Journal-American's* boxing writer, Hype Igoe, that he'd make more money with Boom Boom than he had with Jackie "Kid" Berg. "The nearest thing to Henry Armstrong in action around local rings," proclaimed another sportswriter. "A crowd pleaser," wrote yet another. "Whatever Mancini lacks in ring experience he makes up in viciousness and tireless energy."

He would have eleven more fights over the next year, ten of them at the Broadway. He lost once on account of low blows, and split a pair with the very capable Irving Eldridge, described as "the Bronx Hebrew." He earned a draw against Jimmy Vaughn, though ringsiders thought the decision undeservedly bad after Mancini staggered Vaughn with uppercuts in the third, sixth, and seventh rounds. Shortly after the New Year, he got another shot at Charley Varre, the man who ruined his New York debut with a broken jaw. This time, Mancini put Varre down for a nine count in the opening round. What followed, according to the *New York Times*, was "a clean-cut eight-round victory." It was getting to be a routine: another win, another sellout at the Broadway. The fight mob was talking about a title shot for Boom Boom.

Encased in a tasseled, rectangular shade, the hot lights above the ring endowed the combatants' silhouettes with a phosphorescent trace that seemed almost appropriate for a fighter like Boom Boom. After all, fans at the Broadway Arena had all but sainted him. "They loved him over there," remembered the *Daily News's* late Bill Gallo, a teenage fight buff when he first saw Mancini at Stillman's. "He gave the fans what they wanted: Kept throwing punches, never quit. He took some shellacking even when he won."

Yes, what fans felt for Boom Boom was a kind of love. They knew, quite simply, that he would bleed for them. His instincts were ferociously chivalrous, though never more apparent than in his two bouts with Billy Marquart.

Marquart was a Canadian, nicknamed the Winnipeg Walloper, fighting out of Chicago. He was more experienced than Mancini—41–13, as opposed to Lenny's record of 23–4–2—with a couple of wins over top contenders like Sammy Angott, the lightweight champ recognized by the National Boxing Association. But their records didn't matter as much as their technique, or in this case, lack thereof. As the Cleveland *Plain Dealer* noted: "Neither of the two lightweights knows how to back up."

Their first encounter, according to the *New York Times*, was "a fierce eight-round battle before a sell-out crowd of five thousand three hundred fans at the Broadway Arena." Lenny found Marquart's chin with a left hook in the second round. The Canadian didn't rise until the ref counted nine. In the fourth, Marquart threw two concussive rights, dropping Mancini to his knees. In the seventh, Mancini opened "a deep laceration" over Marquart's left eye. The intervening rounds, as another writer noted, were "crammed with furious punching rallies."

Afterward, in the dressing room, Marquart was informed that he had lost a split decision. "I don't remember a thing after that Mancini nailed me in the second," he said. "Did you ever see a dream fighting?"

The bout instantly gained notice as one of the fights of the year. But Marquart and Mancini would fight again, just three weeks later, a ten rounder in Cleveland. The 4,616 in attendance at Public Hall included a sizable contingent from Youngstown.

At ringside, the *Plain Dealer*'s James E. Doyle saw it as a fight between "squatty" Lenny, who "fought out of a freakish crouch," and the "lantern-jawed Canadian." From Doyle on deadline: "Marquart wasn't long in whaling the Youngstown sawed-off to the canvas. 'Twas early in the second round that he shot over a chin-cracking left hook, and Lenny sat down to think it over.

"Calmly enough, the little guy sat to the surprise of those who thought the punch should have belted at least a small portion of his brains out, but when he tried out his legs again, he was all fury and blaze. A haymaking right reached Marquart's jaw now, and some expected to see Billy topple, but instead the phlegmatic Canadian came over with a double fisted offensive that turned Lenny completely around and made him decide to think once or twice before charging once more."

As the tenth round began, Marquart caught Lenny with a right uppercut that looked for a brief moment like the knockout punch. "But the mad Mancini," continued Doyle, "was right back slinging everything in his bat bag, and he it was who was doing all the punching at the last bell, with Billy shaking off a mild attack of the blind staggers."

This fight had been more savage than their first. But again, Mancini won by split decision. Some moments later, he would be photographed in the dressing room, still wearing his dark satin robe, a terry cloth towel draped over his head like a prayer shawl. At twenty-one, his face is undergoing the inevitable, inexorable transfiguration: from puckish to pugilistic. Its supple features have begun to flatten and purple. His lips are bruised and split. A cut sack of swollen tissue hangs over his left eye. But it's the right eye that catches one's attention: completely closed, clenched like the seam of a mussel shell.

"Yeah," Boom Boom would say, "but you shoulda seen the other guy."

The *Brooklyn Eagle* put the first Marquart fight in context, saying that Lenny had now "moved a step closer to a match with lightweight boss Lew Jenkins." This was welcome news, as Elmer Verlin Jenkins, from what he called a "poor, ridiculous family" of itinerant cotton pickers, was not only a champion, but at the time, a very beatable one. "Famous up and down Broadway," wrote Red Smith, "and in bars and jails all over the country." The key, at least for Boom Boom's handlers, was getting to Jenkins before he drank and caroused his way out of the lightweight crown. But as Jenkins's fight with Bob Montgomery, often referred to as "the Philadelphia Negro," had been postponed to May, Boom Boom was left to fight Angott, lightweight champion of the N.B.A., a private sanctioning body formed to rival the New York State Athletic Commission.

Angott, known as the Clutch for his grabbing tendencies, was not an ideal opponent. "I hope the champeen will try to punch it out with me," said Mancini, "and lay off the Fancy-Dannin' . . . I've been after this shot for a long time. I had to be lucky to get it. . . ."

Judging from ringside accounts of the following evening, luck had little to do with Lenny's performance. Rather, it seemed his good fortune was earned. "In the sixth," according to the Associated Press, "the champion slipped to the floor for no count after a furious exchange." The ninth saw Angott "jarred with three stinging overhand rights to the head."

As it ended, Mancini would recall, Angott was "hanging on the ropes." Still, the ten-rounder went into the books as a split decision. The two judges voted for Angott—a boxer with the sense and skill to take an occasional backward step—and the man in the ring, referee Joe Sedley, for Mancini.

"The verdict was roundly booed," reported the *New York Enquirer*, a Hearst Sunday paper.

The Ring, the Bible of Boxing, noted that Lenny "gave Angott such a going-over that practically every fight fan there, including the referee, thought that Mancini deserved the verdict."

"They gave me the business," is how Boom Boom himself would explain it. *The business*, that invisible hand of hard luck afflicting all fighters. For most of them, the business was more deleterious to their manhood than the blows they took in the ring. Lenny offered to forfeit his purse if he failed to knock out Angott in a rematch. Same for Jenkins. All he needed was a championship fight.

"I'll kayo Angott if I meet him over fifteen rounds," he said.

By August, Lenny was ranked sixth in the crowded and abundantly talented lightweight division. On September 29, he beat Terry

Young in a semifinal at the Polo Grounds. Though most of the forty-six thousand fans were there to see heavyweight champ Joe Louis in the following bout, it was an especially satisfying win for Lenny, who'd fought Young at Dexter Park earlier that summer.

Young had vowed to expose what he called Lenny's "weak chin" in the leadup to their first fight. Such a disparaging untruth, noted the *Coney Island Daily Press*, was rooted in the fact that "Mancini and Young both are ardent admirers of the same young lady." One correspondent had it on good authority that she would leave Dexter Park with the winner. However, as that encounter ended in a draw, her presumed affections would not be gained until the rematch, which Lenny won handily.

"Mancini lived up to his explosive nickname," noted the *New York Times*, "hammering steadily at Young from the start."

Young—real name Angelo De Sanza—kept fighting top contenders as long as it didn't interfere with his day job. In 1943, he was sentenced to two and a half years at Sing Sing for a series of stickups on the Lower East Side. In 1967, someone gave him the business, shooting him to death in a nightclub.

Meanwhile, Lenny's win over the aspiring hoodlum earned him another semifinal date, with a kid named Joey Peralta. It was his first win at Madison Square Garden, which was packed with 20,551 fans to see Sugar Ray Robinson go against Fritzie Zivic. Next stop, the Montreal Forum, where Lenny met a Canadian contender in his hometown. As per Dink Carroll's account in the *Montreal Gazette*, Mancini "came ambling out of his corner like a bear cub . . . parked his chin on Dave Castilloux's chest" and "never stopped swinging punches."

Then there was the matter of Lenny's crouch, which utterly befuddled Castilloux. "Like trying to spear a marble bead with a pickle fork," wrote Carroll.

Yet again, the ten-round decision merited a title shot. But before Lenny could get it, Angott and Jenkins would square off at the Garden. "Looney Lew," as the tabloids had taken to calling him, was still recuperating from a drunken motorcycle wreck that left him with three fractured vertebrae in his neck. Most fans didn't know that; they just knew Lew had embarrassed himself again, dropping fourteen of fifteen rounds to Angott at the Garden. Even his wife was embarrassed.

"If he can't fight better than that the Army won't take him," she said.

If only Boom Boom had been that lucky. On December 18, eleven days after the Japanese Imperial Navy bombed Pearl Harbor. *The Ring*'s reigning number-two contender—already registered in Youngstown in accordance with the Selective Service and Training Act of 1940—announced that he would be inducted into the army. A month later, he reported to Fort Hayes, Ohio, where he was photographed for the *Journal-American* with uniformed personnel admiring his biceps.

By April, *The Ring* finally declared him the lightweight division's number-one contender, a cruel joke for a man whose government now recognized him as merely another private, serial number 35 272 387. Military life did not agree with Boom Boom. He learned how to use a grenade launcher and acquired skill as a marksman, but couldn't train as a fighter. Army food didn't help, either.

His eventual transfer to Brooklyn's Fort Hamilton, where he instructed fellow GIs on the finer points of calisthenics, was a welcome one. At least Max Joss and Frankie Jacobs could get him a little work on the side. Private Mancino's knockouts included Pete Galiano, 33–71–13, at the Fort Hamilton Arena, and Tiger Nelson (record: 5–4–2) at the.Broadway, where fifty wounded veterans attended as guests of the management.

Then there was Leroy Saunders, 2–11–1. Another *bum.* Lenny wouldn't use that word, not about another fighter. But the pugilistic establishment didn't observe such rhetorical niceties. At twenty-four, Lenny's prime was being squandered. He was getting fat and fighting bums.

Meanwhile, he would pick up the paper and read about Sammy Angott, who was still fighting main events at the Garden. No one drafted Terry Young, either. Or Henry Armstrong, the fighter to whom he was often compared (the "White Armstrong," noted *The Ring*).

The leave he took to Youngstown didn't brighten his spirits. Lenny was in uniform when he knocked on the door at 56 Oak Park, where his mother lived with Slick.

"Ma?"

She was in the kitchen.

"Ma."

He saw her face as she turned around. *Marked up*, as Lenny would describe it.

It had happened before, enough for Slick to worry about catching a beating himself. This time, however, Slick was waiting as soldier boy came through the door. He caught Lenny from behind with a chair leg, like a billy club to the back of the head. Lenny would recall buckling, but not falling. Slick wound up again, but as he did, Lenny spun and hit him. Once. Then again.

Stay here . . .

And again.

. . . take care of your mother . . .

And again.

This time, Lenny put Slick in the hospital. Should've killed him, Lenny would say. Private Mancino couldn't wait to ship out.

It was October 1944 when George DeLost, of General Patton's Third Army by way of Youngstown and the C.C.C., ran into Lenny in the Gremecey Forest, not far from the German border. He'd seen Boom's name on a list of much-needed reinforcements, and a couple days later, there he was, "a little bear in a big coat."

"What the hell are you doing here, Lenny?"

Lenny shrugged, not much else. They were under mortar fire. They were always under mortar fire.

Records show that Boom Boom arrived in France on the 17th of September, a rifleman with Company K of the 320th Infantry, a division whose crest, aptly enough, bore the motto "Forward." He soon found himself in the battle for the well-fortified medieval city of Metz, engaged in an endless volley, the ebb and flow of sniper fire, and exploding shells. He learned to crawl on his belly, grenades in tow, inching toward camouflaged machine gun nests. He once spent hours hugging the ground of an open meadow, the German gunners using him for target practice as he waited for Patton's armored cavalry. Clipped by a German bullet or run over by an American tank? For most of that time, it felt like even money.

"You'd be surprised what you see when things get close to your head," says DeLost, a winner of the Silver Star who left the front with a case of frostbite. "Just about everything you've ever done in your life, your family, your home, your girlfriend."

For Boom Boom, it was the Mother of God. He would swear to his children it was her, hovering over his muddy foxhole.

A week or so later, the same day Angott would lose a ten-round main event at the Garden, Lenny relinquished a spot in the forest that seemed to delight a German sniper. Three minutes later, a shell would land exactly where his ass had been.

Then, a telegram for Mrs. Anna Pavone:

REGRET TO INFORM YOU YOUR SON PRIVATE LEONARD MANCINO WAS SLIGHTLY WOUNDED IN ACTION TEN NOVEMBER IN FRANCE YOU WILL BE ADVISED AS REPORTS OF HIS CONDITION ARE RECEIVED

In due course, Private Mancino was declared "totally disabled."

The shell's impact sent Lenny briefly airborne, then dropping, as he recalled, "like a sack of lead."

"I wasn't knocked out; that is, I wasn't unconscious," he said. "I was numb and felt completely paralyzed. After a little while, a buddy crawled over and dragged me to a safer place where he could give me first aid, but it was four hours before the regular medics got me.

"I had a broken shoulder and a compound fracture of my left arm. The shrapnel had torn my arm and my left leg, had hit my right foot."

Then there was the piece lodged near his spine. That's what most worried the doctors over the eight months he spent hospitalized in England, Scotland, and France. After the fear of paralysis passed, it was thought that he would limp. But, in time, his gait returned to normal. And eventually, so did his inclinations, desires, and unfulfilled ambitions.

Toward the end of his rehabilitation, Lenny found himself a couple of sheets to the wind, weaving his way along the Champs-Élysées. The MPs took him back to the hospital.

"Don't tell Ray Arcel," he said.

On July 3, 1945, just days after he was honorably discharged from a military hospital in Indiana, the Veterans Administration ruled Lenny was now considered 70 percent disabled and entitled to an eighty dollars monthly pension. Problem was, at 30 percent able, Boom Boom would never again make the lightweight limit. Sedentary life in army hospitals had caused him to go as high as 195 pounds, this on a man whose discharge form accurately listed him at five foot one and a half.

That's not to say he was without prospects. The fighter was always esteemed by those who fancied themselves men of respect. Some years after the war, for example, Lenny was having cocktails at a Buffalo nightclub when Joe DiCarlo stopped by his table. DiCarlo, also known as Joe the Wolf and Buffalo's Public Enemy Number One, was notoriously camera shy, owing perhaps to his appearance as a famously uncooperative witness before Senator Estes Kefauver's hearings on organized crime. Nevertheless, this very same mob boss would insist on having his picture taken with Boom Boom.

DiCarlo's man in Youngstown was a fast-rising racketeer named Vincent DeNiro. It was DeNiro who offered the wounded war vet employment running a high-stakes barbut game. Lenny tried for a few weeks, but it wasn't for him. He didn't like the idea of staying up all night as *work*. But more than that, he didn't like having to look over his shoulder. He could see the life for what it was. For all the opulence and supposed respect, a guy like DeNiro would have to worry every time he got in his car, wondering if someone had wired his ignition to kingdom come.

So, he returned to New York, and asked Max Joss to get him a fight. By October, he was back at the Broadway, making his debut at 154½ pounds, perhaps the world's shortest junior middleweight. He decisioned the forgettable Baby Sims, then the inestimable Patsy Spataro. Next up was Steve Riggio, a welterweight who had twice beaten boxing's new attraction: Rocky Graziano. Forget Angott. In postwar America, Rocky would be Lenny's prize, not to mention a just reward for his Purple Heart. Boom Boom was back, proclaimed *The Ring*, "and has trained his sights on a match with Rocky Graziano whom he feels he can outslug anytime."

Graziano knew it, too. Why would Rocky fight Boom Boom? As an opponent, Mancini offered risk, but little reward. He posed all the problems, but even as a war hero, lacked the cachet he enjoyed before Pearl Harbor. It was just before the Sims fight that Ray Arcel told the *Journal-American*'s Frank Graham, "He might have become the lightweight champion if he hadn't gone into the Army." But that was just another way of saying Lenny Mancini would never be a champion.

To be sure, his postwar career offered some vintage Boom Boom moments. "The Purple-Hearted Mancini," as the *Brooklyn Eagle* called him, "never took a backward step" in beating Victor Moreno at MacArthur Stadium, "though it appeared at times that a retreat would have been the best course." Three months later, Boom Boom knocked out a 3½ to 1 favorite in the first round in a sellout at the Broadway. He could still pile up wins, nine of them against two losses in his first year out of the service. But beyond places like the Broadway, he had the stink of what if? about him.

Even his admiring hometown columnist, the Youngstown *Vindicator*'s Frank B. Ward, wrote of Lenny now being "a bit on the fat side." "A little chunkier and somewhat slower" was how the *Montreal Gazette* put it.

What's more, he'd started seeing double out of his right eye and cheating on the pre-fight physicals, keeping his left eye only partially covered as the inspector asked him to recite the letters on the eye chart. Seeing two left hooks coming at you was like seeing none. Mancini dropped five of his last six fights, the last four in a row (though the fans raised his arm in victory and carried him to the dressing room after he got the business in Montreal), and the last two to a kid named Rocky Castellani. This Rocky was five foot ten, a natural middleweight. Boom Boom had become an opponent.

It was over. On January 12, 1948, three weeks after his last fight, he eloped with the former Ellen Atreed.

They had met the previous July, literally bumped into each other at the corner of Broadway and 90th Street. Boom Boom was walking home from a bar on Columbus Avenue, not far from the rooming house where he lived with a bunch of other fighters.

She stepped left. He stepped to her right.

She stepped right. He slid to his left.

"What?" said Ellen. "You own the sidewalk?"

"I bought it this morning," he said.

"Fine," she said, passing him. "I'll walk in the street."

A couple nights later, Ellen's friends bring her to the bar. They say they got a guy for her. His name is Lenny. It's his birthday. He's twenty-eight.

She was a good Irish girl, with dirty blond hair and a lot of smarts. Ellen was sixteen when she graduated from a Catholic girls high school in Manhattan. She was the youngest of four, and her uncles did not approve of Boom Boom.

"Guinea bastard," they called him.

"Ellen," he'd say, smiling, "I'm going to have to kick the shit out of your uncles."

She was nineteen when they ran off to Baltimore, where lenient local statutes made it ideal for couples in a hurry.

From there, they went to Youngstown, where it was agreed that they would raise a family. Boom, as she now called him, got a job on the loading dock at General Fireproofing. On June 23, 1948, Boom and Ellen bought a house with a loan of $5,599.95 from the First Federal Savings and Loan Association of Youngstown. A two-bedroom at 807 Cambridge Avenue, it was the kind of tract home popular with those returning from the war: thirty feet deep, thirty-two across, single story, wood frame, concrete steps at the entrance. Aluminum siding would come later.

If Lenny was done with boxing, boxing wasn't yet done with him. On November 14, 1949, the Veterans Administration cited "the existence of the disability prior to aggravation by military service" and turned him down for insurance: "A careful review has been made of all the available records, and we regret to inform you that your application must be rejected because of an old head injury."

In other words, President Truman would settle up for the German grenade.

But not for Billy Marquart.

When the Mancinis finally got a television, Boom would sit in the corner, the right side of his face turned and shaded by the wall, his left locked onto that big Sylvania with the rabbit ears.

It was said that television would kill the fight game. By 1949, Max Joss had shut down the Broadway Arena. His Tuesday night shows couldn't compete with NBC's *Texaco Star Theater.* "Milton Berle was too much," said Joss.

Chapter 3 | Youngstown Tune-up

Though the upper south side was a neighborhood of boys, Little Ellen more than held her own. The first child born to Ellen 'n' Boom, as the Mancinis were now known, played cowboys, not dolls, and everything else from tag to tackle football, the rougher the better. She was very pretty, but not to be tested or trifled with, as evidenced by a kid named Skip Brown from Detroit Avenue, whose nose seemed to burst with a single right hand from Little Ellen.

"I wouldn't mess with her," said Mike Cefalde, who grew up on nearby Avondale Street.

The neighborhood tomboy was twelve, a child at the outset of President Kennedy's New Frontier, when pressed into service as the family's baby nurse. Her brother, Raymond Michael Mancino, was born March 4, 1961. It was Little Ellen's job, when not at school, to give him his bottle, feed him, and change his diapers.

"Look after the baby," said Big Ellen, who spent much of Raymond's first year at her husband's bedside in the hospital. Boom went in for three eye surgeries, none of them successful. Before Raymond's first birthday, his father had lost all sight in the right eye. The pupil remained still, unmoored and unmoved by light or objects.

In Youngstown, the recession of 1960 felt like an echo of the Great Depression. Shortly before Raymond was born, Boom Boom's income was little more than his union medical benefits and army disability, $136.30. He spent most of the previous year

31

laid off from his maintenance job at General Fireproofing. He wasn't alone. There were about twenty thousand unemployed Youngstowners, many of them steelworkers. By 1961, a very good month would be one in which local steel production rose to just 68 percent of capacity. With the mills aging fast and foreign steel cheap, Youngstown became known as "steel's sick city."

It had other names, too, including "Murdertown" and "Crimetown USA," the latter appearing on the cover of the *Saturday Evening Post*. The most well-known victim of "a Youngstown tune-up," as these regular occurrences were called, was a mobster called Cadillac Charlie who, along with his eleven-year-old son, Tommy, died instantly when he turned the ignition key in his '56 Ford. Another son, twelve-year-old Chuckie, was maimed for life.

Going back a decade, there had been eighty-two such bombings in Youngstown. Vince DeNiro, who had offered Boom a job running a barbut game after the war, was now the boss. He owned six cars and changed rides several times a day. At ten minutes after midnight, on July 17, 1961, he died while starting his Oldsmobile convertible. Its hood was found on a roof 150 feet away, which is more than could be said for DeNiro's missing lower half. Boom figured General Fireproofing wasn't such a bad career move, after all.

There were other assassinations for which the weapon of choice was a shotgun. Unlike steel, the numbers and the cheat joints and the barbut games, of which Cadillac Charlie had a piece, were recession proof. In fact, a city like Youngstown suggested that vice and prosperity were inversely proportional. But gambling and pussy, like steel, were industries that required the local establishment's sanction. As one former mayor told the *Saturday Evening Post*, "When you're in politics here, the public expects you to take money." His successor had been disbarred as a lawyer and defrocked as a judge, and met regularly for coffee with a well-known racketeer.

It wasn't always easy telling the cops from the criminals. For a time, the head of the vice squad was a gangster's brother. Another cop's sister ran a whorehouse. According to the maga-

zine, another local mobster, Sandy Naples, "enjoyed such prestige that while serving a six-month sentence in the country jail
he was chauffeured to and from his girl's house on weekends by
a deputy sheriff."

Naples, who drove a bomb-proofed sedan after his release, was
killed with his mistress just as she opened her door to let him in
for a late-night tryst. Police found a twelve-gauge shotgun and
about five thousand dollars in cash, but in keeping with local tra-
dition, not a single suspect. Still, thousands more showed up for
Naples's wake than attended Kennedy's first visit to Youngstown
back in '59.

Kids who grew up on the upper south side understood that their
hometown was a respected nation–state in the gangster empire.
Living within walking distance of those many South Avenue tav-
erns, they knew, among other things, where they would go in
their postpuberty lives to place a bet, throw the dice, or purchase
other illicit pleasures. Cops and robbers were like cowboys and
Indians for grownups. Except in Youngstown, the bad guys were
good. There was high virtue in not ratting. Rare was the second-
generation family that watched *The Untouchables* rooting for that
square Eliot Ness.

Still, as adults themselves, the kids would recall their own child-
hoods in idyllic, almost Rockwellian terms. Little Ellen would
take the baby outside in a wagon or a carriage as she played with
the boys on Cambridge Street. Baseball and football and kick the
can and tag games, like release, were played well into the night.
Life was a ceaseless game, with brief but mandatory intermissions
for mass, dinner, or maybe Boom ambling back from the Wander
Inn, one of his many favorite joints on South Avenue, with a sto-
gie planted in his mouth, a happy stagger to his bowlegged step,
and a cardboard box that filled the air with the steam off a fresh
hot pizza. Everybody got a slice.

Boom Boom was famous, or as close to fame as one got in
Youngstown. The city had produced plenty of fighters. "I remem-

ber being, like, six years old watching the *Gillette Friday Night Fights*," says Cefalde, "and hearing my father talking about all the great Youngstown fighters."

The kids still knew their names: Tony Janiro, Red D'Amato, the Carkido brothers. But Boom Boom started it all. A guy from maintenance at General Fireproofing went to New York and almost became a champ.

"He was so charismatic," says Ellen. "I mean, there wasn't anybody in town who didn't know Boom Boom Mancini."

Before she was a baby nurse or a tomboy, Little Ellen had been a daddy's girl. He took her everywhere, usually by foot, since Boom didn't drive because of his eye. There was the barber shop, and an occasional afternoon at the Wander Inn. Or maybe they'd watch Big Ellen bowl at Champion Lanes, where the Knights of Italy sponsored a league on Sunday nights. That's where they'd run into the former Annie Cannazzaro. On Little Ellen's birthday, she would slip the child an envelope with money inside.

"But it was always on the sly," recalls Ellen, "because she couldn't come visit us at home."

Slick had forbidden it. And Annie knew better than to defy him. He'd still smack her around, even in public.

"My grandmother, for whatever reason, married a son of a bitch," says Ellen. "And left a really great guy."

Grandpa Nick still lived in Buffalo. Little Ellen thought of his visits as events. He gave her money, bought her clothes, and always arrived with the best cannoli she had ever tasted. It was easy to see what her father saw in Grandpa Nick. It wasn't unlike what she saw in her own father.

They would stroll down the block with Little Ellen on his shoulders.

"Who's the boss?"

"I'm the boss, Daddy."

He could put her in a delighted trance just skipping rope, putting himself at the center of a whirring gyroscope.

"Faster, Daddy . . . more . . . do it again."

Even better was listening to him recall the adventures of his youth, the Boom Boom chronicles.

"The stories of his fights, the stories of when he was a boy, stories of when he was in World War II," she says. "I don't care, he could tell them one hundred times. We always loved his stories."

Though no one more than Raymond. As the baby grew, Little Ellen noticed ways in which he was special. He was tiny. Other boys used to hang him down a storm drain by his ankles to retrieve a lost ball, but by the age of two, Raymond could hold a baseball bat like Mickey Mantle. "Athletically," says Ellen, "he could do anything."

Kids couldn't catch him in football or tag. He was fast. He was shifty. And, most of all, he could take a beating. His brother made sure of that. Leonard John Mancino was born on September 21, 1955, making him five and a half years older than Raymond, and seven years younger than Little Ellen, whose responsibilities went from baby nurse to referee.

The boys were very close, tethered in a way that superseded the difference in their ages. Just the same, recalls Ellen, "My mother literally could not leave the two of them home alone. They fought constantly. Lenny was an antagonist, always some button he was pushing. Lenny would call Raymond 'Bucky,' because he had prominent front teeth. Then, of course, to get back at his brother, Raymond would call him 'Len-turd.' Then they would fight: I mean fight."

Unlike the battles between, say, Boom Boom and Billy Marquart, Lenny and Raymond were ungoverned by the Marquess of Queensbury rules, or any other civilizing force for that matter. Hitting below the belt was encouraged. As was the use of foreign objects. Their only limitation lay in the preadolescent male's capacity to do violence.

In terms of personality, Raymond owed more to his mother. "Goody Two-shoes," says Ellen.

The great sin of his youth was stealing red licorice from Wilkenson's drugstore. Upon returning home, Raymond understood he had absolutely no future as a Youngstown gangster. He was over-come with the urge to confess.

Big Ellen had him return to the store, apologize, and pay for the licorice. These acts of contrition made the boy feel better.

"Raymond told on *himself*," says the former Little Ellen. "That's the weirdest thing I've ever heard. I mean, who does that?"

Certainly not Lenny, who exhibited little talent for repentance. Lenny would take in stray cats and dogs. He would stop to help an old lady with her groceries. He was generous to a fault, and had a talent for getting laughs. He was always ready with a smile, at least when he wasn't kicking someone's ass. A dead ringer for his father, Lenny shared Boom Boom's volatile temper and a well-earned reputation as a street fighter. He also had his father's impa-tience with authority. "Lenny was more of a dark side person," says Ellen.

Lenny was just different, or perhaps, in some way, lacking. "Boundaries," says Tank DiCioccio, who grew up across the street from the Mancinis. "We all had certain boundaries."

Except Lenny. The games of release, for example, were usually played between Detroit Avenue to the north and Palmer on the south, with a light pole on Cambridge serving as the jail. When the jailer yelled "Oll-ee, Oll-ee in free!" everybody gave up his hiding place and came in.

"But Lenny never came in," says Tank. "Nobody knew where he was."

They would search. And search some more. But finding Lenny required venturing outside the boundaries of boyhood: past Palmer, past Roxbury, and into the woods beyond the pasture, where, after dark, Lenny Mancini could be seen smoking, the glow on his fingers like a firefly in the night.

Shortly before she left to live on her own, Little Ellen warned her mother: "If you think you're having problems with me, just wait."

Wait until Lenny hit puberty, she meant. As it happened, Ellen 'n' Boom wouldn't have to wait long, as Lenny was kicked out of St. Dominic's in seventh grade. His final offense was getting caught smoking in the boys' room, along with Jimmy Thrasher and Billy Goodall.

Sister Gregory, regarded as the meanest and ugliest nun in all of Ohio, began her interrogation with Jimmy. "Were you smoking?"

"No, sister."

"Let me smell your fingers."

The scent of tobacco on Jimmy's fingers sent Sister Gregory into a rage, as she paddled him right there in the principal's office.

Next, Sister Gregory turned to Billy. "Were you smoking?"

"No, sister."

"Give me your hand."

Now it was Billy's turn to get paddled.

"Lenny?"

"No, sister."

Sister Gregory then asked for the offending fingers, which Lenny presented after sticking them up his ass. "Here," he said.

Soon, Lenny Mancini would matriculate at Woodrow Wilson, where he perfected the look of a rock 'n' roll gangster, circa the early 1970s. He wore his hair long, but favored *purps*, high-waisted, purple, polyester bell bottoms, to go with his platform shoes and leather jacket. Lenny's taste in music ran to Hendrix, Zeppelin, and Hot Tuna. He was glad to be done with sectarian education and its catechisms, as the only use he could have for a priest or nun would be to bless the pot he was growing in his bedroom.

Meanwhile, Raymond insisted that his mom and pop accompany him to Sunday mass, usually at noon, or ten thirty if there was a football game on television, especially one featuring Browns' running back Leroy Kelly. Raymond's was an instinct predisposed to religiosity and belief. More than that, as Little Ellen moved out and Lenny's boundaries expanded toward more felonious territory, Raymond felt a strong, protective urge, the need to keep the family intact and maintain peace.

"My dad drank a lot," Little Ellen says frankly.

"Ray used to get afraid," recalls Tank DiCioccio. "Ray used to stay at our house a lot. He wanted his parents to get along. He wanted his father to, like, do the right things, you know what I mean? He didn't want him to drink. They got in arguments and stuff when he would drink. . . . Ellen and Boom went at it, man. Believe me, they went at it."

The Mancinis couldn't have been much different from most families in a neighborhood where workingmen would report to the bar by six in the morning, order a Gook and a Duke—Guckenheimer rye with a Duquesne beer—and return from their shifts for a triple with a beer wash. Once home, their front doors remained open, and everybody knew everybody's business. Fathers drank and parents argued, quite loudly if the wives were as strong-willed as Big Ellen. But so what? "My parents fought every day," recalls Raymond. "That was their way of communicating." Rather, what would've distinguished the domestic situation at 807 Cambridge was its youngest resident.

Raymond would recall the instances of his father's overindulgence as being rare and benign. "He was a happy drunk," he says. "Never nasty. Never missed a day of work."

Just the same, if Boom Boom were out for the night, as he occasionally was on a Friday or Saturday, little Raymond would stay up worrying.

"Go to bed," said his mother. "Your father will be all right."

"No, ma," he said. "I got to wait."

He knew the bars closed at two, and would not sleep until he heard a car outside, Boom being dropped off at the curb.

By the age of eight, if his father wasn't home by five on a weeknight, Raymond would dial the Wander Inn.

"Is Boom Boom Mancini there?"

"Boom?" he could hear the bartender ask amid the clatter. "You here?"

"Tell him I'm not here," said Boom Boom.

"Not here," said the bartender.

If, in fact, he was not, Raymond would continue dialing. He knew his father's drinking venues in order of preference: the Wander Inn, Coconut Grove, the Hilton Inn, the Diplomat, South-side Civics.

If their bartenders all responded in the negative, the boy would get on his bike, a Schwinn with a banana seat. He would proceed in the same order, starting with the Wander Inn. He'd peek in the window, see if his father was there. Then he'd go inside, amble up to the bar, and tug at Boom Boom's shirt. "Let's go, Pop."

The balls on this kid.

"Boom," the bartender would ask, "you want a drink?"

"Boom ain't having no drink," said Raymond.

Another kid would've gotten a smack. But not Raymond.

"You gonna listen to him?" asked the bartender.

"Ahh," said Boom, "what're you gonna do? That's my baby."

Then they would stagger home, with Raymond leaning on the bike and his father leaning on him.

"Great man, Raymond," said the wobbly Boom. "He was a great man. I loved my father."

At home, Boom Boom was most likely to be found on his corner of the floral-patterned couch. He'd be wearing khaki work pants and a sleeveless tee shirt, his right eye turned to the wall, his left focused on the big Sylvania. Raymond would sidle past his mother, who sat in an easy chair diagonally across from the nineteen-inch black and white, and curl up alongside his father. Sometimes, he'd put his head in Boom's lap. Other times, he'd let his legs dangle over his father's.

Tell me a story.

Didn't matter which one. Raymond knew them all. He knew Sammy Angott ran all over the ring. He knew his old man once got a chance to move around with the great Lou Ambers at Stillman's. He knew that Ambers lost his title to Tony Canzoneri, and that Canzoneri, a dapper New Yorker by way of New Orleans, was his father's idol. He didn't know that Canzoneri, who fought a record twenty-nine times at Madison Square Garden, died in a twenty-one-dollar-per-week Times Square hotel. A bellhop found his body. The former champion in three weight divisions, Canzoneri was fifty-one and destitute, his death attributed to natural causes. The State Liquor Authority would describe Tony Canzoneri's Paddock Bar and Grill, 1634 Broadway, as a front for the interests of a Genovese gangster called Fat Tony Salerno.

Pop, tell me about Rocky again.

Rocky Graziano said he didn't want to fight a guy who'd won a Purple Heart in the war. But the truth, as Boom's progeny knew full well, was that Rocky was afraid. Would've been a big payday, too. But Rocky was a bully. "Once he realized he couldn't knock me out," said Boom, "I'd a beat 'im."

And, Pop, what did Henry Armstrong say?

A friend from Youngstown was visiting Stillman's when Boom introduced Armstrong as "the greatest fighter in the world," he said.

"Can't say that yet," said Homicide Hank, shrugging.

"Why not?" asked Boom.

"I haven't had the chance to fight you," said Hank.

Raymond always laughed at that line. But he believed it, devoutly. Pop was the best. Pop would've been champ if not for the war, the signs of which were still readily apparent to the child snuggling on the couch. There was a spray of pockmarked flesh along his father's left flank, a jagged metal pebble lodged in his bicep, and a reluctance to discuss his time in France.

Pop, tell me about the war.

"Aaahhhh."

Boom Boom was careful to avoid expressions of regret or self-pity, especially in front of the kids. But, every once in a while, as Raymond opened the front door, the boy could feel his father's good eye on him, tracking him across the foyer on his way to the refrigerator, or maybe to put down his books. That eye was like a hand at the back of his shoulder.

"Pop," he said. "What's happening?"

"Aahhgggg."

Raymond could see it on his face. But you wonder what Boom Boom saw, a guy from maintenance at GF.

"Pop?"

"I would've won that title."

When the stories were no longer enough, or when his father finally tired of telling them, Raymond ventured into the basement. It was three steps from the kitchen to the wooden landing, then down another eight to the linoleum floor. There was a rattling old washer-dryer, and a wooden beam from which hung Boom's old army duffel, now packed with rags. The makeshift heavy bag was meant for Boom to get a little exercise, but mostly had been used by Little Ellen, who would swing from it as a kid.

Then, past the duffel, was Big Ellen's Tupperware inventory, which looked like an arsenal to Raymond. Boom didn't opt often for corporal punishment, but on those occasions that warranted it, he went old school with the belt. Big Ellen, on the other hand, could strike from across the room. Using a plastic lid or cup, she could hit either of her misbehaving boys in their most excruciatingly vulnerable places. Worse than that were the straps designed as handles for Tupperware's line of picnic baskets. "When my mom finished with me, I had all these red welts," recalls Raymond. "It spelled T-U-P-P-E-R-W-A-R-E across my ass."

Next to the Tupperware, enveloped in the pleasant scent from a nearby cedar chest, is where he'd find his father's scrapbook, or what remained of it, anyway. The sepia-toned photos and burnt-orange newspaper clippings had been Scotch-taped onto thick paper, which, like the clippings, had begun to crumble. The paper had been hole-punched and bound with twine.

The scrapbook's perishable state led Big Ellen to place it on ever-higher shelves, for fear it would disintegrate with Raymond's frequent handling. But the boy remained undiscouraged, retrieving it standing atop a chair. At night, he'd go through the pages by flashlight. The deteriorating album became Raymond's Bible, his Little Red Book, his instructional, his devotional, his primer of parables.

He learned all about the Broadway and Stillman's and the Garden. He could recite the accounts of his father's valiant victories against fighters like Red Guggino, Joey Fontana, and the "Injun," Chief Crazy Horse, whose complexion was invariably described as "copper colored."

He studied the images: reconciling the maintenance man now slumped on the couch in his Guinea tee with the dapper young man whose hair was slicked back and parted.

Or with Bill Roberts's illustration in the *Cleveland Press*: his father idealized as a cartoon likeness, a Boom in each fist under the headline: ANGOTT'S NEMESIS.

Even as Raymond went to sleep, the headlines would flash in his mind's eye:

MANCINI LIGHTWEIGHT HOPE
"Armstrong" Style Helps Young
Italian on Road to Title Fight

MANCINI GAINED TOP HARD WAY
"Purse" for First Fight Was Broken Jaw and Bus Fare

BOOM BOOM DOES JUST THAT WHEN HE'S IN THE RING
Mancini Dangerous Foeman for Champion Lew Jenkins

MANCINI LOOKS AS JENKINS WATERLOO
Decision to Angott Is Booed

REFEREE CALLS LEN MANCINI WINNER

It got so that Raymond knew his father's career better than his father did, even occasionally reminding him of dates, places, and opponents. "Hey, Pop," Raymond might ask, "remember when you were supposed to fight Bob Montgomery at Ebbets Field?"

Who remembered that stuff?

Raymond did. As if it had happened to him.

The kid had his favorite ballplayers, most of them represented with posters on his bedroom wall: Browns running back Leroy Kelly, Colts quarterback Johnny Unitas, and the Yankee centerfielders, first, Mickey Mantle, and later, Bobby Murcer, who happened to be a natural southpaw like Raymond. At the beginning of a new decade, the Yankees were no longer cool, but Raymond had been a fan since his father told him about Joe DiMaggio and New York. Long before he was Marilyn Monroe's husband, Joe D. had been the most famous and admired American of Italian descent. But as the other sports were mere metaphors for what boxing really is—actual combat—Ray would wonder about the nature of athletic heroism. You never saw pictures of Joe D. with his eye swollen shut. Could DiMaggio have stood up to Billy Marquart?

Nah, he told himself, *only my pop.*

Tank DiCioccio couldn't have been more than five when Raymond showed him the photograph taken after the second Marquart fight. "That's my dad," he'd say proudly.

The boys spent many a day in the basement, and once they were old enough to read, the clippings codified the narrative. Still, the icon of this allegory remained the photograph. The blood and the bruising might have frightened another kid, but they had just the opposite effect on Raymond.

He didn't see a club fighter with a busted eye and dried blood on his lips. Raymond saw a hero. *His* hero. It was the most beautiful image he'd ever see.

"He wanted to be that person," says Tank. "He wanted to be his father. He was in awe of that picture."

It might as well have been Christ on the cross.

At age eight, Raymond began to assemble his own scrapbook, a faux rattan album whose earliest entries include swimming and horsemanship certificates earned in August 1970 at YMCA summer camp. There are records of his Bitty basketball career (as high scorer for the undefeated Elks, he had sixty-two points in the '73 season), and photos and clippings from the Uptown Kiwanis Little League. Raymond's first mention in the *Youngstown Vindicator* is from June 21, 1971; he hit a triple and Tank had a double in a 6–2 loss to East Side Civics. He was even better with Tank as his catcher, throwing twelve strikeouts or a one-hitter on a given afternoon for D.D. Davis Construction.

If the scrapbook was Raymond's way of emulating his father, it was his mother who endorsed the boy's sense of ambition and possibility. "My mother made me believe I was ten feet tall," he says. "My mother made me believe I could be whatever I wanted to be."

In addition to raising three kids and selling Tupperware, Big Ellen enrolled at Youngstown State, where she studied English and earned a certificate qualifying her as a substitute teacher. She was also a great athlete, highly skilled in racquetball, volleyball, and softball. Though she was past forty, coaches at Youngstown State begged her to play softball. Big Ellen had to decline, as she was already too busy with her Raymond, her Boom, her studies, her bowling league, and her tae kwon do class at the Y.

"Never missed a class—big heart, a leader, always in front of the class," says Kae Bae Chun, former bodyguard to South Korean military ruler Park Chung-hee. "Mrs. Mancini became a brown belt, good fighter. The men were scared, definitely."

All the Mancinis were gifted at the combat arts. Little Ellen would become a black belt under Grandmaster Chun's tutelage, and Lenny would fight his way to the finals of the '73 Youngstown Golden Gloves. His trainer was Eddie Sullivan, winner of the 1940 Youngstown Gloves as a lightweight, and a machinist at General Fireproofing, where he worked with Boom. From an old gymnasium on a Navy Reserve base, the trim, bespectacled Sullivan fashioned a host of fine amateurs and an occasional pro. One of them, it was thought, might be Lenny.

"You could hit Lenny with anything," says his friend, Dave Shaffer. "Nothing would bother him."

He was a better boxer than his old man. "There's people who say that Lenny could've been the best fighter in the family," says Mike Cefalde, who recalls him losing a close decision in the '73 Gloves. "He was slick, you know? He had everything. But Lenny enjoyed being Lenny."

He liked to hang out. He liked to party. Before finishing high school, he had a job at Youngstown Sheet and Tube's Campbell Works making more money than Boom. Who needed to fight?

Apparently, only Raymond, who liked what he saw at the Navy

Reserve enough to tap the trainer on his shoulder. "Mr. Sullivan," he said, "one day I'm going to come in and be the best fighter you ever had."

The neighborhood was fertile ground for the gridiron. Bob and Mike Stoops, who went on to become head football coaches at Oklahoma and Arizona, respectively, were from Detroit Street. Ed Muransky, who'd win a Super Bowl ring with the '83 Raiders, grew up on Zedeker.

Those blocks might've been good for football, but were not quite poor enough to produce many fighters. Neighborhood kids were mostly Italian and Irish and Slovak, and went to Catholic schools like St. Dom's and Cardinal Mooney. The fathers had union jobs, and so, it was assumed, would most of their sons.

"A *boxer*?" Tank asked Raymond, thinking at first that it sounded like a job done on a loading dock. "You mean, like box oranges? Box apples?"

"A *fighter*," said Raymond. "Like my dad."

By then, Raymond knew how to throw a hard, straight jab that made a slapping sound as it met his father's meaty palm. "That's nice, kid," said Boom, who, at Raymond's insistence, would fill his old army duffel with more rags, and later, grains of uncooked rice for the boy. Still, Boom figured this boxing business was a phase. As long as there wasn't a Depression, the kid was safe.

Only Big Ellen knew how serious her youngest son was. She gave him her egg timer to clock the endless rounds of shadowboxing and bag work he did alone in the cellar. *Tick, tick, tick.* The boy was marking time, in three-minute rounds, in seasons, and in years. The child knew the time would soon come to put away childish things.

Going into Cardinal Mooney High School, Ray, as most kids now called him, was projected as a three-sport star. He'd never be very tall, but he was fast and canny and unnaturally strong. He was a point guard on the basketball court, a left-handed pitcher and centerfielder in baseball, and the leading rusher for a freshman football team that was undefeated heading into its final game with Ursuline.

"Stay with football," urged Mooney's backfield coach. "We'll get you a scholarship."

The coach, Ace Congemi's boy, Tony, wanted Ray eating and lifting. There was no such thing as a 126-pound running back in northeastern Ohio.

"But then I couldn't make weight," said Ray.

Congemi didn't understand. He was talking about a free ride to college. The kid was talking about starving himself.

"You're going to get all beat up," said Congemi. *Look at your dad*, he wanted to say. "Why do you want to be a fighter, Ray?"

"Because I love it."

It was much the same in baseball, where Ray earned accolades as a pitcher and centerfielder for Local 377's team in the Babe Ruth League. He played for an all-star squad that won consecutive state titles and, a few years later, a Connie Mack team that saw him record the highlight of his baseball career. Against a team from Cincinnati, Ray turned on a hanging curve and jacked it over the outfield fence 320 feet from home plate.

"I weighed a buck thirty-two," he says.

A local scout, Gizzy Gardner, asked if Ray was interested in a minor-league deal with the Toronto Blue Jays.

"No thanks," he said.

Ray had considered himself a fighter—all other endeavors mere amusement—since the age of fourteen, when he first went to train with Eddie Sullivan. The Navy Reserve wasn't much of a gym. Its tiny ring was merely four posts and a mat laid over the concrete floor, maybe fourteen square feet. There was a mirror for shadowboxing, one speed bag, and an old canvas heavy bag. It was filled with sand and, in the dead of winter, felt like punching a wall, as the room's only heat seemed to be generated by the fighters themselves. For a kid accustomed to pastoral fields of play, the Navy Reserve wasn't a particularly hospitable place, but the

Junior Olympics tournament would be held the following spring in Cleveland. For Ray, it was time.

As he began, Ray was good with his hands, not an inconsiderable skill growing up in Youngstown, but had had only one fight with the gloves on. That match had been made a year or so earlier in Stevie P.'s garage up the block.

Stevie was skinny—"strong skinny," as Ray recalls—and a little scary. If Ray was a good street fighter, then Stevie was already a great one: unafraid and seemingly indestructible. His endurance had been learned the hard way, from a father who would get drunk and beat him with boards.

No surprise, then, that Stevie came out throwing raging roundhouses. Ray had learned something from his father, too: a straight 1–2. That's what put Stevie down for a ten count.

Looking back, Ray feels for Stevie. He recalls the bruises inflicted by the father, who was among the crowd counting out his own son in the garage. He remembers Stevie spending the better part of his adolescence as a glue sniffer. As an adult, he lost his teeth. That empathy, however, came later. In that moment, in the garage, Ray felt only ecstasy.

"You feel like Hercules," he says. "Of course, after the fact, you always want the guy to get up after the count of ten. But when you knock him down, it's the greatest feeling in the world. There ain't nothing better than to stand over a man and see him down on the canvas. Nothing."

April 24, 1976, the dressing room at the regional round of the Junior Olympics in Cleveland: Ray can hear the talk as Eddie Sullivan wraps his hands before the fight. He'd be hearing it the rest of his career.

Who the white boy?

I want his ass, yo.

Yeah, talking 'bout you, white boy.

No one give a fuck who you daddy is.

The brothers figured he was lucky to have one.

Still, Raymond knocked out his first opponent in thirty seconds, and the second in thirty-two. A few days later, he tallied another first-round KO in front of eleven hundred at the Campbell Memorial Fieldhouse, just outside of Youngstown. Maybe Ray's was a gift passed through the blood; not for nothing were his forebearers given the Sicilian sobriquet Mancino, or southpaw. Though he tipped the scales at 122 pounds, that left hand was a sledgehammer.

Next stop Detroit, for nationals. Raymond fought all the way to the finals, where he lost a decision to a vastly more experienced kid in what the *Vindicator* deemed "a bruising affair."

Even in defeat, however, the storyline become apparent, at least in Youngstown, where the local paper had run a photo of Ray and his dad playfully squaring off wearing pillowy Everlast gloves. But the truth was, Boom, while flattered, was less than enthused with the singlemindedness of his son's ambition.

"I don't want you to do this," he said. "It's a painful, lonely life. Me, I had to fight. It was a depression. I had to eat. You can do so many other things. You've got so many opportunities."

"Dad, I know," said Raymond, who was already thinking about New York, "but I want to be a fighter."

What was the point, Boom had to wonder, in having a union job?

How does a kid fight if he's not hungry?

Oh, but he was. For his father's love.

"I want to win the world title," said Raymond. "For you."

What do you say to a kid like that?

On Father's Day 1976, fifteen-year-old Raymond wrote his father a poem, "I Walk in His Shadow," which concludes: "I want to be his model, and live with his great name; For I am this man's son, and I'll never bear shame."

It was written on loose-leaf paper and presented to his father in Boom's favorite nook on the couch. Boom read it carefully. And again. Then he went to his bedroom, as Raymond followed him, keeping his distance. Boom closed the bedroom door, but not all the way.

Ray could still see as his father read the poem again. Boom was standing next to the bed, where a little cedar chest housed his Purple Heart and other military decorations. Atop the cedar chest was a cigar box, reserved for his most personal items: the wallet he kept bound with a rubber band, and the photographs of Big Ellen, Little Ellen, Lenny, Raymond, and his own father.

Boom folded the poem and put it in the cigar box. Then, with his back turned to the door, Boom pulled the handkerchief out of his back pocket, and began to wipe at his eyes.

He's tearing up, Raymond thought.

If so, it was the first time since Nick Mancino left for Buffalo.

"Sophomores are the toughest," says Father Tim O'Neill, recalling his years as a young Jesuit, teaching religion at Cardinal Mooney. Tenth graders are jittery, hormonal, and uncomprehending, but never more so than when he instructed them upon first entering his classroom.

"Just be," he said.

Be? thought Ray. Be what?

"Just be," said Father O'Neill. "This is the being room. Being is the absence of doing."

A minute would pass, or maybe two, before the boys were fidgeting ever more frenetically in their seats and the girls were putting on makeup.

Just be? thought Ray. Impossible.

But if Ray could do it, the priest figured, the rest of them would fall into line. He was that most peculiar of students, the jock-moralist, free to proselytize without fear of being accused as a collaborator with clerics or adults. What's more, any kid who came to school with an occasional shiner couldn't be accused of being a nerd.

Abortion. Papal infallibility. Ecclesiastical marriage. Sex before marriage (the only subject about which Ray accepted the inevitability of his doom).

"Ray would take the moral side, not the popular side," says

Father O'Neill, who came to regard his student's pugilistic education as a quest. The priest saw a kid trying to reconcile two very conflicting images: the hero in the scrapbook and the man on his barstool at the Wander Inn. What else could Ray have been but a fighter?

"He had to be," says Father O'Neill. "His dad had been banged up pretty good. Lesser kids would shun a maimed father. Ray had to save his dad from humiliation."

It was enough to turn the priest into a fight fan for the first time since the early fifties, when he would watch the *Gillette Cavalcade of Sports*, otherwise known as the Friday night fights, on a ten-inch Admiral television salvaged from Kelty's bar on Youngstown's west side. Father O'Neill started showing up at the Struthers Field House or the Packard Music Hall, which billed itself as "The Madison Square Garden of Mahoning Valley," or high school gyms from Cleveland to Canton. After each bout, Ray would receive a kiss from his father, and a blessing from the priest. It was the kid who insisted. He had a need to believe.

Of course, Ray had more than benedictions on his side. Eddie Sullivan devised a way to amplify his natural advantages. Converting Ray from a southpaw stance to a conventional one accomplished two things. It got him much-needed sparring (nobody wanted to move around with a lefty). Second, it allowed Ray to lead with his power (as opposed to right-handed fighters who lead with their left).

Any doubts as to the wisdom of this stratagem would have been dispelled on the evening of February 3, 1977, when a crowd of four thousand eight hundred showed up at Struthers Field House to watch the finals of the forty-ninth annual Youngstown Area Golden Gloves. In his last year as a 126-pound novice, Ray floored a kid named Roberto Vazquez within ten seconds of the opening bell. Vazquez managed to get up, only to endure more punishment. "Mancini continued to flail away," according to the *Vindicator*, "until the referee stepped in with exactly one minute remaining in the first round."

Ray then returned to Cleveland, winning the regional Gloves

title by TKO. A month later, at the Packard Music Hall in Warren, a merciful referee interceded on his opponent's behalf to end a fight after all of fifty-five seconds. For the first time, the *Vindicator* referred to him as Ray (Boom Boom) Mancini.

The final fight of his sophomore year saw Ray matched against Leo "Blackjack" Simmons of Akron. Already regional champion in the Open division, Simmons was almost three years older. With a chance to get to the nationals of the Amateur Athletic Union tournament, Ray dropped a split decision in Canton.

Moments later, Eddie Sullivan was seething in the dressing room. "They cheated you," he said.

"No, they didn't," said Ray. "Father O'Neill said I lost. And priests never lie."

Chapter 4 | Black Monday

On September 19, 1977, as workers arrived for their morning shifts, the town's most prominent employer released a statement: "Youngstown Sheet and Tube Company, a subsidiary of Lykes Corporation, announced today that it is implementing steps immediately to concentrate a major portion of its steel production at the Indian Harbor Works near Chicago . . . The production cut-back at the Campbell Works will require the lay-off or termination of approximately 5,000 employees in the Youngstown area."

The day would be remembered as Black Monday. After seventy-seven years, Sheet and Tube's circumstances were even more dire than those of its competitors. Its landlocked location ensured higher transportation costs. Decades of antagonism between management and labor had left its production facilities hopelessly outdated. To make matters worse, Lykes, which took over in 1969, was a New Orleans company whose primary business was ship-building. In their book, *Steeltown U.S.A.: Work and Memory in Youngstown*, authors Sherry Lee Linkon and John Russo describe Lykes as "a highly leveraged conglomerate with . . . no commitment to or history with the local community." Then again, they weren't much different than the other producers who "seemed content to run the old mills into decay and disrepair, until they simply could not compete on a global scale."

The rest of America was about to find out what Youngstown had long known: Steelmaking was just another organized crime. Sheet and Tube's other site, the Brier Hill Works, would close within a year. By 1979, U.S. Steel announced that it would close its Ohio Works and McDonald Mills, eliminating another three thousand six hundred jobs in greater Youngstown. That same year, the Save Our Valley campaign, organized by the Ecumenical Coalition of clergymen and civic leaders, collapsed when the Carter Administration refused to sign off on loan guarantees to reopen the Campbell Works. By the early 1980s, Republic Steel would initiate massive layoffs.

There was a name for the catastrophe inaugurated on Black Monday: deindustrialization. But Boom called it another Depression. He'd been waiting for it, the return of the Hungry City. Now, both his sons wanted to be fighters.

Youngstown's economy was an obstinate beast. For generations, steel was the Mahoning Valley's only legitimate industry, but the mill closings proved a boon for its illegitimate ones, gambling and resultant ancillary businesses like loan-sharking and political corruption. "There's more money floating around now than ever before," a convicted Ohio racketeer told the *Pittsburgh Press*. "People aren't working and they can't go out. But they can borrow, they can gamble on credit. And they're borrowing until it comes out their ass."

"Gambling permeates everything," said Carmen Policy, later the CEO and president of the San Francisco 49ers, but then best known as the lawyer for mob boss Joey Naples. "For its size, I admit, there is no city in America like Youngstown."

Mike Cefalde recalls the mind-set of the unemployed man: "'I got one hundred dollars. What the fuck I'm going to buy my family for one hundred dollars? But, hey, Cleveland is a lock with the points. So I'm going to bet.' Now should they have gambled away the family's money? No. But it happened. You took that shot. I know I did. I would bet."

Actually, Cefalde did more than bet. He started taking action, too. He wasn't the only laid-off steelworker trying to make it as a freelance bookie, but after ten years at Sheet and Tube, he was taking his shot.

Lenny Mancini, Ray's older brother, had only been in the mill since '73. Still, what he lacked in seniority, he'd make up in balls. The shot he took would be an especially long one.

On September 21, two days after Black Monday, Lenny celebrated his twenty-second birthday. On November 12, he hastily married Mary Francis Panno, eighteen, of 968 East Boston Avenue. With the steel business going bust, the husband-to-be decided to make a comeback in the ring.

"I got unfinished business," he told Ray.

Lenny was no longer the star of Eddie Sullivan's stable. That distinction now belonged to Harry Arroyo, a 139-pounder who had already attracted considerable interest as a pro prospect, and his own kid brother, now known as Ray "Boom Boom" Mancini and fighting at 132. Five years after his first Golden Gloves, Lenny didn't weigh much more than 135, but he fought at 147. He did it out of courtesy to Ray and Harry. But, mostly, he did it because he could. Even giving away twelve pounds, he was still banging guys out.

Soon, Boom was dropping by the Navy Reserve, telling Eddie Sullivan not to let Lenny and Ray spar with each other. But, of course, they did. No one else really wanted to spar with them, and they had to get in their work. More than that, though, their conflict was inevitable, in their natures.

"We had wars in the gym," Ray recalls. "Wars."

Ray had become the aggressor, but that only made it easier for Lenny to bait him. "Real slick," says Ray. "He'd feint and move just enough to make you miss, then make you pay: *bing*. Step around you, *bing, bing!* He used to get me with a left hook to the body, then the head. He hit me some shots that made me feel like I wanted to go down."

Lenny had more power than Ray remembered. He put down Arroyo while sparring, and a black kid from Pedro Tomez's Buckeye Elks gym. *Bing*. Ray had seen stars once, moments after his father had cracked him. But these sessions were more disorienting, more grueling.

"We were trying to kill each other," says Ray.

Typically, Lenny drew the first blood, from Ray's nose or lip. Still, the kid brother kept charging. Ray had been defeated before, but this fraternal pairing brought him perilously close to something more terrible and humiliating.

"For the first time," he recalls, "I felt like quitting."

These brotherly beatings endowed Ray with an acceptance of pain he hadn't previously considered. They also changed the emotional calculus between the siblings. Lenny became affectionate, even huggy around his kid brother. "I could tell by how he was with me after we fought," says Ray. "We were more on equal terms. There was a certain sensitivity for me that I didn't remember . . . In other words . . . he loved me."

The Struthers Field House was built in 1951, with enough room for 4,008 high school basketball fans. But never had that seating capacity been mocked as it was during the Fiftieth Annual Youngstown Golden Gloves, the first since Black Monday.

"They broke every fire rule there was," says Chuck Fagan. "You'd have five thousand people in there, easy."

Fagan, not long for his job at U.S. Steel, was just another guy who found himself rooting for the Mancini brothers. He remembered Lenny from '73, and still considered him "a little more natural" than Ray. The younger one had more of a blue-collar style, but he never stopped punching. Still, the brothers' most admirable trait wasn't throwing punches, but taking them.

"Them guys were blessed," says Fagan.

"There were so many fighters," says Mike Cefalde, "but when those two made their entrances, the noise was deafening."

Especially Ray. Years before, the Mahoning County Sheriff tried explaining Youngstown for the *Saturday Evening Post* by saying: "They're sporting-blood people around here." It had been many years, however, since a local guy aroused those instincts. Now, as Ray—with "Boom" stitched on each leg of his satin Tuf-Wear trunks—was introduced for the semifinal round at Struthers, the standing-room-only crowd got up and began to chant:

Boom! Boom! Boom! Boom!

His opponent was a formidable one, Darrell Phifer of the Buckeye Elks. As per Youngstown custom, even amateurs fought without headgear. Ray started punching at the opening bell and at one point, almost knocked Phifer through the ropes. Phifer somehow managed to hold on with his right glove and remain semiupright for three rounds, a feat that earned the audience's respect. "A tremendous bout that thrilled the crowd," reported the *Vindicator*, ". . . Mancini lived up to his nickname . . ."

When Mike Cefalde got home that night, his wife asked him about the fight.

"I ain't ever missing another one," he said.

The finals, held on a Wednesday night in February, were sold out four days in advance. "If you don't have a ticket," one sponsor told the *Vindicator*, "then there's no use coming down." The card featured Harry Arroyo, whom the paper called "Navy Reserve's perennial champion," and a fight between Lenny and the Elks' John Ford, whose own father had won a Golden Gloves title. Still, the evening's most anticipated bout matched Ray with Freddy Bowman, the defending Open champ at 132 pounds. They had sparred before, enough for Ray to know that Bowman was the worst kind of opponent for him: a slick, experienced boxer who knew how and when to clutch and grab.

Bowman danced and counterpunched for the first two rounds. But, at 1:50 of the third, Ray caught him with a right hand that sent his mouthpiece airborne. The ref was slower than Bowman's cornerman, who stormed the ring and shoved Ray, even as, the *Vindicator* noted, "Mancini continued to fire away at the dazed Bowman." Then Eddie Sullivan jumped in, followed by a handful of fans. From his corner, Ray could see one of his neighbors land a tremendous sucker punch. Not to be outdone, a black guy from Tomez laid out a white guy from the upper south side.

After the cops finally cleared the ring, Ray was declared the Open champion, and named the tournament's Most Promising Fighter. From Struthers, he'd go to Cleveland, tallying three more knockouts to win the District Golden Gloves. Such a run inspired the *Vindicator's* Dave Burcham to write that the junior from Cardinal Mooney had "put out more lights than the energy shortage."

Ray did lose twice that year. At the National Golden Gloves finals in Albuquerque, he dropped a decision to Davey Armstrong, who was five years older and a veteran of the '72 and '76 Olympic teams. Then, at the National AAU finals in Biloxi, he lost another decision to Philadelphia's Anthony "Two Guns" Fletcher, a prospect who'd end up on Pennsylvania's death row.

Much to Ray's regret, Lenny didn't make those trips with him. At 147 pounds, he just wasn't big enough, and had been eliminated in his last fight at Struthers.

"I seen Lenny get tagged that night," says Dave Shaffer. "He should've been knocked out. But that boy didn't go down for nothing."

That would be Lenny's last sanctioned bout. On May 25, 1978, just days after his kid brother returned from Biloxi, Lenny became a father. His son was named Nicholas after his paternal grandfather. Nick Mancino, from Buffalo by way of Bagheria, had passed away the year before.

There are several photographs of Ray in the 1979 edition of *Eminence*, the Cardinal Mooney yearbook. He is invariably smiling and partial to prominently collared shirts (some borrowed from his dapper brother). He wears his wavy, longish hair parted down the middle per the prevailing custom. Nothing identifies him as a fighter but the dangling pair of gold-plated gloves that hang with a crucifix just below his throat. Rather, he was voted Most Involved, along with Lori Magazzine (she of the math team and the ski club). He was also elected class president.

"He could've been the principal if he wanted," recalls Paul Gregory, who taught social studies.

The basis for Ray's popularity was obvious. It was his good nature, of course. However, as the town began to cave in on itself, there was also a nascent sense that Ray would represent its people.

A failing industry would transform Youngstown into a multiracial ghetto, with most of the citizenry unable to escape. But Ray was going places.

As a senior, Ray again won the Youngstown Gloves and the districts on his way to the national tournament, held that year in Indianapolis's Market Square Arena. Although Ray won his first two fights there by knockout, Murphy Griffith was sure he'd soon lose a decision. He didn't like Ray's chances to qualify for the Pan-Am Games, either, much less the Olympic team.

It's not that Griffith wasn't impressed, quite the contrary. He just knew Ray was all wrong for the amateurs, where the prevailing system favored stand-up, European-style fighters who could pile up points by tapping opponents with the white part of their gloves. This kid was a natural brawler, and pretty "cute," in fighter's parlance, flinging his elbows. "A little Rocky Graziano," Griffith was calling him, and exactly the kind of prospect he had been sent to find.

In his third fight, Ray drew Melvin Paul of New Orleans, the reigning AAU champion at 132 pounds and a favorite to make the 1980 Olympic team. Paul had considerable international experience, having represented the U.S. at the world amateur championships in Yugoslavia. Ray spent three rounds chasing him around the ring, but finished with little more to show for his effort than a broken thumb.

"Even some of Paul's people who were sitting behind us got disgusted," said Big Ellen. "They said it was a terrible decision."

Less disgusted was Murphy Griffith, who had seen Paul's mouthpiece fly clear out of the ring after a left hook. The trainer wasted little time getting an introduction to the fighter's parents. Boom stayed mostly silent as most of the talking was done by Big Ellen and Griffith, a black man with a shaved head who spoke in the lilt of his native St. Thomas. Soon enough, he was led to the locker room for an audience with an anguished high school senior.

"I was so heartbroken," says Ray. "I mean, my father had come all the way to Indianapolis. I swore I was never going to have another amateur fight again."

He'd be a fool if he did, said Griffith, who argued that Ray was just too aggressive and too much of a body puncher to ever impress amateur judges. "You a *fighter*," Griffith explained. It was in the blood.

"I saw your father fight," he said.

Griffith had come to New York in the early 1940s with dreams of becoming a fighter. As it worked out, he did his best fighting for the United States Navy, winning three Bronze Stars in World War II. After thirty years in the service, Griffith retained his military bearing. His face was chiseled. At fifty-seven, he had none of the fat that afflicts men beyond middle age. He was also the uncle of Emile Griffith, the former welterweight champ, best known for killing an opponent in a nationally televised bout in 1962.

For years, Murphy Griffith had been training amateurs in the navy, most notably Duane Bobick, a white hope who'd go on to be famously knocked out by Ken Norton. But after leaving the navy, Griffith caught on with Joe Frazier's camp, where he met his current employer.

"I represent a man in New York," said Griffith. "His name is Dave Wolf."

Dave Wolf was an unlikely fight manager. He grew up on the Upper West Side of Manhattan, was educated at private schools. A high school sweetheart, Toby Falk, recalls he had a passion for basketball—he was captain of the team at Walden—but not the body for it. He had a stocky wrestler's build, and a propensity for knee injuries.

At the University of Wisconsin, Wolf became sports editor of the student paper and a UPI stringer at the statehouse in Madison. While still an undergraduate, he went to Montgomery, Alabama, to cover the civil rights movement. After earning a master's at the Columbia University Graduate School of Journalism, he accepted a job as a sportswriter for *Life* magazine, where he became best known for a story on the schoolyard sensation Connie Hawkins. From Brooklyn's Boys High, Hawkins was a harbinger of basketball's emerging style, a game to be played above the rim. However, his wrongful implication in a gambling scandal had him blacklisted by the NBA. Wolf's six-month investigation resulted in Hawkins's reinstatement and, in 1972, the publication of a bestseller, *Foul!*

Wolf's next book was to be a biography of heavyweight Joe Frazier. In preparation, he became a *de facto* member of the champion's entourage. "He was around quite a bit," recalls Duane Bobick, whose career was being handled by Frazier and his manager, Yank Durham.

"Whatever he became involved in, he immersed himself completely," says Gina Andriolo, then a law student and Wolf's girlfriend. "He had an incredible eye."

Wolf studied all that he saw. He was in Omaha, Nebraska, in 1972, when Frazier was scheduled to fight a heavy-drinking, ten-to-one underdog named Ron Stander. On a prefight tour of the Civic Auditorium ring, Durham found that a bank of TV lights were not to his liking and, in the words of one writer, "began to rage about a plot to blind Frazier."

The fight was off, said Durham.

"Whaddaya mean?" said Frazier. "The lights don't mean nothin'."

"Shut up and start puttin' your street clothes back on," said Durham.

The offending lights were turned off just moments after Frazier removed his trunks. Frazier then rerobed and took out Stander in five rounds.

The moral of the story: A good manager has to be a prick, obligated to secure every conceivable advantage for his fighter. That's not to say, however, that Durham was always a model manager.

Wolf saw how lax and overconfident Durham had been in preparation for George Foreman, a bout that saw their Frazier lose the title and go down six times in the first two rounds. Wolf also saw how Frazier, Durham, and trainer Eddie Futch lost interest in Bobick after their White Hope was knocked out in South Africa.

"I didn't know it then," Wolf would recall, "but I was serving my apprenticeship."

"I could do this job," he told Gina.

That chance arose soon enough with Bobick, who asked Wolf to manage him after the debacle in South Africa. Under Wolf, Griffith became Bobick's head trainer. He earned eight straight wins against mostly forgettable opponents, and a part in a forgettable South African movie. By the time Big John Tate knocked him out, effectively ending his career, Duane Bobick was ranked fourth in the world.

Not bad for a sportswriter. But a far bigger coup, certainly in terms of publicity, was signing Dallas Cowboys six-foot-nine defensive end Ed "Too Tall" Jones. Jones had been a passionate boxing fan, and remembered sitting on his father's lap back in Jackson, Mississippi, as they listened to the fights on radio. If his dad's guy won, he'd take Ed outside to play catch. At sixteen, Jones fought in the local Golden Gloves, and knocked out his opponent in sixteen seconds.

"Made the front page of the *Jackson Sun*," he recalls proudly.

That KO was about the greatest feeling an athlete could have and even as Jones became the first player selected in the 1974 NFL draft and a leader of the Cowboys' famed Doomsday Defense, he kept telling himself, "One day I'll get it back." That day was January 15, 1978, just after the Cowboys beat the Denver Broncos for the Super Bowl. In the midst of postgame celebration, Jones informed his agent, Don Cronson, that he was going to be a fighter.

"I need you to find me a manager and a trainer," he said.

The Cowboys thought it was a negotiating ploy, but even as Jones played out the last year of his contract, the player and his agent were auditioning trainers and managers. Ken Norton, the former heavyweight champ who beat Muhammad Ali in 1973, recommended Griffith. Cronson, a big fan of the book *Foul!*, was high on Wolf.

"I didn't want a guy enmeshed in the boxing establishment," says Cronson. "I liked that Dave was a hustler. I liked that he stood up to the NBA, and wasn't afraid to take his shot. He was also plenty media savvy. Murphy Griffith could handle the boxing, and Dave could handle what Dave was good at—the story."

It was a big one: a ferocious, oversized football player leaving America's Team to take his chances as a heavyweight, a division whose upper reaches were still considered the most rarefied territory in all of sports. The prospect of Too Tall fighting for a title generated national headlines. CBS wanted to air his debut on a Saturday afternoon telecast. But, of course. It didn't matter if Wolf was typing or managing, he was in the game for one thing: the story.

As he once told John Schulian, of the *Chicago Sun-Times*: "I wouldn't want to manage anybody I wouldn't want to write about."

That was Wolf's test. He wanted a good story even more than he wanted a champion. His plans for a Joe Frazier bio had fallen apart due to journalistic differences with his subject. So what? Now Wolf had something better: this kid Boom Boom and his father. Now *that* was a great story. Better yet, he'd have complete editorial control.

At least a couple of prominent boxing men had already taken a pass on Ray. Angelo Dundee, who became famous working Ali's corner and was now with former Olympic darling "Sugar" Ray Leonard, wasn't too impressed by what he had seen. Nor was Lou Duva, the manager from New Jersey who signed a kid named Rusty Rosenberger out of nearby Warren. Still, Wolf, bankrolled by an aspiring Long Island promoter named Jeff Levine, wasn't the sole bidder for Ray's services. Coming out of Youngstown, it was inevitable that the younger Boom Boom would attract interest from those sporting-blood types.

Chucky George was a bookmaker with a numbers business (the bug, as it was called in Youngstown). But mostly, he was a gambler, and he was willing to bet big on Ray: a weekly two hundred fifty dollars salary just to train. He'd get a car and an apartment, too.

"We'll take it," said Boom the elder.

"Dad . . ."

Maybe the kid hadn't heard. These were tough times.

"Dad . . ."

Ray wanted to know who would get him fights, who would train him, and who had the juice to make sure no one gave him the business.

Chucky George said Eddie Sullivan would train him, of course. He'd hire a booking agent. The rest would work itself out.

Ray thanked Chucky George. He wanted to hear what Dave Wolf had to say.

It wasn't much, actually, at least not compared to what the book-maker had offered. By the time he arrived in Youngstown, Wolf was well versed in the particulars of both Ray's and his father's careers. He could talk Ray Arcel and Stillman's and Sammy Angott all day long. But there would be no salary, no car, and nothing up front. Ray would get a plane ticket, Blue Cross–Blue Shield medical insurance, and, until he got on his feet, a place to sleep on Murphy Griffith's couch. His sparring sessions would be videotaped, and he'd be expected to augment his training regi-men with Nautilus machines.

"You do your job and I'll do mine," said Wolf.

"What's that?" asked Ray.

"I'll get you to the world title," he said.

That was enough for Ray, a promise that he'd get what his father never had. He'd seen what happened to all those fighters from Youngstown to Cleveland. The guys who stayed at home weren't getting many fights, much less title shots. They all became bust-outs.

Eventually, even Boom came around. He especially liked how Griffith kept calling his kid, checking on Ray's hand, how the kid was feeling.

"My trainer never called me between fights," said Boom.

"What do you think, Pop?" Ray knew what people would say: Kid left Eddie Sullivan for a shine *in New York.*

"This man in New York is showing he cares about you," said Boom. "You got to go, Raymond. You stay here, you'll starve."

But it was Lenny, a devoted fan of all the boxing magazines, who became Wolf's most passionate advocate. Lenny had read all about Dave Wolf. "This guy's making moves," he said. "This guy's strong."

Besides, Lenny already had enough of wise guys like Chucky George. He was making a living collecting their debts.

Chapter 5 | The Family Name

In mid-September 1979, the *Vindicator* ran a photo of Ray signing his contract, flanked by his proud parents and his new manager. Then, the parties adjourned for the first shot in a soon-to-be-ubiquitous publicity packet, as Ray stripped down to his trunks ("B-O-O-M" now embroidered down each inseam) while Pop raised his gloved fist for the camera. Later that day, a teary-eyed Ray would stop by General Fireproofing to say good-bye.

By the next morning, everyone in town had seen the banner headline across the morning paper: MANCINI VOWS HE'LL GET TITLE.

The piece hit on all the narrative's salient points, from Sammy Angott and the controversial decision to the wounds that earned "Original Boom," as he was now called, the Purple Heart. It noted that Ray, first photographed with boxing gloves at the age of just eight months, knew every detail of his father's career "just like I was there."

"I'm going to win the title for the both of us," said Cardinal Mooney's class president. ". . . I won't be satisfied with anything less."

The date had been already set for Ray's pro debut, October 18, at Struthers Field House. Ringside seats would go for ten dollars, four dollars for general admission. They could be purchased at locations all over greater Youngstown, including Paul Morris Sporting Goods, Steelworkers Local 1617, Creatura's Barbershop, and the Upstairs Lounge in Austintown.

Great stuff. Wolf couldn't have written it better himself.

• • •

Later that evening, Ray made an appearance at Giants Stadium, where he watched a friend from Warren, Rusty Rosenberger, get his ass kicked for the first time as a pro. Next stop was a one-bedroom in the Park Royal Hotel, 73rd Street between Central Park and Columbus Avenue. Ray put down his bags, one for his clothes, the other his gear, and Griff pointed toward the couch. It was old; that's all Ray would remember of it. The black-and-white television was old, too.

Before retiring, Griff gave him a rundown of what was expected. They'd be taking most of their meals at a diner down the block. Ray's diet would be heavy on roast chicken and steamed vegetables, with a little potato or rice now and then. The preferred breakfast was oatmeal and bananas. Eggs were to be poached. Toast would be rye or wheat. The acceptable sweetener was honey. He was expected at the gym, wrapped and ready to work by one o'clock.

Ray nodded, a little embarrassed now that Griff had taken off his shirt. The trainer was even more cut than the eighteen-year-old fighter.

"I'm not going to be here all the time," said Griff. "I'm not going to get up and tell you to do your roadwork. I'm not going to remind you about playing with the girls, or to get the proper rest. You professional now, Ray. When you get in that ring, it's your ass, not mine."

The next morning Ray ran into Central Park at West 72nd Street. He headed downtown before turning east, a path that provided a view of the world's most magnificent hotels. They stood like nineteenth-century palaces: the St. Moritz, the Essex House, the Plaza, and as he turned up Fifth Avenue, The Pierre and the St. Regis. He continued north twenty blocks, then around the reservoir, where he got a kick out of all those jogger types with their skimpy nylon shorts. Ray always wore thick cotton sweats, his sole concession to the fashion of fitness being the work boots he'd finally forsaken for a pair of Pumas. Still, none of the marathoners or 10K guys could keep up with him. Neither could the fighters.

"I could stay with him," says Randy Stephens, a cruiserweight comanaged by Wolf, "but only for about an hour."

The Times Square Gym, 145 West 42nd Street, between Broadway and Sixth Avenue, was up a flight of stairs that smelled like piss. When founded in 1976 by Jimmy Glenn, a veteran Harlem trainer, there was a tuxedo rental downstairs. By the day of Ray's arrival, Forty-deuce was America's capital of degeneracy, what with all those second-floor signs promising "Live Girls."

The fighter had abided by Griff's admonition not to stand too close to the subway tracks, else some "crazy motherfucker" shove him in the path of an oncoming train. He stared at no one before disembarking at 42nd and Broadway. Then his path was strewn with archetypes from the dawn of New York's hip-hop epoch: bums, winos, and junkies; runaways and throwaways; the pimped out and the fucked over; the horny, the wretched, the ambitious; boom-box impresarios and three-card monte dealers.

Writer Pete Hamill once called the Times Square Gym a "school and clubhouse for apprentices and champions." But it wasn't Stillman's, not quite. Like crime and politics, New York's boxing scene evolved as a story of ethnic succession. The Irish, Italian, and Jewish fighters had been replaced by blacks, Puerto Ricans, and Dominicans. Other than that, gym life hadn't changed too much. Old fight posters were peeling off the walls, which themselves were blistered and cracked. Heavy bags had been beaten into various states of misshapenness and wound with reams of silver electrical tape. There was a squeaky stationary bike, a rusty weight set, and a hissing radiator by the window. The summer's big hit, *Rocky II*, was still going strong at the RKO Cinerama up on 47th Street, but beyond the plate glass window was a twenty-five-cent peep show ("New SEXtacular, SEXciting, SEXational LOVE Acts on Stage"), and a sampling of cinema's most wicked and shameless offerings, porn, splatter, blaxploitation, and kung fu. Still, what caught Ray's eye was the OTB. He couldn't wait to tell the guys back home. In New York, the state itself took your action and kept the vig.

• • •

That night, Wolf and his girlfriend, Gina Andriolo, brought Ray to the Feast of San Gennaro on Mulberry Street. The air was redolent with the smell of frying zeppole and sausage, the night streaked with red and green neon and arcs of silver tinsel. *The future lightweight champ.* That's how he was introduced at Cha Cha's and La Bella Ferrara on Mulberry Street. Who wouldn't like this kid, thought Gina, what with his manners and his smile and the way he crossed himself? It was September 19, 1979. In Little Italy, the Patron Saint of Naples was celebrated with a mass at Most Precious Blood Church. In Youngstown, it was the second anniversary of Black Monday.

Ray swore to God he would make it or remain in exile.

He would not return home another bust-out.

"It was a scary, lonely time for Ray," recalls Gina. "It was just him and Griff. I remember giving him stamps and notepaper so he could write home."

Someone else might have considered it his great good fortune to be young and male in New York as disco merged with new wave. Studio 54, Xenon, and the Mudd Club were pantheons of promiscuity. Neither HIV nor AIDS had entered the conversation. But Ray, who never lacked for female companionship back home, was suddenly as untempted by women as he was by the three-card monte dealers on 42nd Street. A late night saw him turn off Griff's television at ten o'clock. Though still a teenager, he regarded Manhattan as a Spartan mission.

Besides, he had girlfriends back home. One of them, Lisa, now became his pen pal: *I miss you. Can't wait 'till your home . . .*

Then one day, Ray's talking to his brother. "What's up?" he asks.

"Nothing, really," says Lenny, whose marriage had already ended. "Just fucking around with Lisa a little bit."

Then Ray called Lisa. "I really like you, Raymond," she said.

"Yeah . . ."

"But I *love* Lenny."

It was Lenny. Girls loved him. Guys couldn't stay mad at him, especially not his kid brother.

"Ray wasn't a normal kid," says Ed "Too Tall" Jones. "He had no wild in him. I never heard him complain like kids do. He just stayed with Griff. I remember Griff telling me about his old man. Said, 'Ed, that was one tough character.' I believe it, too. The training in boxing is the toughest thing I've ever done. But Ray had maybe the best work ethic I've ever seen."

The Times Square Gym had seen its share of big-name fighters: Ali, Larry Holmes, featherweight champ Wilfredo Gomez, even Roberto Duran, who was now being trained by octogenarian Ray Arcel. But in those last months of the decade, the gym's drawing card, the best *story*, was Jones. Reporters came from all over for an audience with the recently retired Cowboys' defensive end, among them the local sports anchor, Sal Marchiano, who recalls a tap on his shoulder while waiting for Too Tall to finish pounding the speed bag.

"I'm going to be lightweight champion of the world," said Ray.

It wasn't strange for a young fighter to hype himself to a reporter. Rather, what struck Marchiano was the way Ray said it: a simple, declarative statement. The sportscaster gave him a once-over before returning his attentions to Too Tall.

"That's nice, kid."

"Some guys tell you 'I'm the next champ' and you say 'go fuck yourself,'" says the veteran matchmaker Bruce Trampler, who met Ray before Too Tall's pro debut in Las Cruces, New Mexico. "But this kid did not say it in a way that was offensive or annoying. He just strutted up and introduced himself. Cocky little guy, but nice, and ingratiating. You found yourself rooting for him immediately."

A week and a half later, the morning after appearing on the undercard of yet another Too Tall fight, Ray introduced himself to CBS's Mort Sharnik. They were in Phoenix, and Sharnik, the large and literate man who ran the network's boxing division, was having breakfast in the hotel coffee shop when Ray sat down beside him and quickly began telling his family saga.

"He had so much energy and enthusiasm," recalls Sharnik. "There was an ingenuous quality to him you just didn't see in fighters. And the story he told was like a good play: It had tragedy and resurrection. It could've been titled *The Redemption of Lenny Mancini*."

Lovely kid, thought Sharnik, as Ray left to tell the next person his story and its eventual happy ending. *I hope I see him down the line.*

In other words: *I hope the kid can fight.*

Within six months, Ray was 8–0. He opened before a familiar and adoring crowd at Struthers Field House with a first-round KO of Phil Bowen (hyped as 5–2 when, in fact, he was 2–6). "He got scared when I hit him with that first hook on the chin," recalls Ray. "I dropped him. He got up. I dropped him again."

In Phoenix, he dropped a guy named Lou Daniels, then 6–10, in the second round and again in the fourth. Then he heard Daniels's manager-trainer scream at his fighter: "Get up or you don't get paid!" Daniels got up, wearily, and managed, somewhat more gallantly, to lose a six-round decision. Then the Mexican fans pelted the ring with coins in appreciation of the way Daniels stood through his beating.

A less valiant loser was the 1–11 Dale Gordon, whom Ray fought back in Youngstown. "He didn't even look like a fighter," says Ray. "He looked like Charles Manson. Hit him a couple body shots, then he tanked it. That's the only fight I was ever embarrassed."

A week later, Ray went up against 4–0–1 Charlie Evans in Indianapolis. Evans introduced himself during the weigh-in. "You too small," he said. "Gonna whup your ass." Then he caught up with Griff in the elevator. "Gonna knock your boy out," he said.

"Good luck to you, son," said Griff, who couldn't wait to tell Ray, "Man, that boy is scared."

Apparently, with good reason. Eight seconds into the second

round, Evans went down for the last time. According to one account, ten minutes would elapse before he regained even a hint of consciousness.

Finally, the doctor asked Evans, of Omaha, Nebraska, if he knew where he was.

"Kansas City."

"Wake him up in St. Louis," said one of the writers at ringside.

The big problem in those first months was sparring. Ray had a hard time getting any. Before he even debuted, Wolf was paying seasoned pros ten dollars per round (a sum deducted out of Ray's future purses). It was considered a decent wage, especially for working with an eighteen-year-old kid. But it wasn't enough for pissing blood the next morning.

"Bang 'em a couple days, and they don't want to come back," says Ray.

Who could blame them? In Dallas, just a week or so before his fourth pro fight, Ray moved around with David Percifield, whose father, Paul, was a trainer and renowned cutman.

"My son was awful good," says the elder Percifield. "As an amateur, he was top five in the world at the time. He'd fought all over the world. He even got the best of Hector Camacho. He was 135 pounds, even had a style like Ray. I thought it would be good for them to spar."

A couple minutes into their first round, however, the father found himself calling it off. "I knew right then that Ray was above anything I had seen in the weight class," recalls Percifield. "My son had never been hurt before. But he just couldn't take Ray's punches."

Of course, David Percifield protested. Just the same, when Ray was gone, he would confess: "Dad, he really hurt me."

In late January 1981, Ray went to Los Angeles to work out at the famous Main Street Gym. Wolf wanted to get some exposure on the West Coast. Griff wanted to get his guy some work. "We'll finally get all the sparring we want out there," he told Ray.

Los Angeles was a great fight town, and flourishing at the lower weight classes, in which Latin fighters dominated. Among the most beloved southern California fighters was Bobby Chacon. The former featherweight champion had just lost, if gamely, to the great Alexis Arguello, but would soon avenge himself by defeating Rafael "Bazooka" Limon in a dramatic split decision at the Forum in Inglewood, California. Chacon was the kind of fighter other fighters admired, one who regarded violence as a professional responsibility. "A truly honest fighter," remarked the writer Ralph Wiley, "possibly the most honest I had ever met." Sure, Bobby had a Bentley and a charming smile and more broads than he could handle. But the esteem was rooted in his style: occasionally crafty, often reckless, always courageous. He'd take one to beat you. Hell, he'd take two, three or four if necessary. Bobby "School-boy" Chacon would've given an eye to beat Billy Marquart, too.

On the last day of Ray's productive stay at Main Street, Chacon agreed to spar with Mancini. "It was crazy that someone like that would even consider giving me a couple rounds," says Ray. "I mean, this is Bobby Chacon, one of the greats. I saw a tape of him beating Danny 'Little Red' Lopez. I read about him in the boxing magazines. And I was good that day in the gym. He worked with me, but I was coming on strong."

"A tough, energetic kid," Chacon would recall some years later. "The two rounds felt like ten." But Ray would take it as proof that he belonged.

To generate some buzz and exposure with the gaming classes, Wolf sent Ray to Las Vegas that summer to fight at the Silver Slipper, where Wednesday nights saw a crowd of seven hundred to one thousand gather in a second-floor ballroom on the Strip. "Not many tourists, but a lot of dealers and bartenders and small-time degenerate gamblers," recalls Royce Feour, longtime boxing writer for the *Las Vegas Review-Journal*. "They'd stand back by the bar and bet every fight, or every round, sometimes taking alternate corners."

Nothing those bettors saw would've discouraged them from placing a wager on Mancini. He was, like Chacon, an honest fighter: earnest, active, and easy to handicap. In his first fight, Ray "destroyed," to use the *Review-Journal*'s word, his opponent Leon Smith, as referee Richard Green counted out prospect Smithy in the first round. A week later, Ray dropped the considerably more experienced Jaime Nava in the first. But an injured knuckle caused Ray to fight one-handed for seven of the ten rounds. He won the decision, but more important, Ray was getting an education.

"Wolf really did a great job of moving him along," says Feour.

Still, the real action was back in Youngstown and Struthers and Warren, where Mancini's fights were starting to feel like homecomings, celebrations not just for the townspeople, but for what they once were.

"What else did they have?" says Gina Andriolo. "They were so hungry for something good."

Soon Big Ellen's Tupperware sales were dwarfed by the market for Boom Boom souvenirs—tee shirts, key chains, and the like—she sold out of the house at 807 Cambridge. She also did a brisk business in tickets, finding it increasingly common for customers to ask if they could pay with their unemployment and welfare checks.

Businesses on downtown Market Street were now being boarded up, she recalls, but the business of being Boom Boom was just beginning its ascent. Dave Shaffer and Mike Cefalde, both out of work, sold tickets for Wolf out of their cars. Chuck Fagan, now laid off from his mill job and getting part-time money cleaning a bowling alley, caught on as the manager's aide-de-camp in Youngstown. He started off selling round card sponsorships to local bars, then began driving Wolf, who, being a native of Manhattan, couldn't drive himself. A lot of the Youngstown guys dismissed Wolf as a toupee-wearing know-it-all from New York. And Chucky, whose union rep grandfather had been shot at in 1963, was as Youngstown as they came. However, he'd already read *Foul!* and found himself enthralled with Wolf's stories about the Munich Olympics and a Green Bay Packers running back named Jim Grabowski.

"There were times I wanted to kill the motherfucker," Fagan says of Wolf. "But I did like him. He took me under his wing and he started talking about how to promote. One of my jobs was to get all the local papers—the Warren paper, the Niles paper, and Youngstown paper—and cut out any articles on Ray. Then Dave would add them to the press kits and send them all over the world. I mean, when Ray had just six fights, we'd be at the post office for a whole hour."

Wolf made sure the fourth estate would not lack for signs of Boom Boom's imminent greatness, like his first-round knockout of 15–1 Bobby Sparks at Struthers Field House. "A good left hook to the liver," says Ray. "Felt like it came out of his back."

Then he faced undefeated Trevor Evelyn, trained by Murphy Griffith's nephew, Emile. Evelyn was counted out after a three-punch combination in the second round but recalled nothing when he finally came to in the locker room.

"I got knocked out? . . ." he asked.

Ray's next local show, with twenty-two hundred in attendance at Warren's Packard Music Hall, saw him matched with a seasoned veteran, Johnny Summerhays, who, according to the local *Tribune Chronicle*, had "earned a reputation as a master at subtly stretching the rules." Actually, he wasn't so subtle. There were some low blows and at least three headbutts. The first of them came in the fifth round, cutting Mancini's forehead and leaving him temporarily dazed.

"I didn't know where I was," he said.

The second butt, in the sixth, opened a gash above Ray's left eye. The third caused the wound to gush blood.

"It was a bad one," says Paul Percifield, who was sitting in the front row with Randy Stephens. "Once the guy cut Ray, he could see dollar signs. He became a valid opponent."

The recognition of blood is an odd moment for even the most savvy and self-possessed pugilists. He may react in desperation or acquiescence. Either way, says Percifield, "It dents his sense of invincibility."

But Ray was still a kid, which is to say his adolescent confidence was bloated yet vulnerable, and diminished with the taste of each crimson drop that trickled to his lips. "I don't want to say Ray was scared," says Percifield, "but he suddenly realized he could lose."

Worse still, his corner wasn't prepared. Nothing in Wolf's press kits even hinted this was a possibility. Griff was a trainer, not a cutman. Enter Percifield, who rushed to Ray's corner with his bag and expertly applied pressure with an epinephrine solution. The gash still bled, but at a reduced rate, not enough to stop the fight or imperil the fighter. Ray finished with a ferocious rally and a unanimous decision.

Another learning experience. Another cause for celebration. As usual, Lenny was first through the ropes to congratulate his kid brother.

By Christmas, Ray was 16–0 with thirteen knockouts. The eighth-ranked lightweight in the U.S., as *The Ring* proclaimed him, would begin 1981 at the Felt Forum, a five-thousand-six-hundred-seat theater at Madison Square Garden. After that, he expected to fight on one of ESPN's nationally televised shows. Unfortunately, Lenny's prospects as an aspiring strong-arm in rapidly deindustri-alizing Youngstown weren't nearly so flush.

"You don't have to be doing this shit," said Ray, who'd started giving him money from time to time.

"I'm your older brother," he protested. "I'm supposed to take care of you."

Just months before, as Ray embarked on his pro career, Lenny was supposed to be Wolf's man in Youngstown. That didn't last, of course. Lenny liked the idea of Wolf just fine in the boxing magazines. But he wasn't the type to drive him around, listening to Wolf opine as they licked stamps at the post office. Lenny's last known act as a member of Team Mancini came early one morn-ing when he signed a hotel bar tab, "Bang Bang."

At least the girls still loved him. There were so many, too. He'd left his first wife, had a child with another, and was living in a small apartment off Market Street with a third. "Red," he called her. She was a young thing, skinny, cute with curly red hair. She danced topless at Le Chante Clair.

And wasn't that just like Lenny? Ray thought. As a kid, he always took in strays. Lenny was like an adoption service for vagrant dogs and cats.

"What the fuck are you doing?" Ray asked him just before Christmas.

"Ahh, you know," said Lenny. "She needed a place to stay. I got a place. She's making money. We help each other out."

Disgrazia, thought Ray. Disgrace.

"Don't worry," said Lenny. "You're the fighter. You're the one going to carry on the family name."

Chapter 6 | Valentine's Day

According to documents in case no. 81–648, kept on file at Youngstown Police headquarters, the girl known as Red was named Diana Louise Kirkwood. She was born September 24, 1963, in Toledo, Ohio, of ancestry described as Irish-Indian.

She once told a hospital administrator that her parents had died of causes unknown. Her education at the local public schools concluded in the eighth grade, when she "sort of walked out." At age twelve, still the ward of her foster parents, Peter and Goldie Putnam of 316 Manhattan Boulevard, Toledo, she began compiling what police there would describe as an "extensive juvenile arrest record." In due course, Diana would use fictitious birth dates to gain employment as a dancer in several topless bars. By the summer of 1980, the Outlaws motorcycle gang brought her from Toledo—where she had outstanding warrants for receiving stolen property and forgery—to Youngstown, where it operated a safe house for members on the lam.

"It was basically a fortified clubhouse on Caledonia Street," recalls Detective Bill Blanchard, adding that the city's well-earned reputation as a wide-open town made it an ideal destination for fugitives.

A biker named Ralph Tanner broke in Diana as a prostitute. "He said he loved me and that I was his," she explained. "Then he got shot."

Next, she was bought by a fellow Outlaw called Charlie Brown, who put her to work in a Steubenville whorehouse. After about six weeks, she left and made her way back to Youngstown. At seventeen,

Diana Louise Kirkwood was 105 pounds with dyed blond hair, a twelve-inch surgical scar on her left hip, and a heart with Harley-Davidson wings tattooed above her left breast. A fake birth certificate, identifying her as Karen Sue Donovan, twenty-three, enabled her to get work dancing at Le Chante Clair, where she met Lenny.

Later, she would tell a priest "it was love at first bite," as an inspired Lenny made his way onto the stage while she danced and gave her a playful nip. Soon, Red was living in his small apartment on Market Street, a couple of blocks from the club, and Lenny was telling friends how he stole her from a biker gang.

"I loved him more than anything," she said.

By February, Red was of the impression that they would soon be getting their blood tests, prelude to an imminent marriage. Still, whatever their nuptial plans, Red and Lenny had a tempestuous relationship. It became especially volatile when she drank: typically, shots of Black Velvet with 7UP chasers.

"They were always arguing," says Dave Shaffer, who recalls Ray warning his brother that the girl was trouble. "But you couldn't tell Lenny nothing. I mean, Lenny always had a smile on his face. Didn't make no difference to him."

Everything seemed like a goof to Lenny, even the time they got into a spat at the VFW Post 93, a bar on South Avenue. That one ended with Red firing a round from a .22-caliber pistol into the ceiling.

It didn't help that the Outlaws considered her stolen property. Around the same time, she received a visit at work from a couple of the gang's molls, who claimed she owed them fifteen hundred dollars. They beat her up in front of the club.

"Next thing I know she comes running back into the bar, screaming and crying, her face was all bruised," said the bartender, Patty Bartolovich, who remembered Red grabbing a bottle and starting to swing wildly.

"I'll kill those motherfucking bitches," she screamed. "Nobody does this to me. I'll kill them."

Someone grabbed her before she could leave the club. Then she was taken to the office, and a cold compress applied to her face. Finally, as the evening ended, and Patty Bartolovich walked to her car, the bartender saw Lenny trying to console the girl: "She was all upset and crying. Lenny was trying to take her home."

On Friday, February 13, just as Red got off work, a couple of guys showed up and bought her a drink. Then one forced her downstairs at gunpoint. She was held down, slapped, and raped. This was just the beginning, they told her; soon she would be "trained"—biker slang for gang-raped.

Red's account of that night is contested, as Bartolovich said she never saw her leave the bar area. Still, Lenny believed it. She told him later that night. He said he was getting a gun.

Bartolovich saw the couple again the next evening, Valentine's Day, as the bartender returned for her shift at about six thirty. "Red just seemed to stand there in a daze," she said. But Lenny was in a great mood, talking about how he had bought his girl-friend a television.

It wasn't her only Valentine's present. After retiring to his apartment two blocks away, sharing half a joint, and making love, Lenny thought to instruct Red on the use of her other gift, a snub-nose revolver obtained from a wise-guy friend of his. It was for her protection, he said.

"We had sex in bed, then he reached over on the night stand and showed me the gun," she said. "He was going to learn me how to shoot it . . ."

"He told me to cock it back and pull the trigger. He thought it would go in the wall."

The crime scene yielded a paper bag of marijuana, one Universal Enforcer (a pistol with a large wooden handle and twelve-inch barrel), a banana clip with twenty-five .30-caliber carbine shells, a recently fired .38-caliber Smith and Wesson, and one spent shell casing.

When the police arrived, Red told them she might be pregnant or have a tumor. The gun was still on the bed. The body of Lenny Mancini lay on the floor. A postmortem examination revealed an entrance wound half an inch in diameter. It was an inch and a half behind and an inch and a half above his right ear.

At ten twenty-five, Detective Frank Mowery began taking a statement from a woman identifying herself as Karen Sue Donovan.

"I loved him more than anything," she told him. "I didn't mean to shoot him."

It was still Saturday night when Little Ellen called her brother in New York. By then, he was living a flight up from Griff, sharing an apartment with Randy Stephens. It was Stephens who heard the scream as Ray collapsed.

Randy picked him up and held him. He spoke briefly with Ellen, then called Griff, who called Dave Wolf. As they waited for Wolf, Randy read to Ray from the Book of Revelation.

Though the angle and placement of the entry wound suggested something less than innocence, Diana Kirkwood denied killing Lenny on behalf of the Outlaws. Per the second theory of the homicide, she also denied allowing them into the apartment to kill him. Finally, under questioning from Mahoning County Juvenile Court Judge Martin Joyce, she testified that her birth mother was hospitalized in Tucson, Arizona, and that her father's whereabouts were unknown.

It was Joyce who called to brief Father Tim O'Neill, believing the girl could use some counseling with a religious bent. "She didn't look like a go-go dancer," recalls Father O'Neill, who met Diana in a visiting room at the juvenile jail. "She didn't look like a murderer. She looked like a little girl: white as a sheet, shaking like a leaf. The important thing to her was that I brought her favorite candy bar. I think it was a Snickers."

Diana pleaded guilty to negligent homicide, a misdemeanor, and was remanded to the custody of the Ohio Youth Commission, where, technically, she could be held until the age of twenty-one. More likely, with evidence of rehabilitation, she'd be out in a few months. Still, the biggest factor in her merciful sentence was neither the juvenile justice bureaucracy, the priest, nor the court. It was the siblings of the man she killed.

"What do you want us to do?" the cops had asked.

"Nothing's going to bring him back," said Ray, who agreed with his sister that a vigorous prosecution and public trial would only add to the family's anguish. "I don't want my parents going through any more."

"That was very clear to us," says Ellen. "It was more about grief than revenge."

The grief was already overwhelming. Ray and his sister insisted on seeing Lenny on Monday, soon after the body arrived at Rossi Brothers funeral home. The morticians hadn't even begun their work.

"We walk into the room and they bring him in," says Ray. "He was naked except for a towel and cold as ice. Ice. His mouth was open, and his eyes weren't all the way shut. There was dried blood on his face and his mouth and on his hair. I saw where the bullet entered. I put my hands there and felt it."

Meanwhile, Big Ellen was breaking down, her tears flowing steadily since Saturday night when she had gone to St. Elizabeth's hospital and stood over Lenny's gurney, trying to talk him back to life. She had been inconsolable since having to be escorted out of the emergency room.

Not long after she returned from the hospital, a high tide of sympathy washed over the lower South Side. Tank DiCioccio got home from an evening of partying and saw his own mother weeping. Mrs. DiCioccio and Big Ellen had had an argument of unspecified nature years before. They had suddenly stopped talking to each other, and so did their younger sons. "You just didn't ask why in those days," Tank remembers.

But now, Mrs. DiCioccio told Tank that they were going across the street to pay respects to their neighbors. Mrs. DiCioccio would try to comfort her old friend. Their sons would be like brothers once more. "It was like nothing ever happened," says Tank, who read a poem at Lenny's funeral.

It was bone-chillingly cold that day, Wednesday, February 18,

1981, as mourners heard all manner of hymns and lamentations sent heavenward with the sound of Big Ellen sobbing. Still, Boom remained as he had been. "Like a rock," says Chuck Fagan. "I watched him for three days. I watched him at the Mercy dinner, and at the funeral. And he never broke, the whole time, just had this stone look on his face."

On Thursday, Chuck volunteered to take Ray to the Pittsburgh airport for his flight back to New York. Big Ellen drove him to Fagan's house, with Boom in the passenger seat. Chuck stayed in his own car as Ray said good-bye.

"I'm just sitting there," he says, "and then I hear this horrible, screeching, high-pitched sound. It was something I never heard before. Lenny was finally losing it. It was strange because the old man had this deep, gravelly voice, and he was crying as loud as a man could cry. He had his arms around Ray, hugging him real tight."

"I'll stay, Dad."

"You have to go, son."

"I don't have to go."

"You have to. You have to go now."

Looking back, says Ray, "I don't know how I ever got in that car with Chucky."

The ride to Pittsburgh seemed to take days. As he drove, Chucky looked over at Ray. He looked like he was twelve, what with the tear-streaked face. Then the flight was delayed. Chucky sat next to him until the plane was finally ready to board.

"He was lost," says Fagan. "I felt like I wanted to be his brother."

Upon Ray's return, Wolf asked him how much time off he needed. Ray told him to stay with the plan. Training was easier than grieving. Besides, if Ray was possessed of pugilistic genius, it was in his capacity to train. No one worked harder. After all, he was motivated by more than money or fame. His was a quest for family honor. But as he advanced, the stakes only got higher. It was tough enough to tell the world you're going to win the title for your father, but now his big brother had been killed. "Now he's going to win for his dad *and* Lenny?" remarks Father O'Neill, who was worried that the pressure would be too much for a still nineteen-year-old kid.

Redemption wasn't a game of chance; you couldn't double down. Or could you?

In his next fight, March 12, at Madison Square Garden's Felt Forum, Ray faced Stormin' Norman Goins, an experienced puncher who had once knocked down former Olympic gold medalist Howard Davis. "The consensus," noted the *New York Times*, "is that this will be Mancini's toughest fight in two years as a professional."

It wasn't. Ray hit him with two left hooks—first to the liver, then the head—and knocked him out in the second round.

"Just like his father," said the sage Ray Arcel, whom Wolf had conspicuously positioned at ringside. "He's going to be quite an attraction."

Also at ringside was the father himself. Less than a month after his older son's death, Boom found himself beaming with pride.

"I was awed by New York City, the buildings, all of it," recalls Chuck. "But you could see Lenny felt like he belonged there. Just the way he carried himself, the way he wore his hat, cocked just a little bit to one side, his suit. It was a burgundy pinstripe. I mean, he looked like New York in the 1940s."

Lenny Mancini was introduced in the ring that night as Boom Boom's father, the Original Boom Boom. Then, after the fights, everyone went to the bar on Seventh Avenue. Chuck studied the old-timers as they drank. There was Boom and Tony Janiro, a former middleweight contender from Youngstown whom Boom delivered to Ray Arcel. Rocky Graziano was there, too. They were wisecracking, laughing, telling stories.

At one point, though, Boom got serious. "You," he said, pointing at Janiro, "I *made* you." Then to Rocky: "And you, you were scared to fight me."

"Boom Boom," said Rock, "you were the only guy got pissed off when someone swung and missed you."

Chapter 7 | # The Kiss

Among the young ESPN's best-rated shows was a weekly collaboration with promoter Bob Arum called *Top Rank Boxing*. It was hosted by former New York sports anchor Sal Marchiano, who flew into Chicago early April 2 to conduct preliminary interviews for that night's card live from the Conrad Hilton. It was routine stuff, talking to the fighters, fleshing out their usually sketchy bios, and asking production assistants to fetch coffee. Then Ray took the photograph of his father from his wallet.

Marchiano needed a moment to recognize him, the kid from the Times Square Gym. But now he knew exactly what he had: a great story. It didn't hurt that the card, which also featured noted middleweight bleeder Vito Antuofermo, was billed as Italian Night. "We took the picture and blew it up into a full-screen shot," says Marchiano.

It was that shot, a sepia-toned fighter's pose, combined with Marchiano's voice-over, that introduced Ray to the national cable audience. "It's almost like a scenario for a John Garfield movie," Marchiano began. "It's 1942 and Lenny 'Boom Boom' Mancini is the number one contender amongst the world's lightweights. He gets a contract to fight the champion. However, he is drafted by Uncle Sam . . . The allies need him against the axis powers . . . mortar shot . . . Purple Heart . . . can't fight anymore . . .

"Now we wipe to 1981, his twenty-year-old son, Ray 'Boom Boom' Mancini, is undefeated in seventeen pro bouts, fourteen by knockout, and he says he wants to win the title that eluded his father."

Ray's opponent, Al Ford, an African-Canadian, was 54–12, and known to show well even in a loss, as he had in knocking down lightweight sensation Aaron Pryor and going the distance with then-champion Ken Buchanan. Ray wore red, green, and white trunks ("the colors of the Italian-Americans," proclaimed the ring announcer). As the fighters went forth from their corners, Marchiano informed viewers that Ray was also an honor student who wrote poetry.

"A very sensitive young man," he said.

Such sensitivity was lost on Ford, who took a merciless beating in the fourth round when he crumbled from a series of thunderous body shots, took an eight count, then upon rising, an overhand right. Within moments, Ford was being held up by the ropes, a wobbly target suspended in a velvet net. It was enough for Marchiano's color man, Al Bernstein, to remark that the ref, not the fighter, "must be unconscious in that ring."

Ford somehow managed to go the distance, losing a unanimous decision. If it wasn't close, the level of honest violence and the inexorable manner of Mancini's forward progress made for compelling television. The postfight interview wasn't bad, either.

Ray held his mother tight and blew a gloved kiss to his father, who was back in Youngstown recovering from vascular leg surgery. "I love you, Dad. That's for you," he said. "And for all of Youngstown."

"We had a new star," says Marchiano.

By then, Ray knew all about John Garfield. After just his seventh pro fight, occasioned by a Too Tall undercard in Jackson, Mississippi, fifteen months before, a reporter mentioned Ray reminded him of the movie star, who died suddenly of a heart attack in 1952.

The next day, Ray called home. "Ma," he asked, "who was John Garfield?"

How could she forget? *Body and Soul* came out in 1947, the year she met Boom. It was classic noir, and considered the first great boxing picture, with Garfield in the role of Charley Davis, whose cutthroat quest for a title shot makes him an easy mark for a mobbed-up promoter.

"So handsome," said Big Ellen. "All the girls loved him."

Of course, Sal Marchiano wasn't the only one who understood how and why Ray would resonate on television. Just a month past his twentieth birthday, Ray possessed advantages his father couldn't have conceived. With Arum signing on as his promoter, a driven manager in Wolf, and a medium that would adore him, Ray had *juice*, that mysteriously invisible elixir that protected fighters against "the business."

Arum, a Harvard-trained tax lawyer by way of Brooklyn, was a former federal prosecutor. His *Top Rank* company had spent the better part of the seventies promoting heavyweights, including Muhammad Ali, and cultivating an archrivalry with a fellow superpromoter, an ex-con named Don King. By the eighties, however, Arum had seized upon the idea that smaller weight classes would be more cost effective, and found a new niche promoting welterweights and middleweights like Sugar Ray Leonard, Marvin Hagler, Thomas Hearns, and Roberto Duran, now trained by Ray Arcel.

Assisting him in these endeavors was matchmaker Teddy Brenner. In the fifties, Brenner had turned Brooklyn's Eastern Parkway Arena into a nationally known "House of Upsets." In 1959, he went to Madison Square Garden, staying there for nineteen years until going to work for *Top Rank*.

"Wolf was telling Teddy we had to get this kid Boom Boom," recalls Arum. "And Teddy remembered the father from the forties. So he made some inquiries with people in Youngstown, which was really a mobbed-up town, and the word came back that the kid was something special."

Regarded as boxing's greatest matchmaker, Brenner understood more than the betting odds. He understood the sport's uniquely fervent sense of tribalism. Says his protégé, Bruce Trampler: "If you look at the shows he did at *Top Rank*, almost every one is a mixed match. Say, black against white, Dominican against Puerto Rican, whatever. He'd rarely put in two white guys, two black guys, or two Hispanics. It was *vive la difference.*"

In this regard, Ray Mancini was a matchmaker's fantasy. He wasn't merely *white.* Rather, his presence remedied an even greater dearth in the fight game, that eternal lack of Italian stallion class presidents from the rust belt, intent on redeeming their pug fathers. And now that Ray had a big-time promoter, he was ready to receive that highest blessing in American sports, that consecrating kiss of network television.

The history of boxing on television was an endless cycle of success and scandal, of sensation and outrage. NBC's run with Friday night fights ended not long after the Supreme Court upheld a ruling that Madison Square Garden, which typically supplied the venue, and the International Boxing Club, which supplied the fighters, were engaged in an illegal monopoly. Of course, fight fans had known for years that the IBC was a front for the mob. Back in 1953, when Ray Arcel began promoting *Saturday Night Fights* on rival ABC, he received a call telling him to "get out of the TV racket, if you know what's good for you!" Shortly thereafter, he was cracked in the head with a lead pipe after leaving a synagogue on Yom Kippur. Arcel didn't return to boxing until 1972, when he took on Roberto Duran. The game hadn't changed too much. The networks were still the networks.

For most of the 1970s, television interest centered on the heavyweights, with Muhammad Ali as the grand protagonist, around whom all storylines revolved. But as the decade wore on, Ali went into decline. An ABC tournament to identify his successor—a Don King production rife with kickbacks and phony records— ended only in scandal. Hence, Arum's decision to focus on the lower weight classes seemed especially prescient. "Each of the networks became known as specialty shops for certain weight divisions," says Arum. "CBS zeroed in on the lightweights."

Such was Mort Sharnik's design. In his capacity as "consultant" for the Tiffany network, Sharnik became what *Sports Illustrated* would call "boxing's silent kingmaker, the ultimate gray eminence . . . rarely seen, never heard, always felt." As kingmakers went, Sharnik was a decidedly big (six foot two, two hundred fifty pounds), benign, and literate one. He was himself an alum of *Sports Illustrated*, having been a feature writer and investigative reporter through some of the magazine's most glorious seasons. But his abiding interest was boxing.

Sharnik was the last man to talk to Davey Moore. That was March 21, 1963. Moore was sitting on a rubbing table in the bowels of Dodger Stadium, just minutes after losing his featherweight title in a savage fight with Cuban expatriate Sugar Ramos. Moments later, Moore called out for his trainer, Willie Ketchum: "My head, Willie! My head! It hurts something awful!" Moore then collapsed, never to regain consciousness. It was a horror, though one Sharnik wrote about well, turning in a classic piece titled "Death of a Champion."

The Moore–Ramos fight inspired condemnation across the globe, from the pope, who proclaimed that boxing was "contrary to natural principles," to Bob Dylan, who penned a famous protest song, "Who Killed Davey Moore?" Still, none of it dissuaded Sharnik from covering more boxing. "I had a good eye for it," he says. "I liked the fighters, and the fighters liked me."

Even Sonny Liston, who, during the early 1960s, was demonized as the surly Negro thug of the heavyweight division, opened up to Sharnik. "A boxing match is like a cowboy movie," Sonny told him. "There's got to be good guys, and there's got to be bad guys."

Sharnik never forgot that, as Liston's precept would inform his tenure at CBS. If ringside commentator Gil Clancy, former trainer of champions (Emile Griffith among them), saw the fighters as cute or aggressive, as boxers or punchers, Sharnik saw them as protagonists: cowboys and Indians, good guys or bad, babyface or heel.

"I looked for good stories," says Sharnik, who now remembers that kid from the coffee shop in Phoenix as a marvelous confluence of circumstance, both plot and protagonist. "Ray fought like he came out of the Forties. He was a movie fighter. 'Boom Boom' was a Hollywood production. It was John Garfield in *Body and Soul*. It was Wallace Beery in *The Champ*."

It was all of them, even those just too pedestrian to warrant Sharnik's mention: *Rocky*. And still it was more: a unique combination of innocence and arrogance. "Ray had his own feeling of manifest destiny," says Sharnik.

Mancini's first CBS fight, broadcast May 16, 1981, from the Concord Hotel in New York's Catskill Mountains, was against Jorge Morales, the world's sixth-ranked lightweight as judged by the World Boxing Council. From Ponce, Puerto Rico, Morales was said to be 27–5–1, and held the North American Boxing Federation's championship, a belt that put him in line for a WBC title shot. Play-by-play man Tim Ryan hit all the right notes to set up Mancini's network debut: telling viewers of the fighter's devotional poetry, that his father was "promised a title shot he never got," and his resultant quest, which forced Morales, who called himself "Kid Dinamita," to spend most of the first nine rounds absorbing punches with his back to the ropes. With Morales's left eye closed, with a hematoma the size of a jumbo egg on his brow, the doctor stopped the fight before the tenth round. Ray, who'd thrown an average of 110 punches per round, was hoisted into the air by exultant Youngstown friends who had stormed the ring. Next, the moment most remembered: Ray kissing his father on the mouth.

"Done!" wrote *Sports Illustrated*'s William Taaffe. "Star is born!"

"I didn't understand what the big deal was," says Ray. "I did it after every fight."

But this was national television. This was Saturday afternoon. American sons did not kiss their fathers, much less on the mouth. Unless they were Ray Mancini: "My dad used to tell me, 'You're not a man if you can't kiss your father on the mouth.'"

After the commercial break, Ryan interviewed both Boom Booms at ringside. Ray had his arm around Lenny.

"I'm going to keep this belt," he said, referring to his new NABF title, "because the world title goes to my father."

"Lenny," said Ryan, "you gotta be a proud daddy today."

The father was white-haired and still disheveled from the celebration. He wore a light blue sport jacket, an open-necked shirt with an assortment of pens in the breast pocket, and thick horn-rimmed glasses. Ray stroked his hair as he tried to answer.

"Oh yeah," said Boom. "Very proud of him."

"Did he do everything you expected?" asked Ryan.

"He done everything the way I expected." Boom had the voice of a bullfrog. "He threwed 'em. Threw uppercuts and everything. Like we talked."

"Did you throw punches nonstop like he does when you were fighting?"

"Well, ahh . . . I threw 'em fast."

"A little more," said Ray, stroking his father's hair again. "He threw more of them."

"He's much smarter than I was," said Lenny.

The exchange resonated, recalls Ryan, because "it was so genuine," which is to say televised but uncorrupted by the artifice of television. The CBS people had been around the family enough to know what was authentic, though none of them more than David Dinkins, Jr., a young producer doing pieces on Ray for *Sports Saturday* broadcasts. They played basketball and racquetball and made an occasional trip to the China Club in New York. But Dinkins's affection for the Mancinis came by way of his visits to 807 Cambridge Avenue. There, he found himself awed by the former Ellen Atreed's mastery of Italian cuisine and the amount of family-style quantities that came forth from her "itty-bitty kitchen."

"It didn't end," says Dinkins. "There was wine, manicotti, a chicken dish, then fish, and sauces with everything. I don't know how Ray ever made weight."

Still, those dinners did less for his stomach than his heart. Dinkins, whose father would be elected mayor of New York before the decade's end, came from a prominent Harlem family. He was educated at prep schools and private colleges. "Ray and I were from different worlds," he remembers. "I had absolutely nothing in common with these people. But I felt like a member of the family."

Dinkins understood the dead brother was not part of the script. Every so often, Ray would speak of him vaguely, but it was plain to see the pain was still new, and ran deep. The stoicism only ennobled Ray.

"He was the son everybody wanted to have," says Dinkins, who suddenly found himself producing a kind of family show in the guise of boxing.

"It became a phenomenon," says Sharnik, citing the ratings. "Boom Boom did great numbers."

"It had gotten beyond boxing," says Gina Andriolo. "He started getting fan mail from nuns, telling him they were praying for him. Something was happening. You could feel it. I mean, Joe Six Pack was watching on TV, telling himself: 'I wish my son could do that.' And his son was saying the same thing, 'I wish I could do that for my dad. I wish it was like that between us.'"

For all their violence, Ray's fights weren't merely redemptive. They became an affirmation of family values. Two generations of Boom Booms would invert all the time-honored clichés about television families, from Bill Cosby's to Archie Bunker's to the Cleavers. "It was like *Leave It to Beaver*," says Andriolo. "Except Beaver was knocking guys out."

Even before Morales was taken to Monticello Hospital, Wolf was campaigning to get Mancini a title shot. "His showing convinces me," said Wolf, "he's really ready to go after a world championship."

That meant going after Alexis Arguello. Not only was Arguello the WBC's lightweight champion (the WBA title, held briefly by Sean O'Grady, would soon be vacant), he was among the world's great fighters. Still, the sanctioning body, CBS, and Arum wanted a preliminary match first, with the winner to get Arguello. Hence, Mancini's next opponent would be a southpaw, Mexico's Jose Luis Ramirez. Not only did Ramirez have a record of 71–3, he had already knocked down Arguello, losing a very close split decision in Arguello's adopted hometown of Miami.

The Ramirez camp didn't mind fighting at the Packard Music

Hall in Warren, as it would only ensure television exposure and hype the rematch with El Flaco Explosivo, the explosive thin man, as Arguello was called. And if Ramirez and his handlers didn't consider the twenty-year-old Mancini a serious threat, they weren't alone.

Such was the presumption against white hopes. Oddsmakers considered fighters, not their backstories, knowing that what sounded too good to be true usually was. Now, as Ray broke into the ranks of top contenders, there was talk that his newfound fame was less deserved than contrived, scripted by Dave Wolf, sold by CBS, and bankrolled by its corporate sponsors from Michelob to Grecian Formula to Armor All. As a young black producer, Dinkins was particularly sensitive to the whispers that Ray was "another telegenic white guy who was basically a fraud."

Even Tim Ryan concedes: "We had doubts about his actual ability. How far could he go once he stepped up in class?"

Ray didn't understand why he was such a prohibitive underdog. But it pissed him off when he heard from old-school Youngstown guys that Vegas wasn't even taking action on the fight.

Once again, training camp was held in the Catskills, a vacation spot two generations of Jews referred to as "the mountains." Now the host hotel was Grossinger's. Long considered the Ritz of the Borscht Belt, its clientele had aged. Ray loved the *alter cockers*, members of a tanned and wrinkled tribe who would interrupt games of shuffleboard and gin rummy to wish him luck.

"I'm from Brownsville," they would say. "Tuesday nights at the Broadway Arena. I saw your father."

In all ways, the Catskills were an ideal training locale, endorsing his sense of destiny. Previous occupants of the training lodge included champions from Barney Ross to Rocky Marciano to Muhammad Ali. Chuck Fagan, an avid distance runner, would accompany Ray on his morning miles over the hilly terrain. By now, the inner circle was set, a cast of four: Wolf, Griff, Chucky, and Tank. At the beginning of each camp, Chucky and Tank set out to procure the training aids Griff had requested. These would include a baseball bat and a used truck tire (usually available at a gas station) for Ray to pound at three-minute intervals, until it felt as though his arms would fall off. Then there was sand, sold in fifty-, seventy-five-, and one-hundred-pound bags for sandboxes at Toys "R" Us. Griff would have them harnessed to the fighter's back, as Ray sprinted up hills and performed the requisite number of push-ups. The first task of each camp, however, was for Tank and Chucky to scour the forest and find boulders and logs suitable for Griff's regimen, which transformed Ray into a pugilistic Sisyphus, endlessly pushing boulders and logs up very steep hills.

Griff's methods might've been old school, but Ray embraced them with a sense of fidelity and duty. He never cheated on training, not a rep, much less a round. "There wasn't a person on the face of this earth who worked harder than Ray," says Fagan.

July 19, 1981: The mood in the dressing room was thick with tension, as Ray punched himself into a lather. But now, waiting on the call to march forth, it occurred to Griff that his fighter might be too coiled, his desire too great.

"This is what we all worked for," he began in his soft island accent. "Ray, you trained hard, boy. So, here's what I want you to do . . ."

Ray still sweating and snorting.

"Knock this boy's dick into his watchpocket."

It took a few moments for everyone to stop laughing. Even as Wolf got the call from the network—lights, camera, action—Tank and Chucky were still suppressing grins, wondering *What the fuck is a watchpocket?*

The event had been expertly stage-managed for television. The nefarious Roberto Duran, a huge curiosity coming off his *no más* fight with Sugar Ray Leonard, was ringside. So was one of the combatant's next opponents, the dapper and gracious Alexis Arguello. "He looks like a Nicaraguan Omar Sharif," wrote the *Chicago Sun-Times'* John Schulian, "handles himself like a diplomat, and sounds like he ought to be selling Monet originals to Palm Beach dowagers."

The fighters were joined by three thousand fans who jammed the Packard Music Hall beyond capacity. They rose to cheer with rabid gusto as Mancini entered the ring and blew them kisses.

"It's really like fighting in one of the old fight clubs," Ryan told the viewers. "The atmosphere here at this moment is electric."

Ramirez had reason to feel confident. He had Ray by more than three inches in reach and, having turned pro at fourteen, a wealth of more experience. But those advantages seemed negated by the sixteen-foot ring Wolf had written into the contract. Griff's plan to beat the southpaw was to apply constant pressure; the tiny ring ensured that Mancini wouldn't have to chase him to do it.

By the end of the second round, Ramirez's manager was complaining that his fighter couldn't get his footing, as there was no rosin tray. Actually, there was a rosin tray. But after learning that Ramirez would wear leather-soled boxing shoes (as opposed to Ray's rubber-soled ones), Wolf instructed Chuck to get rid of it.

"I put it under the ring," he says.

In truth, all the rosin in the world wouldn't have changed the outcome. By the twelfth round, three thousand fans were standing, punctuating their "Boom! Boom!" chants with staccato claps. Without taking a backward step, Mancini easily outboxed and outpunched Ramirez for a unanimous twelve-round decision. The referee had it 120–108. The two judges saw the fight 119–110 and 119–112.

"We learned something," says Tim Ryan. "Mancini was better than we thought. He was in great condition. He threw eight million punches a round, and he never backed off."

At fight's end, Ray prowled the ring looking for his father. "Dad!" he called. *"Dad!!"* Finally, Lenny was helped through the ropes. The ensuing kiss elicited another round of applause. At twenty, Ray would have his title shot against the great Alexis Arguello.

"Just to be in the ring with him is going to be a great opportunity, a great thrill," Ray told Tim Ryan. "If God willing, I beat him, it will be the greatest thing in my life."

Then Arguello himself appeared in the ring, resplendent in a navy blazer with peaked lapels and a striped tie. "I hope it will soon be my pleasure," said Arguello, responding to the interviewer's question about Mancini. "He demonstrated to his people he's a great, great fighter."

It was uncommonly gracious for life in the ring. But even as Ryan ended the broadcast and kicked it back to Brent Musburger in New York, there was reason to wonder if the challenger was too awestruck for his own good. Almost a head shorter than his opponent, there was something perilous in all the good manners, in the beaming, fawning way Ray kept thanking the man who would try to separate him from his senses.

The championship bout would be held October 3, 1981, at Bally's Park Place in Atlantic City. Arguello was 72–5, and a three-time world champion. Ray remembers a reporter asking if he was ready after only twenty fights.

"Why don't you ask my father how many title shots you get?" he said.

In private, the question made him fume. "I beat the number six contender," he says. "I beat the number three contender. What am I supposed to do? Say 'no thanks'? How the fuck can you call yourself a fighter and say no to a world title? How is anyone going to believe in me, if I don't believe in myself?"

This belief was Mancini's essence, of course, even if his supporters couldn't all share it. "This is a hurt business," says Dinkins. "It isn't like missing a putt or a foul shot or getting struck out. You can get hurt bad."

Dinkins wasn't merely concerned for his friend's health, but for his confidence. He knew anything that fractured Ray's belief could fracture the man, as well.

"When you get that close to somebody," he says, "you feel for him."

For his part, Sharnik recalls imploring Wolf not to take the Arguello fight. There were plenty of good lightweights, he argued, but this test was too soon for Mancini. Wolf would hear none of it.

The manager was many things: a control freak, a unique combination of neurosis and arrogance, ferocious in defense of his fighters, but insecure about himself. The slightest disagreement would cause him to whine, "I guess you guys don't need me anymore." Even his admirers would agree: Dave Wolf was a huge pain in the ass.

"He would drive people absolutely mad," says Arum.

His West Side apartment was stocked with a seemingly inexhaustible supply of pills, for his sinuses, his ulcer, his anxieties, his migraines. There was also pile upon pile of magazines. "Every issue of *Sports Illustrated* that ever came out," says Fagan, who recalls Wolf telling him he needed a lift to the barbershop.

Only two problems with that. They were training for Arguello at Grossinger's, and the barbershop was 120 miles away in Brooklyn. Second, Wolf wore a none-too-convincing toupee, a fact that Chucky, Tank, and Ray would note with some mirth behind the manager's back. Still, Fagan drove him—two hours in traffic before Dave mysteriously got out somewhere in downtown Brooklyn—for the same reason he couldn't tell Wolf to send his hair by UPS. He knew, as they all did, that Wolf had Ray's back.

Negotiations for the Arguello fight were painstaking, as Wolf argued points that no one had ever heard before. He broke everything into strict intervals: how many minutes and seconds Ray would have to put on his robe, to make his entrance, to warm up. He marked off the number of steps from the dressing room to the ring, with right and left turns written into the contract. The national anthem could not exceed an allotted time. Should the network balk at any of his demands, Wolf had a standard response:

"Put on a movie," he'd say. "Fight's off."

Training for Arguello went well, with Ray sending sparring partners home at an alarming rate. There was the Dominican champ who left with a couple of cracked ribs, the two-time Golden Gloves winner who split after three days, and the guy whose eyes looked like a raccoon's after some ring time with Mancini. His most reliable sparring partner, according to *The Ring*, "a game kid from Mexico," took to "wearing a ply of foam rubber around his tender middle."

Just the day before, Wolf had threatened to pull out, objecting to the use of Mexican "Reyes" gloves. "We have a contract that says these gloves will not be used," he said. "If they are, he won't fight."

The Reyes gloves were scrapped in favor of Everlast. But Wolf, upset about the selection of two Hispanic judges and a Puerto Rican referee, kept threatening until Brent Musburger came on at four thirty and informed viewers that the show would go on. CBS's taped lead-in began with the champion's take on his opponent: "He has the stronger ambition to give his father something life has taken away from him."

"This is the moment I waited for all my life," countered Mancini. "This is the chance my father never got. I'm here to do it for him and after this we'll be one happy family."

Salvation through violence. What could be better? The network was happy, as were the sponsors, whose commercials extolled the virtues of Budweiser, Mr. Coffee, and Republican tax cuts. Even Boom, sitting in a wheelchair at ringside while recovering from bypass surgery, had reason to feel encouraged by the way the fight started.

At first glance, the opponents didn't look evenly matched: a praying mantis versus a waterbug. The graceful Arguello was almost a head taller, with a seven-and-a-half-inch reach advantage. Ray appeared to be crouching even when he wasn't.

Through the middle rounds, Ray did more than hold his own. He was getting inside behind his jab. He was scoring with hooks to the body and the head. He was even connecting with right hands. What's more, he demonstrated a great chin, able to absorb Arguello's viciously precise hooks without any tremor in his legs. "I think Arguello was absolutely mystified that this kid was holding him at bay," says Ryan.

By the ninth, Arguello's eyes had begun to blacken. The challenger was beginning to tee off, pushing the bigger man back into the ropes. By now, Ray's own corner had begun to believe their man could actually win.

Then, with Arguello pinned and the round coming to a close, the fighters clashed heads. Arguello pawed at his eye, as if to look for blood. Was it con artistry or capitulation? Ray would never know. Determined to outgentleman the gentleman, he stopped fighting. Instead of pressing his advantage, Ray found himself apologizing just before the bell sounded, relinquishing the moments of his greatest advantage. It was good manners, but in the fight game, a cardinal sin.

"He had been so respectful of me and my father," says Ray. "He was one of my heroes growing up. To be honest, I didn't know what to do."

"Griff went berserk in the corner," says Fagan. "Fucking berserk."

After eleven rounds, the fight was even on the judges' scorecards. But as it went into "the championship rounds," Arguello's advantage was beyond quantification. At the end of the twelfth, he put a right hand on Mancini's chin. Ray's head swiveled and his legs buckled, as if to curtsy, but he didn't go down. Instead, as the blow rendered him momentarily stupid, he walked off to the nearest corner, which just happened to be his. Only then did the bell ring.

By then, Ray had a small cut over his left eye, and a deep laceration in his mouth. He was swallowing a lot of blood, though earning great credit as he did, leaping off his stool to run at Arguello for the fourteenth round.

"He may not walk out of the ring with the championship of the world," said Gil Clancy, "but he's a champion as far as I'm concerned."

"He's won my heart," said the other color man, former WBA champ Sean O'Grady.

Then, as if taking his cue from the broadcast, Arguello connected, in succession, with a leaping left hook, a right to the solar plexus, another left hook, and a long, straight right that sent Ray to the canvas. Referee Tony Perez quickly stopped the fight. Mancini had been stopped for the first time.

It seemed as if Big Ellen was first in the ring, tears streaming down her face as she sought to comfort her son. She wasn't alone, though. Tank, who also found himself crying, was struck by the number of adults who were suddenly weeping.

"I want to apologize to the people of Youngstown," said Ray.

Later, in the dressing room, he would tend to the more diffi-cult part. His bid for redemption—to save all the Mancinis—had ended in humiliation. He got what his old man never had, only to fail in a way Boom never did. Couldn't even finish on his feet. That's how Ray looked at it. Thirty stitches were needed to close the gash behind his lip. But his mouth didn't hurt, not really. It's not pain fighters fear. It's shame.

"I'm sorry, Dad."

Now Ray put his head down and began to weep. Boom took him in his arms. "Don't you apologize for nothin'," Boom told him. "You fought great."

That was the consensus, of course. Even as he wept, Ray was bigger, better, and more marketable than ever. *CBS Sports Satur-day* recorded a rating of 9.7 that day, a number that translated to almost a million televisions. He'd been blessed. And as Ryan con-ducted the postfight interview, it was the mellifluously accented Arguello who pinched Mancini on the cheek, assured him he'd be a great champion, and delivered the kiss.

"I love your father," said Arguello. "That's the most beautiful thing you have."

Chapter 8 | Title Shots

There is great concern for a slugger in the wake of his first loss by knockout, as that maiden voyage into fistic insentience punctures his self-belief.

"If they're tested prematurely, it kills some kind of fire in them," says Sharnik. "They become blighted—unconsciously, of course—and unable to take the next step. They start thinking 'What if?' Like, 'What if I throw the left, and he counters me?'"

Or, *What if I get knocked out?*

What if . . .

As this creeping self-doubt tends to afflict big punchers (given to delusions of invincibility early in their careers) more than the craftier boxers (who've already been forced to acknowledge their limitations), one feared the worst for a twenty-year-old like Ray. To that point, he had considered only destiny, not consequence. Sure, bad things happened in the ring, but only to other fighters. Freddy Bowman, for example, Ray's long-time rival in the amateurs, had been knocked out in the same ring where Arguello TKO'd Ray. Now Bowman, from the east side of Youngstown, lay comatose in the Mahoning County Nursing Home, where he would eventually expire, in 1982, thirteen months after the fight.

Ray was saddened by the news, but willfully ignorant of the details. Truth was, he didn't want to know anything about Freddy Bowman's death. It wasn't insensitivity. It was self-preservation. Still, Ray's handlers wondered how long before he started pondering the what-if question. Ray's sense of his mission might've bordered on the divine, but at some point he'd start wondering,

103

"Where but for the grace of God go I?" For a fighter, the only thing worse than getting knocked out, is having time to think about it. Hence, the decision was made to get Ray back in the ring as soon as possible.

By December 26, when he knocked out journeyman Manuel Abedoy in the second round of an ESPN show in Atlantic City, he was already signed to fight Ernesto Espana, the WBA's number-one contender. If he couldn't have Arguello's WBC belt, he'd go after the World Boxing Association title.

"That's when a lot of the fun started," says Arum. "I was pretty well connected with the WBA."

Boxing in the 1980s was no less corrupt than it had been in the 1940s and '50s, when the conspiracies emanated from mafia figures like Frankie Carbo and Blinky Palermo. But if the old IBC represented organized crime, then the WBC and the WBA were disorganized ones, more closely resembling banana republics. The WBC operated out of Mexico City, and its president, a Don King ally named Jose Sulaiman, considered his title a lifetime position. The WBA, with headquarters in Panama City, had titular presidents in Rodrigo Sanchez and Venezuela's Gilberto Mendoza, who won the office he still holds with Arum's backing. But the real power was a Puerto Rican manager, Pepe Cordero, a fat man with good taste in suits.

"Looked like a hit man," says Ray.

Hall of Fame trainer Emanuel Steward and his lawyer once traveled to San Juan for an audience with Cordero, hoping to get their fighter a title shot. The meeting began with Cordero putting a gun on the table between them.

"Now, gentlemen," he said, "how can I be of service to you?"

All told, a 1980 title shot for Steward's guy, lightweight Hilmer Kenty, cost $300,000.

It was a bargain compared to what Cordero charged Arum, who'd bristle at the oft-stated charge that he controlled the sanctioning body. "There's one bagman in the WBA and that's Pepe Cordero," he told an interviewer from *The Ring*. "And anytime you want a fix in the WBA you 'bribe' Cordero and he takes care of it . . . It's bullshit that I control the WBA. When I want something done I have to pay off Cordero also."

Shortly after New Year's 1982, Espana backed out of his January 23 fight with Mancini to face the new champion, Arturo Frias. Apparently, Cordero had prevailed upon the WBA to grant Espana, whom he managed, an immediate title shot. This left Mancini without an opponent, and more important, a direct claim to a title shot.

Instead of fighting Espana—the five-eleven number-one contender he had prepared for—he got short, fast Julio "El Diablito" Valdez. It was difficult to look good against a guy like Valdez, a sturdy-chinned Dominican with a good right uppercut. But Ray eventually sent his mouthpiece flying with a left and knocked him out in the tenth.

A week later, Frias beat Espana at the Olympic Auditorium in Los Angeles. After an accidental headbutt opened a huge gash below Frias's left eye, the fight was stopped in the ninth with the champion ahead on all the judges' cards. Now it was widely supposed that Mancini would fight Frias, as that was the bankable fight for CBS. But Cordero appealed to the WBA, claiming that the gash had been caused by a punch, not an accidental butt, and that his fighter should be declared the winner or get an immediate rematch.

"So, we went to the WBA executive committee, go through the tape frame by frame, and *prove* it was a headbutt," says Arum.

The committee's esteemed members remained unconvinced. "The *banditos*," as Arum likes to call them, "told me to go to Puerto Rico and work out a deal with Pepe."

Said deal was payable by check to Cordero's company, Salinas Productions. It included $250,000 for Espana to step aside and allow Mancini to fight Frias. If Mancini won (his purse would be $100,000), Espana would get yet another title shot for another quarter million.

"Cordero took me to the cleaners," Arum testified years later. Half a million bucks and Pepe didn't even have to show his gun.

• • •

Training camp for the Frias fight was held in Tucson, Arizona, where Mancini's crew stayed at a Howard Johnson's and trained a few blocks away in a local gym. If Ray's sense of pure purpose insulated him from most distractions, Chuck Fagan was a nervous wreck. He wasn't concerned about Frias, not with the way Ray was taking out sparring partners. He was worried sick that the title shot itself was jinxed.

First Ray hyperextended an elbow. Then came word that Frias, still recovering from the headbutt he suffered against Espana, kept getting cut in sparring. Such news convinced Chuck that a cancellation was imminent.

Finally, one afternoon at the gym, Chucky gets a tap on the shoulder.

It was a Tucson cop, who explained that they just got a call from the Howard Johnson's, where two Hispanic males—one with a handgun, the other toting a rifle—were reportedly looking for Ray.

"You have any idea why?" asked the cop.

"I have no fucking idea, officer."

Chuck and Ray then returned to the hotel with the cop and spoke to the chambermaid. "She said a guy came up to her on a second floor balcony and asked where Mancini's room was," recalls Fagan. "She said she pretended not to know anything, but they kept asking her questions. Finally, they went to their car and she saw a third guy. He was the driver. She said he had a rifle, too."

That night, Chuck told Ray, "We got to call Wolf, tell him what happened."

"No, I don't want to get him upset."

"We have to."

"No, he'll want SWAT teams on the roof," said Ray. "He'll call out the fucking National Guard."

It was as close as Ray and Chuck ever came to blows. But Ray was the boss. They didn't call Dave. Then, as they got ready for bed, Ray heard something outside the door of their suite.

"Jumped about five feet in the air," recalls Fagan, who told Ray to go to hell and promptly called Wolf, who said he was calling the National Guard and getting a SWAT team to follow Ray while he did his roadwork. He also had them go to Vegas, where they would share a suite at the host hotel, The Aladdin. Given the circumstances, it was prudent to finish training camp in a city where they knew the gangsters.

Neither the aim nor the identities of those rifle-toting male Hispanics ever became clear. At first, Ray and Chuck thought they could've been Pepe Cordero's boys. But Cordero had an interest in Ray's victory, as it would ensure a payday with Espana. Maybe they were Mexican Mafia. Or, perhaps, just guys from East LA who had money on their homeboy, Frias.

Chucky didn't know who they were, but he knew who to call. There was no shortage of expatriate Youngstowners in Vegas, some of them wise guys who had found employment at the Tropicana. "I had two friends of mine brought guns over," says Fagan.

They were .38s. He kept them in a duffel bag with his dirty laundry, and never told Ray. The kid was ready to blow as it was. "I don't know anything about guns," he says. "But I could figure out how to shoot one."

Once they had arrived in Vegas, Ray's distractions were minimal. Even Wolf was eventually pacified. "I'll never forget it," says Arum. "He was driving everyone crazy. So much so that Teddy Brenner, who'd seen it all, couldn't take it anymore and called somebody in Youngstown"—a veteran wise guy, no doubt—"and that person called Wolf and told him that unless he stayed in his room and didn't say a word for the rest of the promotion, he wouldn't be around anymore."

Meanwhile, Mancini had been honed into great shape, mostly by a game young featherweight named Freddie Roach. Also the son of a fighter, albeit a domestically abusive one, Roach refused to acquiesce as Ray's other sparring partners had. It was the best and most arduous preparation Ray had endured since sparring with his own brother at the Navy Reserve gym.

Speaking of which, it struck Tank DiCioccio that Ray had gotten a perm just before the fight. Lenny got a perm the week before he died. Coincidence? Probably. But the closer it got to the title bout, the more the inner circle of Mancini family and friends thought of Lenny. On the eve of the fight, his presence could almost be felt in certain suites of The Aladdin hotel. It was unmistakable, unspoken, and again, edited out during preproduction.

That's not to say CBS didn't do an especially artful job. Mancini–Frias was framed as a continued celebration of the virtues displayed in Mancini–Arguello. In fact, Arguello made a guest appearance at ringside. Especially dapper in a white suit and Panama hat, he predicted a Mancini victory.

By now, Ray's story was known to millions. "This has been my life's mission," he said. ". . . So I can look at my father in the later years and know that I've finally given him the thing in life I wanted to give him." The unexpected star of the prefight production was Frias, who came on camera with a flannel work shirt and a semifresh wound on the bridge of his nose.

"We still go to church every Sunday," he told Tim Ryan.

At twenty-one, Frias had married a widow with two daughters and took them in as his own. Now, when he wasn't sweating in the gym or bleeding in the ring, his days were spent ferrying his girls to and from practices and games. His youngest had recently snagged a game-clinching rebound, he explained, and the older one was just selected captain of the cheerleading squad.

"That's where my happiness is, with my family," said Frias.

Now twenty-five, this self-described "kid from the barrios" had a house and a car and figured he was three fights away from being able to send his daughters to UCLA and give them the education he never had. He was dedicating the fight to the girls and their mother, of course.

In Frias, America had yet another knight in the crusade for family values. If he was no less valiant than Ray, his valiance was to be short-lived.

"These are two of the finest young men I've met all the years I've been in boxing," began Gil Clancy, noting the shame that "only one of them is going to walk out as champion of the world today."

To most people, that translated as, *too bad Frias has to get his ass kicked.*

Here, then, as Ray crashed into the ropes just seconds after the opening bell, was the unimagined possibility.

"Oh, shit," thought Chuck.

"My fucking heart," says Tank, "almost fell to the ground."

"A thousand deaths," said Boom.

As it happened, the father had taught his son a means of escape. *Spin 'em, spin 'em,* Boom would say. And as Frias moved in to attack, that's exactly what Ray did: ducking and grabbing his opponent above the right elbow and turning him. In a split second, the fighters had exchanged places. Now Frias's back was on the ropes. What followed wasn't subtle, but it was entertaining.

"Possibly the single most concussive round in ring history," wrote the *Los Angeles Times*'s Richard Hoffer. "An eternity of violence, blows non-stop, bombs bursting every second."

Ninety seconds into the fight, Ray had a cut above his left brow. Frias was a bloody mess, though most of it coming from a gash on his cheek and the bridge of his nose. In the third minute, Ray floored Frias with a left hook.

"Place goes apeshit," says Ray. "I feel a surge."

Frias rose at the count of seven, with referee Richard Green inspecting the fighter before allowing him to continue. It was the correct decision. Surely, the champion had something left.

Unfortunately for Frias, Ray wouldn't let him show it. What followed the fight's resumption were thirty-six unanswered blows. As the onslaught began, mere eagerness gave way to frenzy, with Ray hauling off, throwing roundhouse punches and Frias again on the ropes. Frias's last moments as a champion were helpless ones. Green stopped the fight with six seconds remaining in the round. Those six seconds might've put as many years on Frias's life. "I don't care how many seconds were left," said the referee. "I looked into Frias's eyes and they were going round and round. I notice he didn't complain when I stopped it."

In Ray's recollection, Green's raising of his hand initiated something almost biblical. "Like the parting of the Red Sea," he said. In fact, it was a human deluge. Suddenly, it felt as if all of Youngstown were there in the ring: Chucky and Tank, who, like Ray, kept flashing on Lenny, and Tank's brother, Jumbo, and Chris who owned the all-night diner and Congressman Williams and Father Tim and Little Ellen who was weeping, convulsing with joy.

"The ring almost collapsed," she says.

Ray kissed his parents and held them tight. Then he, too, began to sob.

"I have finally served my one purpose in life," he said.

Boom's boy was the champ. The Aladdin's sportsbook could have given you odds on the fight, but not the journey: from Bagheria, Sicily, to Las Vegas, Nevada, from regret to redemption, a cure for the family curse.

"I wish my father was alive to see this," said Boom.

The weeks that followed the Frias fight felt like an extended coronation. Upon their return home, the Mancinis were taken by motorcade down Market Street, which was lined with thousands of screaming fans. Mayor George Vukovich presented Ray with a key to the city and thanked him for always plugging Youngstown in the press. A street near Cardinal Mooney was renamed Ray Mancini Drive. Finally, the new champion himself, who had come to consider jewelry and clothes his only vices, commissioned a local merchant to make a crown jewel, a gold piece with "Pride of Youngstown" written in diamonds.

That's what they called him. That's what he liked to be called. Still, by the spring of '82, even as Mancini's procession came down Market Street, there was a sense that Youngstown's favorite son now belonged to the world.

As the *New York Times* declared: "Mancini has the ebullient boy-next-door personality and exciting nonstop punching style to become a superstar." Actually, the way the storylines were falling into place, he could become more. The day after Mancini won the title, Sugar Ray Leonard went in for surgery to repair a partially detached retina in his left eye. If the speculation were true — if Sugar had thrown his last punch — Mancini would become the most marketable star in the game. He already had a sponsorship deal with Sasson jeans. Now he was ready for something bigger, more mainstream, say, Coke or Pepsi. Madison Avenue always favored ebullient boys next door. But wholesome white kids who could punch were especially rare. At twenty-one, Ray was that most anomalous form of boxing life: a happy fighter, the pug without pathos.

Just weeks into his reign as champion, he flew with his family to Italy, courtesy of *Top Rank* and Italian promoter Rodolfo Sabbatini. Seeing his parents in business class, fiddling with the headphones, asking if the drinks were really free, added immeasurably to Ray's sense of accomplishment.

"It made me feel I was a good son," he says.

They landed in Milan, where Ray did an interview show. Then it was on to Bagheria, Sicily, ancestral home of the Mancinos and the Cannazzaros. Now, for the first time, they met Aunt Pietra, Uncle Vincenzo, cousin Leonardo, who was in the computer business, and a smoking-hot interpreter named Marina.

"I explained that I was the grandson of Nicola Mancino," says Ray. "And they made me feel like I was home grown."

The townspeople told him they would get up at four in the morning to watch him fight on television. Now, they would honor Ray with a feast that ended around that time. The following afternoon, the new champ appeared on a balcony from the local city hall to wave at fans and family.

"The whole town was there," recalls Ray. "I felt like the pope."

The Espana fight was set for July 24 at Warren's Mollenkopf Stadium, a high school football facility that could accommodate more than twenty thousand fans with folding chairs arranged on the field. Top tickets were priced at $100, until Ray protested to Arum and Wolf's money guy, Jeff Levine.

"You can't do that," he said. "These people can't afford it."

The adjusted price scale, with tickets running between ten

and fifty dollars, would ensure a massive gate. "This is the biggest event we've ever had here," said one local official, who expected the fight to generate up to eight million dollars for the Warren-Youngstown economy.

The idea of Boom Boom as an agent of relief was already part of the storyline. According to the U.S. Department of Labor, Youngstown—ground zero in America's industrial recession—led the nation in joblessness. Unemployment would reach 21 percent that summer. But this depression wasn't merely economic. As Boom Boom became ever more symbolically potent, a personification of milltown virtue, life in the Mahoning Valley became more wicked.

The political climate went from merely corrupt to literal lawlessness. Where else in America would the chairman of the county Democratic Party call police to arrest FBI agents for trespassing at a mob boss's restaurant? Never mind that the party boss had been caught on tape at Jimmy Prato's Calla-Mar Manor. So had Mayor Vukovich and the county treasurer been heard on surveillance equipment the feds had planted at Calla-Mar.

Then there was the sheriff, Jim Traficant, already the subject of a federal grand jury investigation. Traficant would admit taking $103,000 in campaign contributions from Charlie Carrabia, the Cleveland mafia's man in Youngstown. He'd also admit taking $55,000 from Pittsburgh's guy, Prato, although he claimed to have returned that sum. Unbeknownst to the sheriff, however, a Carrabia associate named Joe DeRose had taped their meetings. Those tapes eventually found their way to the FBI, and Traficant was indicted for bribery and tax evasion.

Defending himself at trial—another humiliating spectacle for Youngstowners—Traficant argued that the bribes he took were part of his one-man sting operation, his grand strategy to play the Pittsburgh and Cleveland factions against each other and finally rid Mahoning County of its mafia scourge. Jurors believed enough of it to acquit Traficant. Of course, his case—not to mention his subsequent election to Congress—was helped immeasurably by Carrabia's disappearance and DeRose's murder.

DeRose had been the tenth killing in a mob war between the Pittsburgh and Cleveland for control of the Youngstown-area rackets. Ten murders over several years did not, in itself, make a crime wave. But news of the dead gangsters, like news of corrupt politicians, set a tone. Like Boom Boom Mancini, they, too, represented something larger to the locals. Things were bad enough when the mills were running and people were fighting over the spoils. Now they were fighting over the scraps.

"People just got a lot meaner," remembers Tank DiCioccio. "Everybody was on edge. That's what happens when you don't have work and you don't have food."

The population of Youngstown proper decreased from almost 133,000 to 115,000 between 1979 and 1981. Assault numbers went up for five straight years, beginning in 1977, the year Sheet and Tube shut its doors. By 1982, assaults had almost doubled, from 573 to 1,133.

Meanwhile, Mike Cefalde and Dave Shaffer were driving around town selling tickets for the Espana fight. "The office," as they referred to it, consisted of three steel lockboxes in the trunk. In one box, there were tickets. Incoming cash was stashed in another. The third held a loaded .45-caliber automatic.

"You didn't need nothing to carry one," says Cefalde, "so I just told the cops: 'I ain't paying back that money if someone tries to rob me.'"

The ranks of aggravated Youngstowners apparently included old Boom himself, who finally, the day before the fight, got in Wolf's face. Apparently, Ray hadn't told the manager he was taking his parents to mass at St. Dominic's. With his star's whereabouts unaccounted for, Wolf was about to file a missing persons report.

"Don't you ever," said Boom, poking two fingers into the manager's chest. "Don't you ever" — poke — "ever" — poke, poke — "get my kid upset before a fight."

As Boom could still be scarier than your average Youngstown wise guy, Wolf again made himself scarce until fight time. Besides, all the prep work for Ray's first title defense had already been done. Once again, Ray had trained, in the words of *Sports Illustrated's* Ralph Wiley, "as if he were preparing for a holy war."

Griff had him do countless push-ups and sprint sixty-degree inclines with ninety-pound sacks of sand on his back. He had him bash truck tires with a baseball bat for four-minute rounds. The ring had been imported from Indiana's Market Square Arena, as per Wolf's specifications. A mere eighteen by eighteen feet, it favored Ray. "You don't like it?" said Wolf. "Play a movie."

No sooner had the ring been assembled, than Wolf dispatched Chucky and Tank for a reconnaissance mission. The fight would go off under a high, hot July sun. And though the ring itself would be canopied, Dave would make sure Espana had the corner unprotected by shade, with the sun right in his eyes.

That same day, a crowd of 2,500 attended a Mancini pep rally at Warren G. Harding High School. "The All-American boy, with a touch of mozzarella," said Irving Rudd, *Top Rank's* PR man. Rudd was an old-school publicist, which is to say equal parts vaudevillian and gray eminence. His first press release, it was said, had been occasioned by Cain and Abel. Fetching young women were known to hear him say: "If half the horses I bet on were in as good shape as you, I'd be a millionaire." Still, as it concerned Mancini, Rudd's unabashedly cornball conception charmed even the most grizzled and irascible fight correspondents.

"A pep rally for a boxer," marveled the *New York Times's* Mike Katz. "Cheerleaders for round card girls. Marching bands and 'victory pasta pie.'" The concession stands, operated by Harding's Panther Moms and boosters from rival Western Reserve High, would sell popcorn and lemonade with a selection from Big Ellen's line of Boom Boom souvenirs, including shirts, sweatbands, seat cushions, and posters.

It was more than a PR stunt (though it was that, too). The manner of celebration hearkened back to a time before the mills had closed, before the corrupt nexus between crime and politics had

rendered Youngstown the butt of more jokes. Mancini's major-
ettes signified a temporary suspension of the cynicism, a moratorium on the ever shitty news.

"It sounds corny to say that Ray saved the town," says Tank.
"But that's kind of what it felt like. Ray came along at the exact
right time. People actually had something to look forward to."

"It was such a down time, we were being called a ghost town,"
recalls Little Ellen. "Ray was like this bright light."

"Everybody there wanted to be part of it, to have some of that
reflected glory," says Gina Andriolo, who recalls Mrs. Bagnoli, the
seamstress, working on Ray's robe for the fight. "It was like she was
making a wedding dress."

For Youngstown's last virgin.

The crowd, which CBS estimated at nearly twenty thousand, was
especially impressive as viewed from the network's aerial camera.
Any outdoor fight feels like a profane revival meeting. But this
was an undulating mass, in terms both literal and metaphoric,
swelling with devotion for its champion, who entered the ring
in Mrs. Bagnoli's hooded robe, white silk with red trim. The
fans included a great number of shirtless men, who, no doubt,
had tried to cool themselves with something other than lemonade. Temperatures were in the high eighties—"hotter than hell,"
recalls Little Ellen—by fight time, shortly after *Sports Saturday*
went on at four thirty.

Espana entered the ring squinting, almost painfully, it seemed,
into the oncoming sun. The WBA's perennial number-one contender was almost five-eleven with a six-inch reach advantage.
"Like a giraffe," marveled Gil Clancy. "His legs are almost as tall
as Mancini."

It was interesting, then, to see Ray begin by outjabbing the
longer man, throwing stiff, high leads that established both pace
and dominance. Then came the usual Mancini body punches,
an assortment of rights and long left hooks directed to the organ
meat, liver, and kidneys.

"I started ripping those shots to the body and I heard him moan," said Ray. "I knew it was just a matter of time."

The third round saw Espana land some uppercuts and a good short right, but to little effect. By the fourth, Pepe Cordero's man was weak in the legs. After round five, wrote Wiley, "Mancini looked over his shoulder to see if Espana would make it to his stool."

At the end of six, Ray was battering him on the ropes. But even as Espana's corner threw in the towel, no one seemed to hear the bell. Referee Stanley Christodoulou stopped the fight, with Espana taking four punches after the sixth round. It didn't make much difference. He was done anyway.

Espana immediately announced his retirement. "Maybe he should have retired before," said Cordero, "but he made a couple of nice paydays."

If Espana was finished, Ray was still at the beginning of something glorious. With an arm around his father, he told Tim Ryan: "We're gonna be around for a while."

Among the throng of cheering, if still-shirted fans, was Sylvester Stallone. His debut as John Rambo, a Vietnam vet who'd returned from Southeast Asia as a one-man vigilante squad, would not be released for months. But *Rocky III* was still in theaters. Taking in almost $130 million in U.S. box offices, it would be the fourth-highest grossing picture of 1982. In addition to a chart-topping theme song, "Eye of the Tiger," it transformed a former bouncer calling himself Mr. T into a cultural icon.

"If we do a *Rocky IV*," Stallone told the delighted crowd, ". . . we'll do it here."

As it pertained to popular culture, Youngstown wasn't different from the rest of America. Fans observed little if any distinction between Stallone and Rocky. Now, his presence in the Mancini fable blurred the lines between sport and entertainment, fighting and acting, fantasy and reality.

In a matter of days, Ray would receive that highest of honors: the cover of *Sports Illustrated*. It featured a photograph of Ray finishing a left hook, Espana reeling, and the crowd in the background like a watercolor. It read:

BOOM BOOM BOOMS!
Lightweight Champ Ray Mancini Wins Big

Still, the headline in the next day's *Vindicator* was more to the point: Mancini Upstages 'Rocky' in TKO Before Multitude.

Ray had seen *Rocky* in 1976 at the Newport on Market Street, an old, balconied theater with thick velvet curtains drawn back to reveal an irresistible boxing fantasy. But "the trippy stuff," as Ray calls it, didn't begin until Stallone attended the afterparty at VIP 2000, a club/restaurant on Route 224 in Niles. That's when he let his real purpose be known. Stallone wanted to produce a movie about Ray and his father.

"I thought it was crazy at first," remembers Ray. "I mean, I'm a fighter."

Tank and Chucky and everybody else in the makeshift VIP room seemed awed by the presence of a movie star, but Ray pegged Stallone as a "straightforward guy and a real fan of boxing." He'd also done some homework, and knew all about the poem Ray had written for Boom on Father's Day 1976.

What Stallone had in mind was a TV movie. CBS would be a natural, no? Again, the network's imprimatur would provide another way for the original Boom Boom to get the acknowledgment he never received. Better yet, Ray could play himself . . . if he wanted.

Play himself?

Actually, the more Ray thought about it, the less crazy it sounded. After all, didn't he remind people of a young John Garfield?

Later that summer, after the press had declared him "boxing's new superstar," Ray visited the set of *Staying Alive*, the *Saturday Night Fever* sequel Stallone was directing in New York. The movie, which, like the original, starred John Travolta, was something of a dud. But the prospect of Stallone's involvement left Mancini inspired.

"Sly is not going to act in it," Ray told the boxing writers, "but *produce* it."

Who do you want to play you? Ray was asked. There was an assortment of fighting actors from Robert De Niro, who won an Oscar for *Raging Bull*, to Tony Danza, who had considerably more success with an ensemble series, *Taxi*, than he had as a pro middleweight.

"De Niro?" said Ray. "Yeah, he could play anything. But Tony looks more like me. He's a better fighter, too."

Then again, his schedule permitting, there was one best casting choice. And it was Stallone's idea.

"I was a born actor," said Ray. "Besides, who can play me better than me?"

With jewelry and clothing as his self-proclaimed, if modest, profligacies, Ray was just beginning to sample life as a star. His taste in early bling was only slightly less subtle than his taste in cowboy boots, of which he now had seven pairs, including those of lizard, ostrich, and python.

It was an even more bountiful season for women. Under the disco ball at VIP 2000, they unwittingly disclosed their various aspirations to be Olivia Newton-John or Sheena Easton, or, at least a few of them, Joan Jett. Ray would recall Marvin Gaye's "Sexual Healing" as that summer's song. It usually came on late at night, courtesy of the DJ or a quarter in the jukebox, and signified the beginning of yet another conquest. Ray was still only twenty-one, blissfully unattached, longer than he ever had between fights. If, for some reason, the championship belt didn't work, he'd also been blessed with one of the world's best pickup lines: "Sly says I should play myself."

Of all the girls, however, one qualified as special, a blonde from suburban Boardman named Gina. If what they shared wasn't quite love, it was an exquisitely high state of smitten.

Aspiring Miss Americas usually don't consort with fighters. Then again, Ray wasn't merely an all-American boy. For Boom Boom Mancini, the prophecy of superstardom had come to pass. He could be found on the cover of *Sports Illustrated* and in a fashion layout in *Penthouse*. His fights, as Arum was quick to remind people, did "humongous ratings."

Now strangers would come up to him and ask: "When you gonna fight that Mr. T again?"

This kind of fame had mercantile advantages, too. After Sasson, there was a deal with a Chicago-based toy company for a line of kids' boxing gloves and punching bags. Dave and Gina (who, by now, handled Ray's contracts) were already in the midst of discussions with Coke and Pony, makers of then-popular athletic shoes.

Corporate America was seeking a replacement for Sugar Ray Leonard, whose retirement seemed more of a foregone conclusion with each passing day. The reigning welterweight titleholder, Leonard had now pulled out of his second consecutive fight, a bout with the 140-pound champion, Cincinnati's Aaron ("The Hawk") Pryor. Pryor, known for dissolute living and devastating punching, then signed to fight Arguello. It was considered a superfight. Though in economic terms, it was just a prelude to an even bigger payday. All roads to big money, to maximum earnings, now went through Mancini.

"Mancini drew twenty thousand in a football stadium," Pryor would acknowledge. "I'd never draw that many in Cincinnati."

It was widely supposed that Ray would fight Pryor, as a war between black and white sluggers from Ohio was too lucrative not to happen. Unlike the boxing press, Mancini liked his chances with the Hawk. First, he wouldn't have to find him. Pryor, like Ray, stayed right in front of his opponent. Second, and more important, he had a habit of sticking out his chin, making for a very inviting target.

Still, Ray was upset with the news that he'd have to wait for a rematch with Arguello. The single gift boxing had not yet bestowed upon Mancini was a rematch with El Flaco Explosivo. As deep as his affection and respect were for the Nicaraguan champion, he wanted even more to celebrate over his prone body.

"That's what I want, more than ever," Ray told the *New York Post*.

"Stay away from Alexis right now," said his father.

"What, you're telling me I can't beat him?" asked Ray.

"That's not what I'm saying, Raymond."

"You don't believe in me?"

It was the only time Chuck Fagan saw Ray genuinely pissed off at his old man.

"Of course not," said Boom. "It's just that you're my baby."

In lieu of Arguello, the WBA gave Ray its new number-one contender, Duk Koo Kim. Fighting out of South Korea, where the WBA had especially strong ties, Kim held the Asia and Pacific lightweight championship. While the distinction earned him some respect in the eastern hemisphere, he remained anonymous in the states. To the extent that Kim was noticed, the boxing press cast him as an obscure, marginally qualified product of the WBA rating system.

"All that was done by Cordero," says Bruce Trampler. "Probably to assuage Korean members of the WBA."

"They insisted on Kim," says Mort Sharnik, referring to Wolf and the WBA.

That's not to say men like Trampler and Sharnik bought into the talk that Mancini–Kim was a mismatch. In fact, they expected a good fight, certainly better than they would get with former Olympian Howard Davis, whose handlers spent the summer campaigning for a shot at Ray. Unlike Davis, an expert defensive fighter with a cautious style that bordered on European, Kim was a brawler. Hence, Sharnik figured his bosses would be happy. If the Kim fight were merely the latest installment in a televised serial, there was also reason to believe it would be, in programming parlance, action packed. For those who considered Ray as protagonist in another CBS hit not unlike *Dallas* or *Magnum P.I.*, it wasn't a bad way to promote his eventual showdown with Arguello, a 2–1 favorite to beat Pryor in Miami the night before.

As it happened, relations between the Mancini and Arguello camps were so cordial they shared a training camp, the fighters taking turns working out in a ring under a big white tent at the Americana Canyon Hotel in Palm Springs. There was no question Arguello was the more accomplished fighter. Just the same, there was no doubting the identity of the more popular one.

Suddenly, Ray found himself a darling of the performing classes. Every day, it seemed, another celebrity would arrive like a pilgrim under that great white canopy for an audience with Ray. There was Sonny Bono and Kirk Douglas. There was Dodgers manager Tommy Lasorda, and Kansas City Royals third baseman George Brett, then in the prime of his Hall of Fame career.

Still, the most talked-about guest wasn't even famous in his own right. Jilly Rizzo had long been Frank Sinatra's right-hand man.

"Jilly Rizzo!" says Tank. "Immediately, I call my parents, because Sinatra's like a God to our family, and to everybody we know. I tell them, 'Jilly Rizzo's here,' and they don't even believe me at first. So I said, 'No. I'm telling you the truth. Jilly Rizzo's right here.'"

Not only that, he had been dispatched by The Man himself.

"Frank wanted me to apologize," Jilly told Ray.

"Apologize?"

"He wanted to be here in person," said Jilly.

"Oh. Thank you."

"Also, Frank wants to know if you need anything while you're here."

"No. I don't think so."

"He wants you to know he's a big fan, and that he'll be at Caesars for the fight."

"Thank you. Thank you."

"He'll be playing in Vegas that week," said Jilly. "He'd like you to be his guest."

"I'd be honored."

The invitation only made Ray work harder. He could not train like Arguello, who surprised Ray by bringing a blonde (certainly not his wife) with him to camp. Arguello would send her home ten days before the fight. Such a regimen, he told Ray, had never failed him before. Still, Ray figured the time for sexual healing was over. While Arguello was out prowling, Ray was in his room studying Kim's fights on a VCR.

The rest of the world might be taking the Korean lightly, but not Ray. He didn't like what he saw on tape, either, though it certainly seemed familiar. Kim, like Ray, was a natural southpaw. He was willing to take a punch, or two, just to give one. What's more, he never took a backward step.

Fighter and trainer watched until they were bleary eyed. Finally, Ray spoke up. "Griff," he said, "this guy's going to be a headache."

Chapter 9 | The Desire for
a Harmonious Family

Duk Koo Kim was born July 29, 1955. At the age of two, he survived the virus that killed his biological father. When he was not yet five, his mother, Sun-Nyo Yang, whom he'd remember as "a woman of great misfortune," left his stepfather, a bean-curd peddler.

His oldest son had become violently abusive. And on the morning Sun-Nyo fled with Duk Koo and his two younger siblings, she carried all their possessions on her head. "That first day we walked seventy lis in the hot sun," Duk Koo wrote years later in his journal. "We didn't have anything to eat the whole way."

Finally, at sundown, they stopped in a town eighteen kilometers from the demilitarized zone that separated North and South Korea. Banam was a poor fishing village. But to Sun-Nyo and her children, the townsfolk must have seemed well off. "I was not embarrassed when I saw my mother begging for food because I was so hungry," wrote Duk Koo.

It was in Banam that Sun-Nyo met her last husband. His name was Kim, the most common of Korean surnames. He was a farmer and a fisherman, with a small patch for rice, and an old boat he would take out into the East Sea for mackerel, cuttlefish, and octopus. Home was a block from the shore, in a ramshackle house with a thatched roof and walls fashioned of mud and plywood. A partitioned cinderblock structure in the yard served as both an outhouse and a shelter for the family's most valued possession, a cow.

Kim had three sons and a daughter but like many Korean families in the 1950s, his had been fractured by the civil conflict. After spending years imprisoned in North Korea, he returned home to find that his wife, believing she would never see him again, had moved in with another man. Taking Sun-Nyo off the street and into his home was Kim's attempt at restoring the balance of domestic life.

His youngest son, Kun Yeung, was eleven or twelve the day he came from school to find Sun-Nyo there with her children. "My father said she was my new mother," he recalls.

In short order, Duk Koo's siblings were sent to live with relatives. But Sun-Nyo established herself as the household's maternal figure. "She had a warm heart," says Kun Sik Kim, the eldest brother. "But she was very assertive about everything she did, and she served her husband well."

Banam was nominally Buddhist, but not religious. "People here in the countryside would go to the temple on Buddha's birthday, but that's about it," said Kun Sik, noting that the state of one's belly was usually a more pressing concern than the state of one's soul.

"We were all poor," he says. "We lacked food."

Duk Koo Kim, as he was now called, became the fourth and junior most brother. In the summer, he would swim out under a blazing red sun to catch fish and scallops. In the autumn, he'd fry locusts to eat as a snack. In the winter, with snow covering the mountain that rose behind Road Number 7, he and his brothers would corral rabbits and bludgeon them with sticks.

To get to school, Duk Koo would walk four kilometers along the railroad tracks each morning. Elementary education was another shameful experience, as his tuition fees were usually in arrears. "I would ask my mother for some money, and each time she would say she didn't have it," Duk Koo recalled. "She would hit me every time I asked."

He didn't fare much better with his fellow students. Duk Koo fought often, but not well. These fits of ill-temper would often conclude with a teacher pinning a letter to his shirt, a mark denoting his shame, and parading him around the school. The other kids laughed at him.

Kun Yeung was disgusted at the sight of his stepbrother returning home with yet another bloody nose. "When I told him to fight back, he tried to resist," recalls Kun Yeung, who himself had a martial temperament and liked to raise fighting dogs. "I think he wanted to avoid fighting. But I told him . . . 'If you don't fight back, they will only hit you again. So you should chase them and hit them first. Hit them in the nose because when they bleed, it puts an end to the feud.'"

Years later, Duk Koo had a different recollection in his journal: "One new brother used to drag me around forcing me to fight with other village kids. The older kids enjoyed watching our fights, and I despise them even today for it."

Either way, Duk Koo was learning to fight. He didn't like it. But he didn't like himself, either. Poverty alone was cruel enough, but in a culture that valued pale skin, Duk Koo bore the additional stigma of a dark complexion. In a society that equated patriarchy with one's standing and honor, he'd been told his own father was dead, and given another man's name. He would look back on his youth as a state of humiliation. "I never had a happy home, and I was deeply unsatisfied," recalled Duk Koo. "Every now and then, I would become uncontrollably angry."

Nevertheless, this seemingly unremarkable boy vowed big things: "I always repeated to myself that I shall live to make it big."

He left Banam as a teenager and found employment at a bakery in Sokcho, twenty-six kilometers down the coast. Then he found his way to Seoul, where he worked as a welder, a career that ended with Duk Koo getting into an argument with his boss. Soon, he was sleeping under a bridge and subsisting on crackers. Eventually, he held jobs as a waiter (fetching plates of roast chicken and draft beer) and a peddler of chestnuts, pogo sticks, palm-reading manuals, and ballpoint pens.

But it wasn't until he found his way to the Dong-Ah boxing gym that he found a place where he could exploit his rage and ambition. What Stillman's was to New York in the 1940s, Dong-

Ah was to Seoul four decades later: the country's premier gym, and a supplier of fighters for the popular weekly cards televised on Korea's MBC network. It was located on the third floor of a building in downtown Seoul, and run, in an iron-fisted way, by a former fighter named Hyun-Chi Kim.

"Hyun-Chi Kim's word was that of God," says Sang-Bong Lee, a featherweight who befriended Duk Koo.

Those who ran afoul of Dong-Ah's master were forced to kneel, then bend over as younger fighters struck them as many as 100 times across the buttocks with a mop handle. The boxers, Hyun-Chi Kim concedes, "were scared of me." Just the same, he took some pity on Duk Koo, a homeless country boy who managed to stand out even in the fraternity of Dong-Ah's poor young men.

"I noticed he was worse off than the others," says Hyun-Chi.

The boss, who also managed and promoted Dong-Ah's fighters, allowed Duk Koo and Sang-Bong to sleep on the gym floor. Unfortunately, it was easier to provide shelter than ability, of which Duk Koo seemed to have little.

"I didn't think he was fighter material," says Hyun-Chi Kim.

He wasn't alone in this assessment. Duk Koo didn't have heavy hands. He wasn't fast, or possessed of great stamina. Worse still, in the beginning, he didn't even show much courage.

"In my opinion," says Seo In Seong, another Dong-Ah fighter, "he was a bit of a coward."

In fact, Duk Koo's problem wasn't fear. Still, as a kid who'd just come in off the street, his aptitude for pugilism remained difficult to discern. Yoon Gu Kim, who fought as a welterweight, couldn't figure it out until the first time he really hit Duk Koo. Bigger, stronger, and more athletic, Yoon Gu put a lot into that punch. But unlike most young fighters, Duk Koo didn't take it personally. He just smiled. It was as if he expected to get hit. Finally, Duk Koo's talent had become evident in sparring. He didn't train so much as endure.

"He was more strong-willed and ruthless than others," says Yoon Gu.

Or, put another way, Duk Koo was less easily discouraged. After all, he had nothing to lose but a life spent selling pens on city buses. If his dream of fighter's glory seemed far-fetched, it was all he had.

As he'd write in his journal: "Poverty is my teacher."

If the depth of Duk Koo's aspirations remained unknown, then so did the full depth of social standing. He didn't speak of his step-brothers in Banam, or the circumstances that led to his mother begging in the street. "It would have hurt his pride," says Yoon Gu.

"I think he was able to perform well," says Sang-Bong, "because he was an extremely lonely person."

Such isolation, however, wasn't a permanent state. Dong-Ah was up three flights of stairs. The fourth floor housed a tea company, which employed a bookkeeper named Young Mee Lee. She was pale and proper, very pretty, and very Christian. For a poor, dark-skinned boxer like Duk Koo, gaining her favor seemed slightly less probable than winning the championship of the world.

"She looked feminine and smart," says Seo In Seong. "Way out of his league."

They bumped into each other in the stairway. She was on her way down; he was going up. She nodded, motioning for him to pass first. Young Mee could feel his eyes on her. But with a cap pulled over his brow, she didn't recognize him as the one who kept pestering the tea company's receptionist for an introduction. It wouldn't have mattered anyway. Young Mee wasn't the least bit interested.

"My parents weren't so ambitious as to wish to have a doctor or a lawyer as a son-in-law," she says. "But they wanted me to marry a regular salaryman."

Definitely not a fighter. Several times, she refused his request for a date.

But again, Duk Koo remained undeterred, if slightly deluded, with a talkative arrogance that belied his station in life. Duk Koo would bargain for secondhand gym clothes at an open-air market. Still, he spoke as if he were destined for fame and fortune, in love and boxing. His manner was immodest, un-Korean, and dumb-founded even Sang-Bong, with whom he now rented a tiny apartment near the gym.

"He was exaggerating things in his behavior to hide his status," says Sang-Bong.

"I refused to see him," says Young Mee. "I avoided him."

Duk Koo responded with love letters. Good ones, too.

"They opened my heart," she says, recalling a line from the first one she received:

... When a man cries because his heart aches, the whole world, heaven and earth, cries with him ...

Finally, in anticipation of their first meeting, the rough-hewn young man from the gym gave himself a makeover. He wore an ill-fitting suit and read a book, as he waited for Young Mee in a cafe. "I walked right past him," she says. "I didn't recognize him."

She wasn't alone. By now, several years into his tenure at Dong-Ah, Duk Koo's own stablemates were having trouble reconciling the itinerant hillbilly who arrived in 1977 with the fighter now challenging for the Oriental and Pacific Boxing Federation title. Kim hadn't become a great fighter, not by any stretch of the imagination. He didn't scare anyone. He didn't beat up sparring partners, even those in lighter weight classes. But in acquiring a reputation as a crafty southpaw, he was better than expected.

"He worked harder than anyone," says Seo In Seong.

And with work, came the gradual acquisition of confidence. By winning his first amateur tournament, Duk Koo qualified as a "special talent student" at a local high school. His trophy, a standard-issue school uniform, was a great source of pride. And for a time, he never took it off.

"He liked to show off and say 'I'm a student, too,'" says Seong. "Before that, he had never been to high school. We don't even know if he went to middle school."

Duk Koo's professional career began with unremarkable success, against unremarkable opposition. His first win of note, or at least, something of a personal milestone, came on October 6, 1979, with a six-round decision over Young-Dae Kim, who had beaten him twice in the amateurs. The following summer, in his first fight outside the country, he stopped a Filipino in the eighth round of a scheduled ten in Manila.

That made him 9–1–1, with three knockouts. Still, Hyun-Chi Kim found him too raucous and unrefined, as both a boxer and a man. Some fighters talk loudly to quell their own fears. But fear didn't qualify as an excuse. "I had to control Duk Koo from acting over the top, and strongly reprimand him," recalls Hyun-Chi Kim.

Finally, when a full-of-himself Duk Koo reported late to the gym, Hyun-Chi, whose dead-eye stare could inflict both fear and shame, told him to leave. As punishment went, this was infinitely worse than being caned with the mop handle. Duk Koo wasn't merely being told to go home. He was being banished, cast off in disgrace. He packed his gear and left with his head bowed.

"Without boxing, Duk Koo was nothing," says Sang-Bong. "If the gym master does not accept him, wouldn't that mean the end of him? Everything was lost for Duk Koo. That is why he attempted suicide."

He left notes for Sang-Bong and Hyun-Chi Kim. Then he took the pills. Upon regaining consciousness, he found himself in Youngdeungpo Hospital.

"He created a scene," says Seo In Seong, who believes the attempted suicide was a bid for Hyun-Chi Kim's attention.

If so, it worked. Not only did the manager-promoter take back Duk Koo, he got him some good fights. Duk Koo, for his part, did more than rededicate himself. He envisioned victory as redemption, a way to mitigate the condition of his birth, a cure for every curse passed through his blood.

"Now I understand my mother and feel sorry for her," he wrote. "That's why I want to be a good son and bring her happiness. In order to do that, I must reach the top . . . I shall run and fight until I am covered with blood and sweat."

"He didn't have enough to be a world champion," Hyun-Chi Kim says flatly. "But we thought that if we honed his skills, he could do well enough to perhaps win an Asian championship."

On February 28, 1982, Duk Koo fought Kwang Min Kim, 21–3–1, who held the Oriental and Pacific Boxing Federation title, a belt that earned fighters standing with the WBA. Even Kim's friends considered him an underdog against Kwang Min, nicknamed "Tank."

Duk Koo kept to a crafty southpaw style, constantly hitting and turning his opponent. "The strategy was to wear down Tank," recalls Yoon Gu Kim, who by now was Duk Koo's trainer. "It was quite shrewd."

The unanimous twelve-round decision gave Kim more than a title. He used the proceeds to purchase a real suit and rent a two-bedroom apartment for him and Young Mee.

Korean fighters were not supposed to have girlfriends. It was considered bad form, as romance was thought to corrupt the fighting spirit. Hyun-Chi Kim considered disciplining Duk Koo when he found out about Young Mee. Just the same, neither he nor anyone else at Dong-Ah could deny the strangely salutary effect the relationship had had on the new Oriental champion.

"He was even more diligent once he got a girlfriend," recalls Yoon Gu.

Again, diligence was born of devotion. Duk Koo needed both to overcome the odds against him. After all, the courtship, like his career, hadn't begun with much promise. Before agreeing to a date, Young Mee issued a test: "I made him pledge then and there, he wouldn't box again."

He swore he would not.

By then, Young Mee had no intention of actually making him quit. "I could see how much he loved boxing," she says. "It was the thought and the commitment that counted—that he could even *think* about quitting."

Still, the testing wasn't done. Young Mee's quite disapproving father would soon invite him to the family's home. "Since my father was always very eloquent, he started talking to convince Duk Koo to give up," she recalls.

But Duk Koo, an avid reader of novels and histories like the *Samgukji*, the history of China's three ancient kingdoms, was articulate and convincing in his own right. Now he presented his own history, as he'd begun to keep a journal.

"He was quite persuasive," recalls Young Mee. "My father had fled from the north during the Korean War and experienced much hardship. So after hearing about the life that Kim had, he gave in."

Next, Duk Koo and Sang-Bong invited themselves to a lunch, where they sat down across from Young Mee and another young man. He was a military policeman, and considered himself her boyfriend.

"I told him to yield, to give up, since Duk Koo likes Young Mee," recalls Sang-Bong. "The fool couldn't even say anything."

With the soldier gone, the courtship was ready to begin in earnest. For the first time in his life, Duk Koo had some money in his pocket. He brought her to buffet restaurants, which Young Mee recalls as being precious for kids in their early twenties. He had her try foods she had never tasted. Still, the delicacies themselves are more difficult to recall than the feelings they evoked.

"He was soft, tender, considerate—and very affectionate toward me," she says, blood rushing to her face years later. "He did everything I wanted. I don't think I was ever happier than I was then."

Duk Koo won his next four fights, two by unanimous decision, two by knockout. "He suddenly changed his style," says Seong. "He transformed into a real fighter."

He'd become less cute, and more courageous. He would talk for hours with Sang-Bong, arriving at a pugilistic philosophy not unlike the ancient Hwarang warriors, who eschewed the idea of retreat in battle.

"Stepping back was shameless," says Sang-Bong, who noticed that his friend was experiencing a sudden interest in Christianity.

The Bible study, like Duk Koo's newfound courage, came as a result of his relationship with Young Mee. By the spring of '82, the couple was discussing marriage. They had engagement parties for her family in Seoul and his in Banam. But Duk Koo was never happier than the day he hosted a barbecue at the apartment he now shared with his fiancée.

"He was full of confidence, and so much pride," says Seong. "He believed that the whole world was his."

Kim had seen his highest aspiration in his fiancée's protective, patriarchal clan.

"He was thirsty for that," says Sang-Bong. *"Thirsty."*

"The desire for a harmonious family," says Young Mee, who knew better than anyone, was what moved her man.

That autumn, early November 1982, she found herself on a second-floor balcony at Incheon International Airport. In observing the Asian convention—that ancient prohibition against fighters taking lovers—she could not be seen with Duk Koo's modest entourage, or by the gaggle of reporters following them as they boarded their flight to the states. Not only was her fiancée now the WBA's number-one contender, he had made news with intemperate remarks that he would beat Mancini, that only one of them would return home alive.

"Either he dies," said Duk Koo, "or I die."

And now Young Mee was forced to watch without saying goodbye. She could not so much as wave. Even as tears streamed down her face, the dance had begun, the ballet of blood and light in her tummy. She was pregnant with Duk Koo's son.

Chapter 10 | Heaven

However improved and inspired he was, Duk Koo's newfound status as the WBA's number-one contender—and, therefore, a mandatory challenger for Mancini's title—came as something of a surprise that September.

The rankings, of course, were sanctioned by Pepe Cordero. But the Korean and Japanese boxing establishments had long been enmeshed in the sanctioning body's corrupted bureaucracy. In the mid-1970s, a new WBA president was besieged with Asian promoters and managers trying to give him cash. "Are you the man we now pay for the ratings?" asked one.

However it came to pass, the prospect of a Mancini–Kim fight was first broached in a meeting between Hyun-Chi Kim and Bob Arum at the Waldorf-Astoria in New York. Hyun-Chi had a middleweight who was supposed to fight Arum's great champion, Marvin Hagler. When that bout didn't come off, Hyun-Chi inquired as to Arum's schedule and booked the grandest room he could find to impress his American counterpart. If Hagler was unavailable, he reasoned, perhaps they could still do business.

"It was a very easy negotiation," Arum recalls. "The dollar was very, very strong. And the money I had to work with from CBS and Caesars Palace"—which had decided to christen its new outdoor ring with a now-vintage show of Mancini-mania—"meant that Kim would probably get his highest purse ever."

Kim's purse, reported as twenty thousand dollars, was actually much higher, and most of it untaxable, according to Arum. Unlike a fighter's purse, a promoter's fee was not subject to withholding.

The bulk of Duk Koo's payment, says Arum, would have come directly from Hyun-Chi, who'd be paid by *Top Rank*. "That's the way we did it in those days," says Arum.

American sportswriters knew little about Kim, other than he didn't have a chance in hell. "People knew how crooked the WBA was, and how they overrated foreign fighters," says Royce Feour. "That number-one ranking didn't mean anything."

Just because a fight was cynically conceived, however, didn't mean it lacked merit. Mort Sharnik spent at least five hours reviewing tapes of Kim before accepting him as an opponent on CBS. "We took a lot of flack for putting on that fight," he says. "But I remember thinking what a great fight it would be, that Mancini and Kim deserved each other, both of them long on intensity and enthusiasm of the heart. It was *never* a mismatch."

"Ray was better," says Bruce Trampler. "But not by much."

What's more, Hyun-Chi Kim had devised a strategy to close that gap. Fighters don't typically like engaging versions of themselves. Duk Koo, then, would try to out-Mancini Mancini. He would keep pressing forward. He would crouch even lower than his opponent. He would go to the body, and counterpunch from the angles that naturally presented themselves to a southpaw. The idea wasn't to knock Ray out so much as wear him down. "Kim does not have the height of Arguello," Hyun-Chi told an American reporter. "He has to get inside to use his strengths. Pour it on—that's the way to fight Mancini."

Meanwhile, some in Duk Koo's camp worried that their fighter might wear himself down first. He was training in a way that engendered concern. "His drive was way over his ability," says Seong. "But he looked unhappy and depressed. I think he was overdoing it. He was different than before. This was a once in a lifetime chance."

With a child on the way, Duk Koo had begun to think of the fight as life itself. Winning the championship would grant a kind of eternal life without shame. Conversely, he equated defeat with death. As one man had to lose, that man would die, as well.

"If he doesn't die," Duk Koo said of his opponent, "then *I* will come back dead."

To watch him train at Seoul's Sejong Hotel was to see a man trying to brag away his fear. Kim would direct his taunts at a poster of Mancini, its eyes poked out. "The title belongs to me!" he would shout.

Duk Koo even had a carpenter build a small mock coffin, which he said was intended for Mancini. "I will bring him back in here," said Kim.

Disgusted, Yoon Gu stomped it into pieces. Duk Koo's behavior might have come from cowardice or nerves. It could have been a way to psyche himself up, or a misguided attempt at showmanship. But after a while, Yoon Gu and Hyun-Chi had enough.

Finally, Hyun-Chi halted a training session and ordered Duk Koo to strip naked and stare at himself in the mirror. "Be humble," he said. "There is no other way for you to become a champion."

The rest of the camp proceeded without incident. In fact, as it concluded, Yoon Gu now considered his fighter only a very slight underdog. Mancini was a little slow, he figured, and his fighter had a natural advantage as a southpaw.

Sang-Bong was of the same mind. He had been training with Duk Koo for years now and could remember feeling obliged to let his friend "win" as they sprinted up Nam San mountain. But no more. They sparred many rounds in preparation for Mancini, and Duk Koo stood down. If this were the chance of a lifetime, Duk Koo was ready.

On the night of Sunday, November 6, 1982, the challenger and his handlers landed in Las Vegas. They were in awe of the wide roads and the immensity of the blinking neon Strip. Caesars' casino was so bright it felt like broad daylight, its shimmer accentuated by big-breasted cocktail waitresses sporting Roman tunics and high-piled ponytails of fake blond hair. Sudden converts to kismet—the religion of all gamblers—they went straight to the slot machines.

"This is like heaven," said Duk Koo Kim.

• • •

Duk Koo and his small retinue took photographs by the statue of Venus and the famous fountain out front. The ersatz grandeur only fed the fighter's sense of destiny. He even found an old silver Rolex in one of the casino's bathrooms. Obviously, it was a harbinger of his good fortune.

Kim received at least two American journalists in his suite that week. Ralph Wiley, of *Sports Illustrated*, entered a darkened room, the air heavy with incense, the drapes pulled back just enough for Kim to gaze out into the desert. Wiley inquired as to the condition of the fighter's chin. Finally, after deeming the translated grunts insufficient, Wiley grabbed his own chin and moved his jaw from side to side.

"Seeing this," he wrote, "Kim's expression changed. I would like to say he smiled, but it was something else. Scorn. He gently touched his jaw with two fingers of his right hand, then without averting his gaze, he reached over and touched the marble windowsill with the same two fingers, just as gently. He turned to face the desert. The interview was over."

Royce Feour, of the *Las Vegas Review-Journal*, encountered a more glib fighter. Feeling good about himself, Duk Koo told the reporter he was the son of a rich man. Being the scion of a wealthy farmer, he didn't fight for the money, but merely for love of the competition. The newspaper photographed Duk Koo in his hotel room, interrupting his self-imposed studies to look up from an imposing volume of Korean history.

As the interview ended, Feour asked the translator about the neatly lettered Korean characters on the lampshade by the fighter's bed.

"Live or die," he was told. Or, as an American colloquialism, "Kill or be killed."

"Duk Koo," recalls his trainer, "wrote very good calligraphy."

In the middle of the week, Tank DiCioccio scouted one of Duk Koo's workouts.

"What's he look like?" Ray asked.

Tank was happy to report the Korean had been wearing a sweat suit, meaning he was trying to cut weight.

"What else?" asked Ray.

"He looks good, tough," Tank conceded. "Guy's doing nothing but body work."

"Yeah, and?"

"Guy keeps coming forward."

Actually, he charged. He practiced for the beginning of each round by running across the ring to deliver a straight left, punctuated by a kind of battle cry. Like something out of a kung fu movie, Tank thought.

Mancini nodded knowingly. He'd been trying to tell the sportswriters: "We're going to have a war, no doubt about it." Let the rest of the world be surprised by this Kim. Mancini had refused to be. The stakes were too high now. Caesars had just completed a ten-thousand-seat outdoor arena in anticipation of the event. The house of Mancini had grown in stature since those days of the Broadway Arena. Now Boom Boom was right under Sinatra on the marquee outside Caesars.

"How you feeling, champ?" asked Sinatra, who invited Ray to his set after the fight.

"Thank you," said Ray. "Feel good."

"I've been following you," said Frank. "You're making us real proud."

Us. It was clear whom he meant: the great Italo-American tribe whose ancestors weren't even considered white people when they arrived, like Nicola Mancino, in steerage.

Ray had become one of their heroes. But still, he was more than that, more than another White Hope, a term he detested. What was long suspected had become official. Just days before the fight, Sugar Ray Leonard hosted a massive press conference at Baltimore's Civic Center. Among the crowd of nine thousand was a prospective opponent, middleweight champ Marvin Hagler, who listened as Leonard announced his retirement due to the effects of retinal surgery and diminished desire. Just that quickly, Hagler lost the biggest payday in sports while Ray became the fight game's most bankable star. Dave Wolf had already received seven different offers, each with purses in excess of a million dollars for the WBA lightweight champion.

On the eve of Mancini–Kim, Alexis Arguello faced Aaron Pryor in Miami's Orange Bowl. Through thirteen rounds, it was an even, if epic evening. Before the fourteenth, trainer Panama Lewis admonished his assistants to have Pryor drink from a particular water bottle. "The one I mixed," he said.

Shortly thereafter, Arguello found himself helpless against the ropes. Pryor delivered at least fourteen consecutive blows to the head before referee Stanley Christodoulou stopped the fight. Then, as their man slumped, Arguello's cornermen ran into the ring, placing a towel on the mat and laying him down, quite carefully.

Arguello, noted the Associated Press, "remained motionless in the ring for several minutes."

That was the photograph that traveled around the globe: a tight shot of the fallen champion, his eyes closed, his face expressionless, as if lying in state. It was a horrifying image, and it filled Arguello's friend with great regret.

"I always wanted to be the one to do that to Alexis," said Ray.

Not long after Arguello regained consciousness, Bob Arum took a charter to Vegas. His guests included none other than Mr. and Mrs. Henry Armstrong, still regarded as the greatest lightweight in boxing history. Armstrong, in attendance at the Orange Bowl, had asked Arum if he could see Mancini fight.

"I remember his father," said Armstrong. "And he reminds me of myself."

Armstrong only added to the number of dignitaries and celebrities already on hand at Caesars. There was Willie Stargell, who had led the Pittsburgh Pirates to two World Series victories; George Brett, perennial American League All-Star; Robert Goulet; Lou Rawls; Bill Cosby, the voice of TV's "Fat Albert"; and of course, like an old married couple, front and center, Jilly and Frank.

Before the fight, Ray could hear Duk Koo pounding the lockers on the other side of the dressing room wall. The accompanying screams were even more disconcerting.

"War cries," recalls Ray, who was surprised to see so many Korean flags as he made his way into the ring. Kim's countrymen, most of whom had made their way from Los Angeles, would not be disappointed. At the opening bell, Duk Koo came across the ring and hit Ray flush on the chin with a straight left. Then, some seconds later, another left to the heart.

"They're landing bombs!" exclaimed Gil Clancy, one of two analysts in the three-man CBS booth that also included Tim Ryan and Ray Leonard.

The template was established in that first round. The fighters would stand toe-to-toe, their heads perilously close, and wing punches. Ray threw thudding hooks to the body and the head, and right uppercuts aimed at Kim's heart. Kim would return fire with wide, sweeping rights. More surprising, however, were his remarkably accurate left leads.

"He's really getting nailed," Clancy said of Ray.

As the broadcast went to commercial, the network's erudite, bow-tied matchmaker couldn't help but be pleased with himself. The prognostications of a mismatch had already been proven wrong, if not foolish. "I'm thinking it was a great fight, exactly what I figured," says Mort Sharnik. "It was like boxing yourself in the mirror."

It was southpaw against converted southpaw. Each man was listed at five-six with a reach of sixty-five inches. Kim weighed in at 134¼, a half-pound lighter than Ray. But more than that, the fighters seemed united in their willingness to give and receive pain.

Each man had a tactical advantage. Ray liked to fight low, but Kim's crouch was even lower. Ray had the shorter, crisper, superior hook. In fact, his strategy was to "break off the hook" at the first sign of Kim's left lead, figuring his punch would find its target first. Sometimes it did. And sometimes not.

"I knew I'd have to eat a few," he says.

A furious exchange near the end of the third round—Kim connecting with looping right hooks, then Mancini inflicting a series of body shots—concluded with the Korean pushing Ray back, as if the champion were a little kid. Kim raised his arms and pumped his fists. He had now taken Mancini's best shots.

"Bing, bing, bing, bing, I'm hitting him with everything for like a minute," Mancini would recall. "And then he just backs off, like, celebrating. He just took my best shots and he's putting up his arms in triumph.

"That'll take your heart away."

A lesser fighter, a bully, would have folded right then. Instead, Mancini trudged back to his corner, clearly the more wounded man. Paul Percifield went to work on the left ear, which was split open and spouting blood. Less easily treated was Ray's left hand. After throwing a left hook that literally bounced off the top of Kim's head, it was swollen and throbbing with pain.

Even more swollen than Ray's fist, which would balloon to twice its normal size, were the hearts of Kim's countrymen. "I was so exuberant," says Kun Sik, his eldest stepbrother, who recalls most of Banam cheering wildly around a tiny black-and-white television.

"Duk Koo was enchanted," says Sang-Bong, who watched the MBC broadcast in Seoul. "Some spirit must have taken him over. I think he thought it would be his last fight."

"We thought he could become world champion," says Seong. "It was the only one of his fights that I did not see him back up."

"They both run across the ring to get to each other," Ray Leonard said admiringly shortly after the fourth round began. "I'm surprised that no one's been sent to the canvas . . . those are big bombs."

"There's no give," responded Clancy. "They're not slipping the punches. They're not moving. They're there to get hit."

The longer it went, this accrual of stubborn brutalities, the more it seemed like an homage to the Original Boom Boom. Little Ellen remembers trying not to hyperventilate at ringside. Chuck Fagan recalls thinking, *What's Ray got to do? Kill this guy?*

Waiting on the bell for the sixth, Clancy felt uneasy. He had been in the corner March 24, 1962, at the Garden, when his fighter, welterweight Emile Griffith, beat Benny "Kid" Paret into a fatal coma. Now the former trainer spoke in an ominous aside to his fellow broadcasters. "Something's going to happen in this fight," Clancy said quietly. "Either one guy's gonna get busted up, or nail the other guy very badly."

The fight settled into a rhythm. Ray would win the first part of a round, then, when it seemed against all probability, Duk Koo would answer with shots to the belly and straight lefts, one of which, at the end of the eighth, snapped back Ray's head. They would breathe and bleed and lean on each other, achieving a state of violent intimacy that, looking back, seems almost fraternal.

"I knew him better than his mother," says Ray, adding that, for the first time since sparring with Lenny at the Navy Reserve, "I felt like quitting."

If his body wanted to shut down, his mind would not allow it. Then again, his mind wasn't all there, either. As the fight approached the championship rounds, Ray had reached some hallucinatory edge.

What is Bill Cosby doing in my corner? he wondered. *And why's he screaming at Chucky in that Fat Albert voice?*

Am I dreaming?

"What happened is Bill Cosby comes up and starts tapping me on the shoulder, telling me to tell Ray to throw the right hand," says Fagan. "I couldn't believe it. I mean, my parents bought me every album he ever did. But now I want to tell him: 'Bill, I love you, but get the fuck out of here.'"

• • •

At the end of nine, Ryan, Clancy, and Ray Leonard all agreed that the fight was dead even. By the eleventh, it seemed as if each fighter were wearing a sickly blueish mask. The engorged right side of Duk Koo's face looked as if a chunk of mouthpiece had broken off, settling between his molars and his cheek.

"Never mind how many rounds," said Clancy. "It's the pace that's been torrid. This is like a thirty-round fight."

Finally, Ray shot an uppercut to the heart that caused Duk Koo's left knee to touch the canvas. It might have been ruled a knockdown if Kim hadn't regained his footing so quickly. By now, Kim was clearly the more fatigued fighter, as tired as he was suddenly admired. Fans rose in appreciation after the twelfth.

The next round began with Ray running across the ring to deliver a straight right. It was the first of forty-four consecutive punches, an onslaught that slowed only when Kim found enough of his opponent to grab. Then, after breaking free of that grasp, Ray got off seventeen more, most of them hooks to the body. The announcing team was now anticipating the knockout. Seventy-nine seconds of the thirteenth round would elapse before Duk Koo threw his first punch.

There was a left, followed by a series of belly shots.

"Look at him punch back!" exclaimed Ryan.

The pummeling, with Mancini on the receiving end of most of it, continued until the bell.

In between rounds, as the fighters accepted their mouthpieces, Ryan reminded his audience whom they were watching. "This is the challenger, Duk Koo Kim," he said. "You may not have heard of him before. You will remember him today."

Again, Ray ran across the ring. But this time, he stepped right and stunned Kim with a left hook. In a matter of moments, Ray had a clear shot, driving a straight right into Kim's face. The challenger fell as if blown back by an explosion: head, torso, hips, then finally, the limbs. The back of his head came to rest briefly on the ring apron. Then Duk Koo managed to turn himself over and grab the ropes, scaling the lower rungs as if they were a mast of a ship, finally pulling himself up.

The Padrone, Nick Mancino, center; the former Annie Cannazzaro at his left; their son, Lenny, below. Courtesy Ray Mancini

Lenny with the Civilian Conservation Corps in Ely, Nevada, 1937. Courtesy Ellen Kosa

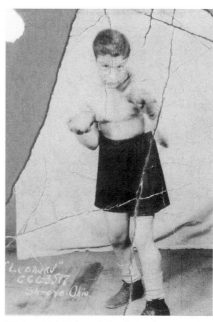

He would fight anybody.
Courtesy Ray Mancini

The original Boom Boom posing
with manager Frankie Jacobs.
New York, 1939.
Courtesy Ray Mancini

Ray Arcel, teaching him the
left hook at Stillman's Gym.
Courtesy Ray Mancini

"That's my dad." Boom after
the second Marquart fight, 1941.
Courtesy Ray Mancini

Buck Private.
Courtesy Ray Mancini

From left:
Vincent Mancino,
Boom, Joe "The
Wolf" DiCarlo,
Ellen, Vincent's
wife, Mary Ann.
Buffalo, c. 1949.
Courtesy Ray Mancini

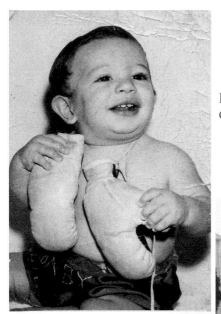

Raymond, eight months.
Courtesy Ray Mancini

From left: Boom, Raymond,
Lenny, Little Ellen. Easter,
1969. Courtesy Ray Mancini

The amateurs: with trainer Eddie
Sullivan at the Navy Reserve gym.
Courtesy Ray Mancini

Lenny, Boom, and Raymond, Navy Reserve, 1979. Reprinted from *The Vindicator*, © The Vindicator Printing Company, 2002

White Boy: training at the Buckeye Elks Gym.
Photo by Rob Engelhardt/(Warren, OH) *Tribune Chronicle*

Boom Boom, the sequel: turning pro, 1979. Courtesy Ray Mancini

In the driveway on Cambridge Street. Reprinted from *The Vindicator*, © The Vindicator Printing Company, 2002

With Murphy Griffith, before the title fight against Art Frias.
Copyright Linda Platt

Hometown Hero: defeating Ernesto Espana at Mollenkopf Stadium. AP Photo/Gus Chan

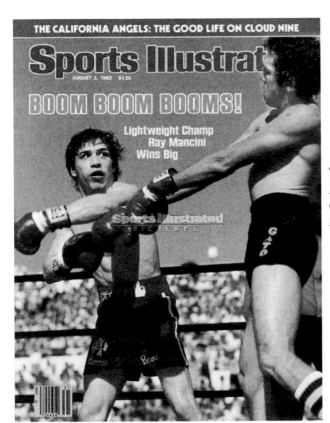

The cover of *Sports Illustrated*, August 2, 1982.
George Tiedemann/*Sports Illustrated*/Getty Images

Flanked by manager
Dave Wolf and Father
Tim O'Neill on Boom
Boom Mancini Day,
Cardinal Mooney
High School, 1982.
Courtesy Ray Mancini

"You're not a man if you can't kiss your father on the mouth." Boom, Ray, and Big Ellen after the Espana fight. Photo by Rob Engelhardt

Famous friends:
"Sly says I should
play myself." With
Sylvester Stallone.
AP Photo

With another big
fan, Frank Sinatra,
at Caesars Palace.
Copyright Linda Platt

Father and son
watching Pryor-
Arguello—
November 12,
1982—the night
before Ray fought
Duk Koo Kim.
AP Photo/Jeff Scheid

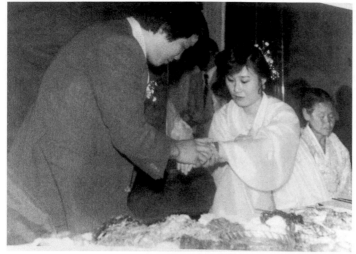

"The desire for a harmonious family": Duk Koo Kim and Young Mee at their engagement party in Seoul. On the right is Kim's mother, Sun-Nyo. Courtesy Young Mee Lee

"I knew him better than his mother": Mancini vs. Duk Koo Kim. © Bettman/Corbis

Duk Koo trying to rise in the 14th. "One of the greatest physical feats I had ever witnessed," said Ralph Wiley. Copyright Bettman/Corbis/AP Images

The morning after: Ray praying at the mass for Duk Koo.
AP Photo/Scott Henry

Legally dead: Sun-Nyo weeping at her press conference, November 17, 1982. To her left, Dr. Lonnie Hammargren; right, Kun Yeung Kim.
AP Photo

"Your father is in America." Young Mee with Jiwan, 1984. Courtesy Young Mee Lee

The rematch with Livingstone Bramble. Reno, February, 1985. © Bettman/Corbis

In a pretty good mood for a guy who needed seventy-five stitches. At left, cutman Paul Percifield. © Bettman/Corbis

That's entertainment: with Tony Danza in *Who's the Boss*, 1985.
American Broadcasting Companies, Inc.

With Nick Turturro and Holt McCallany in *The Search for One-Eye Jimmy*.
Copyright Brooklyn Search Productions

Carmen and Ray, expecting.
Courtesy Ray Mancini

Nina. Courtesy Ray Mancini

Mickey Rourke giving baby Nina her bottle, 1990. Courtesy Ray Mancini

Leonardo. Courtesy Ray Mancini

Ray-Ray. Courtesy Ray Mancini

Ed O'Neill and Ray at Il Forno.
Courtesy Saint Sophia Productions

"I think it was not your fault." Ray and Jiwan. Courtesy Saint Sophia Productions

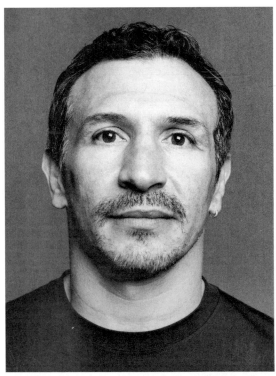

Ray "Boom Boom" Mancini. Copyright Holger Keifel

"One of the greatest physical feats I had ever witnessed," Ralph Wiley would recall.

Once upright, Duk Koo fell back against the ropes. Richard Green wasted no time taking him into his arms. Nineteen seconds into the fourteenth round, the fight was over.

"I felt like Hercules," recalls Ray, whose seconds hoisted him into the air.

In the celebration that followed, Ray blew kisses to the crowd and tried to congratulate his opponent. But Kim's corner was suddenly too thick with human traffic for Ray to see what was happening. Hyun-Chi and Yoon Gu kept trying to prop up their fighter, but Duk Koo kept slipping off his stool.

Boom and a weeping Big Ellen made their way into the ring, where they assembled arm-in-arm for the now-standard live shot. Before Tim Ryan could begin the postfight interview, someone called for a stretcher.

It was under the ring apron, at Royce Feour's feet. The reporter handed it to an EMT and watched as Duk Koo was strapped in and carried to an ambulance. He was taking four breaths per minute.

Six thousand miles away, on the outskirts of Seoul, Young Mee was at a friend's house. Finally, when the suspense became unbearable, she asked her to turn on the television.

No, the friend told Young Mee, the television isn't working.

Upon his arrival at Desert Springs Hospital, Duk Koo was given a CT scan revealing a subdural hematoma—a blood clot—on the right side of the brain. Dr. Lonnie Hammargren, the neurosurgeon who reported to the ER, saw from the scan that most of the blood had settled in the parietal lobe. He estimated its volume to be 100ccs.

"Enough to fill between three and four one-ounce shot glasses," he says.

Duk Koo was wheeled into the operating room, and given a dose of Mannitol to reduce the pressure in his brain. His head was shaved. Ice water was squirted into his ears, a test for brain-stem response. There was none.

This would be Hammargren's fourth such surgery on a fighter. The previous three had survived, with relatively little impairment, but the extent of the brain trauma in those cases wasn't comparable to this. There was little cause for optimism as the surgeon readied his drill. The first hole in Kim's skull was made with a 5/32 bit. The spurt of blood that followed was recorded at five times normal pressure.

From Dr. Hammargren's account, based on his notes of that day: "Significant bleeding occurred from the skin and from the muscles in the temple area because of the thickness of swelling from high blood flow from the bruises encountered during the fight . . . The blood was removed but the brain swelled from the bruising, rapidly filling the cavity where the blood clot had been removed. Three separate drains were used to remove any residual or subsequent bleeding . . . his prognosis was still extremely poor."

Ray's own convalescence began back at his suite. His sister held ice bags to his left hand, his left ear, and his left eye, now closed. His still-weeping mother tended to the right hand and right eye.

"Don't cry, Ma," said Ray. "We won."

Considering what he had just endured, Ray was feeling pretty good, even elated. It had been the most hard-fought and dramatic victory of his career. But as the euphoria dissipated, his body became a feverish mass of hurt, with bruises of every shade from mauve to lilac to violet to plum. He slept briefly before the strangely somber visitors began arriving in his suite.

"Look at me," he told Father O'Neill. "I don't think it's worth it."

"Ray," said Father O'Neill, "the kid's in bad shape."

"Did I break his jaw?"

The way Mancini remembers, it was Griff who informed him of Kim's condition.

"So taxing," said Griff. "The fight was so taxing. I think it just took its toll on that boy."

"What do you mean?"

"It don't look good, Raymond. It don't look good."

Soon, Dave called from the hospital. He instructed Ray not to speak with the press. Kim's brain was swollen, he said, and probably beyond repair.

"What are you saying?" asked Ray. "What the fuck are you telling me?"

Duk Koo Kim would be all right. Ray was sure of that. To believe in Kim's demise was, at some level, to believe in his own. He recalls disregarding the admonitions of his handlers to shower and dress. He had a show to attend. Sinatra asked personally. It might as well have been the pope inviting him.

The opening act that night was comedian Charlie Callas, a *Tonight Show* regular known for his entertainingly elastic faces. Then Frank and Nancy Sinatra took the stage, for the ninth of their thirteen-night engagement at the Circus Maximus Showroom.

Ladies and gentlemen, Frank began, *this afternoon I saw the greatest fight I've ever seen . . . And here he is with us, my friend, the lightweight champeen of the world, Ray "Boom Boom" Mancini . . .*

That's how Ray would recall it, word for word. But as the spotlight found him in the audience, he felt like a perpetrator. The glint off his sunglasses and his jewelry cut through the nightclub's haze as he stood to wave. Ray could feel the weight of his own counterfeit smile.

Sinatra didn't know what had happened, nor did the audience members who seconded his sentiments with hearty applause. But Ray, just beginning to comprehend, was already shrouded with grief and guilt. Two and a half hours on the operating table hadn't changed anything for Duk Koo Kim. Death was inevitable; the body would go the way of his brain.

The crooner's remark was intended as a kind of benediction. Even as Sinatra spoke, though, Ray couldn't help but think of what his father had told him. Boom had only meant to comfort him, father to son, one fighter to another. But the words were more haunting than any Ray had ever heard.

"Thank God," said Boom. "It could've been you."

Ray was turned back at the Desert Springs emergency room, with Hammargren informing him that neither Kim nor his entourage were in any shape to receive visitors, however well-meaning they might be. Still, Ray ran into Yoon Gu back at the hotel.

"His eyes were like chestnuts," says Yoon Gu.

They shook hands and half-bowed at each other, but did not try to speak. "Our body language was meant to convey that it was a good fight," says Yoon Gu.

The trainer had already been ordered to gather Duk Koo's belongings and take the next flight home, as his services were needed back at the Dong-Ah. Among the items Yoon Gu found were Kim's boxing shoes and hand wraps, the fighter's good brown suit, some jewelry, and American cosmetics he had purchased in the casino's Forum shops for Young Mee. But Yoon Gu could not find what he was looking for. The Rolex had disappeared.

After boarding the flight to Incheon airport, Yoon Gu locked himself in the bathroom, where he would spend the better part of his next twelve hours, and began to cry.

"There are no signs of any brain function," Hammargren told the press late Saturday. "What little there is left will stop working after a short while . . . The pressure in his head will go up and up, and that will be it."

The neurosurgeon also ventured an educated guess that the coma resulted from a single blow, quite possibly the last. "The hemorrhage was quite fresh," he said. "The trauma was caused by one punch . . . They tell me he fought like a lion in the thirteenth round. Well, nobody could fight like that with a blood clot in his brain."

By Sunday morning, newspapers around the world were describing Kim as "just about dead." Ray rose without waking. The pain made sleep difficult, but then, so did those goblins of suggestion and doubt that now invaded his consciousness. Yes, what his father said was true:

It could've been me.

He said as much in the couple of interviews he granted that day. David Dinkins did a piece for CBS News. Peter Alfano came for the *New York Times*.

"It was a terrific fight and I saved my title but what am I, a hero?" he asked Alfano. "I was in there with him, and who's to say it couldn't be me? And yet, how can I say, 'It was better him than me'?"

Those were divine questions. But so that His purpose might become known, Father O'Neill presided over a ten o'clock mass at a ballroom in the Tropicana hotel. Most of the attendees were Youngstowners, either expatriate wise guys or card-carrying members of the entourage. Ray, his left hand bandaged, bowed his head as Father O'Neill asked them all to pray for the everlasting soul of Duk Koo Kim.

Our Father, who art in heaven, hallowed be thy name . . .

By now it was Monday in Seoul, and Young Mee had been apprised of her fiancée's condition. "I thought the sky fell down on me," she says.

Chapter 11 | Ghosts

Sun-Nyo Yang's arrival was heralded by her quote in a UPI dispatch from Seoul. "My heart has been broken apart," she said.

She hurriedly flew to Los Angeles, where she was met by a delegation from the Korean consulate. Her son was on life support, she was told, and the decision to disconnect the respirator would be hers. By the time Sun-Nyo deplaned at McCarran International Airport in Las Vegas, the cameras and reporters were poised and ready. Though Duk Koo remained alive in the legal and, arguably, theological senses, her procession to the gate had the air of a funeral cortege. Hyun-Chi Kim held her by the right elbow. Kun-Yeung Kim, her stepson, who had once admonished Duk Koo to bloody bullies' noses, walked a step behind.

In the glare of such sudden and intense inspection, Sun-Nyo's gait seemed unsteady, as if she were suffering from vertigo. She wore a plain white robe, a traditional *han bok*. At sixty-five, she was weathered, obviously frail, and strikingly small, not close to five feet tall.

"A little bitty thing," recalls Hammargren, who had complied with the family's request for Duk Koo to be examined by Korean doctors with expertise in acupuncture and medicinal herbs.

At the hospital, Hammargren showed the mother and stepbrother the images of Duk Koo's brain. Kun-Yeung instantly understood them as harbingers of his stepbrother's inevitable demise. Still, he announced Sun-Nyo's arrival at bedside in the ICU. "Mother is here," he said. "Please open your eyes."

Then Sun-Nyo took her son's hand. "Open eyes," she repeated.

"It's not your fault. Open eyes, your brother and I are here. Please, wake up."

After fifteen minutes, she was led from the room, weeping.

"What will happen when they disconnect the respirator?" she asked one of the consulate officers.

"Your son will die," she was told.

Neither the needles nor the herbs improved the prognosis. Asian doctors were as helpless as Hammargren to heal her stricken son. "I am not optimistic," said Dr. Chang Bin Lee. "He belongs to the dead."

At the five-thirty P.M. hearing the next day, Nevada District Court Judge Paul Goldman declared Duk Koo Kim legally dead. Surgeons from Stanford University harvested his kidneys for transplantation, but declined to take his heart as the designated recipient feared the publicity. The respirator was then detached.

Then Sun-Nyo, "tiny," as she was described in the *Review-Journal*, held back tears long enough to read a statement that was translated for the media: "The American doctors and nurses have done their best to rejuvenate my son. In spite of all our efforts, we cannot revive him. If I continue to let the doctors and the staff supply medical treatment, it is a burden to them.

"My son has shown his bravery in fighting Mr. Mancini. My true reason for the transplants is that my son can live forever and have everlasting life in this world. Through the transplants his fighting spirit can be given to others."

In the days that followed, Duk Koo was eulogized by Korean Protestant ministers in an open-casket service at Las Vegas's Palm Chapel. Those who paid their respects in person included Dr. Hammargren, U.S. Senator Howard Cannon, and the referee, Richard Green. The casket was then draped in a South Korean flag and flown to Seoul, where Duk Koo would lie in state at the headquarters of the Korean Boxing Commission.

Before the body was repatriated, Hyun-Chi Kim was on the phone, instructing Duk Koo's friends not to let Young Mee go public, lest it damage the dead fighter's image. However, as the news enveloped Seoul, Young Mee decided to make herself known. Her baby with Duk Koo was due in six months. "If it's a boy, I will make him a boxer to follow in his father's footsteps," she said.

She was also quoted vowing to marry Duk Koo posthumously. "I will marry Duk Koo's spirit and no one else, and I will live with him for all my life," she said. "I believe that is the only way to console him."

Duk Koo might've been surprised to know he had two life insurance policies at the time of his death. One was the standard policy for any boxer fighting in a *Top Rank* show. The other, also a standard policy, was underwritten by the Korean Boxing Commission. The sum of the death benefits, according to Hyun-Chi, was approximately one hundred thousand U.S. dollars, then a small fortune for most Korean families.

"In the beginning, Young Mee and her father, an elder at the church, didn't appear," says Hyun-Chi, who was charged with dividing the insurance monies. "Then, when the media wrote about the existence and the amount of insurance money, they finally appeared. They claimed that they needed to receive (a bigger) portion of the money because they needed to raise a child. I said that this is not the time to talk about these sorts of things and that I would be fair. I thought that I also needed to give some money to his mother who had raised him. So I told Young Mee and her father that they should put their concern to rest because I will be very fair—that I wouldn't take even ten won. But whenever they saw a reporter, Young Mee would cry and shed tears."

"She married him posthumously for the money," says Kun-Yeung Kim. "It was an act to draw public opinion in her favor."

Young Mee, for her part, remains deeply hurt and offended at the suggestion. Yes, "people around her" suggested that she marry Duk Koo posthumously. But she never did, and says her quotes were a fabrication. "It snowballed into an unfounded rumor," she says. "My pastor said that posthumous marriage was against the Christian faith."

• • •

For Ray, the accuracy of Young Mee's remark was immaterial. He believed in spirits: his father's, his brother's, and now Kim's. In fact, they would not leave him alone. Sleep was no relief, either, as they now populated his dreams.

Like Young Mee, Ray relied on his Christian faith. It would deliver him through this period, as it had delivered him through his brother's death. But his religiosity—his own literal construct of heaven and hell, guilt and ghosts—made temporal life more difficult. Though he spoke with Father O'Neill several times a day, Ray now found it impossible to abide by the priest's admonition from sophomore religion class.

Just be.

How? The media's slow-moving infantry met him at the airport. His name, as that of the man who died at his hands, was on Walter Cronkite's lips. He couldn't pick up a newspaper or turn on the television without being reminded of what had happened. It didn't help that there was an NFL strike, and that Kim's death now became fodder for the news hole in America's sports sections. Alone in his Boardman apartment, Ray was reluctant to answer the phone or gaze in the mirror. Rather, he would stare in horrified disbelief at the fatal instruments. He still couldn't make a fist with his left hand.

"I must have hit him a thousand times with it," said Ray.

"He goes from periods of denial, as if this never occurred, to periods of depression," Dave Wolf told the *New York Times*. "We don't want Ray to become the second tragedy here."

The easy, if somewhat erroneous comparison was that between Ray and Emile Griffith, who beat Benny Paret into a fatal coma twenty years before. Emile, Murphy Griffith's nephew, had been trained by Gil Clancy.

"I don't think Emile ever got completely over it," said Clancy. "He was never the same fighter and as sorry as I feel for Kim, I feel sorry for Mancini."

"You don't forget," said Murphy. "Some can handle it, some can't. How it will happen in Ray's case, only time will tell."

"I'd like him to quit," Little Ellen told the Associated Press.

Ray Arcel, on the other hand, who knew two generations of Mancinis, recommended the young fighter's hasty return to the ring. "If he broods about it he'll start thinking it can happen to him," said the trainer.

In fact, that had already happened. Three days after the fight, Ray held a press conference in Youngstown, telling reporters how much he identified with Kim. "I have realized that I am the same way," he said. "I would fight to my last breath. The same thing could happen to me . . .

"Look at me now. I'm a physical wreck. I'm mentally beaten up. My hands are swelled up like balloons. My eye is closed. You can say, 'Yeah, Ray, go on. This is just something that happened.' But I don't know if I want to go on . . .

"I've reached my goal. I've achieved it for my father. There's nothing else to achieve, in my eyes . . .

"My family, my lawyers, and my friends are all trying to console me. They can't. I was the one in that ring with him. I was the one that hit him."

The candor and ingenuousness that won Ray so many fans were now liabilities. He'd turned a mere press conference into a public confession. Worse still, were the sins to which he admitted. Sure, he was only human. But he was a fighter, too. And as such, declarations of fear and doubt were permanent and unpardonable.

As the fight became national news, the venue shifted from Caesars to Desert Springs Hospital, site of what Mort Sharnik called the death watch. There, soon after Kim's surgery, Bob Arum called for a suspension of boxing while a federal panel looked into the state of the sport.

"The old excuses that prevailed in the past don't prevail now," he said. "We have to ask some serious questions."

Of course, some of the same prognosticators who had predicted a mismatch now snickered that Arum's proposed moratorium coincided with a busy stretch of championship fights promoted by his archrival, Don King. The fight game justified such cynicism, but the fight itself did not. There had been no tragic mistake, no lapse in judgment by the referee (as had been the case with Ruby Goldstein, who waited an inexplicably long time to intervene with Paret trapped in the ropes), no suggestion that either the fighters or their cornermen conducted themselves with anything but valor. If not for the postscript, Mancini–Kim would have gone down as a great fight. Instead, within hours, it had become the flashpoint in a raging debate about boxing.

"The beast has struck again," wrote *New York Times* columnist George Vecsey. "The tragedy in Las Vegas comes at a time when boxing is flourishing all over the United States. With the pro football players out, probably for the season, television has sent out the recruiting message to every gymnasium in America: Uncle Beast Wants You."

Vecsey hadn't been alone watching in horror the previous night, either, as an oxygen mask was pressed over the face of an unconscious Arguello. "Is there anything that can be done to keep people from being punched into unconsciousness and sometimes to the brink of death?" he asked.

Eleven days later, heavyweight champ Larry Holmes squared off against the overmatched Randall "Tex" Cobb in Houston's Astrodome. By the ninth round, the swollen ridges along Cobb's already pronounced features gave him an unmistakably tragic look, that of a bloody Cro-Magnon warrior. Howard Cosell, more famous than any athlete but the now-slurry Ali, described Cobb's face as being "like hamburger meat."

As it went on, Cosell told the ABC audience that the fight had lost its sporting status and now qualified as "an assault on the sense of any civilized human being." Still, the broadcaster reserved special contempt for the referee, who let the "brutalization" go the full fifteen rounds. "Doesn't he know," asked Cosell, "that he is constructing an advertisement for the abolition of boxing?"

Some days later, under the headline FIGHTING MAD, COSELL WALKS AWAY FROM SPORT TURNED SPECTACLE, the *Washington Post* announced that he would no longer cover professional boxing. The fight game needed full federal regulation, Cosell told the *Post*'s Dave Kindred: "Either that, or abolish the quote-sport-unquote."

In a matter of weeks, the American Medical Association would announce its official position on boxing: Ban it. "Boxing seems to me to be less a sport than is cockfighting," wrote Dr. George D. Lundberg, editor of the association's journal. "Boxing is an obscenity. Uncivilized man may have been bloodthirsty. Boxing, as a throwback to uncivilized man, should not be sanctioned by any civilized society."

Of course, even an organization as august as the AMA would have to admit that its concern was sudden. After all, brutalized boxers weren't exactly a new phenomenon. Nor were ring deaths. At the time of the Kim fight, *The Ring Record Book* listed 337 pro fighters who had died from boxing-related injuries since World War II. One hundred and twenty were in the United States.

"You could," argued veteran columnist Jerry Izenberg, "point out that eight young men have died this very year from injuries directly related to football or that a sport like hang gliding had forty-eight deaths last year as opposed to four for boxing—and there are a hell of a lot more fighters than gliders."

The World Boxing Council—the sanctioning body affiliated with Don King—responded to the criticism by shortening the length of championship fights from fifteen rounds to twelve. There was, as yet, no evidence that this would make fighters safer. But longtime boxing *aficionados* like Izenberg, a close friend of Ali's since the early 1960s, understood that the uproar had little to do with the public's concern for pugs. Rather, it served as another illustration of Marshall McLuhan's theorem: "The medium is the message." There was a sense that the horrors of November 1982, Kim's death first among them, were made distinct and amplified by the power of national television.

Arum nailed it in the waiting room at Desert Springs. "How terrible this is to have 20 million people in the US see the kid get killed on television," he said.

In fact, *CBS Sports Saturday* scored an 8.7 Nielsen rating that afternoon, a twenty-one share, and was seen in 7.25 million

homes. Fatal fights had been televised before, Emile Griffith–
Benny Paret being hitherto the most famous. Eighteen years later,
a Mexican bantamweight named Lupe Pintor knocked out a
painfully thin Welshman during a CBS broadcast from Los Angeles's Olympic Auditorium. Johnny Owen, known as the Merthyr
Matchstick, went down in the twelfth round and never got up.

Interestingly enough, for men who began their dying on television, both Paret and Owen were mythologized in prose. "Paret
died on his feet," wrote Norman Mailer, who'd watched from ringside. "He was still standing in the ropes, trapped as he had been
before, he gave some little half-smile of regret, as if he were saying,
'I didn't know I was going to die just yet,' and then, his head leaning back but still erect, his death came to breathe about him. He
began to pass away. As he passed, so his limbs descended beneath
him, and he sank slowly to the floor. He went down more slowly
than any fighter had ever gone down, he went down like a large
ship that turns on end and slides second by second into its grave.
As he went down, the sounds of Griffith's punches echoed in the
mind like a heavy ax in the distance chopping into a wet log."

In Owen's case, the London *Observer*'s Hugh McIlvanney
watched from ringside as the young Welshman was all but mar-
tyred by the "extreme depth of his own courage." Just hours after
Owen lapsed into a coma, McIlvanney wrote of his own dread
going into the fight: "There is something about his pale face,
with its large nose, jutting ears and uneven teeth, all set above
that long, skeletal frame, that takes hold of the heart and makes
unbearable the thought of him being badly hurt."

Owen, as McIlvanney reported, would die a virgin, "a boy so
obsessively dedicated to a fighting career that he has never once
allowed himself to be distracted by a girl, never as much as kissed
one in earnest."

And what of the killers? What of Griffith and Pinter?

Very little, actually. Emile Griffith was gay, black, and from the
Virgin Islands. Lupe Pintor was from Cuajimalpa, Mexico, and
did not speak English. To the Nielsen audience, they remained
abstractions. Ray Mancini, by contrast, was boxing's equivalent of

the boy next door. Americans *knew* him. Unlike anyone else in the fight game, people trusted him. Now they had to reconcile their trust and affection with the idea that he had taken a life. It was a difficult enough task for Ray himself. It was impossible for the fans.

Gina Andriolo, who by now was writing Ray's contracts, understood the implications when negotiations for his endorsements came to an abrupt end. There would be no soft-drink deal, no shoe deal, no apparel deal. "Those CBS afternoon fights reached so deep into Middle America," she says. "But now those same people had seen the Kim fight."

"Not only was it a tragedy," says Mort Sharnik. "It was the end of boxing, certainly on network television. The ratings dropped like a rock after that. After a few years, boxing was no longer on the networks."

"The fight game was on a roll and Mancini was a tremendous part of it," says Arum. "To have him associated with this tragedy cast a pall on the sport. It didn't kill it, but it stopped the momentum. A lot of sponsors had second thoughts, and once that happens, there's no money. The advertisers were throwing around huge dollars. If you're an advertiser, you don't want to see death."

The Mancini fable—the story Ray so carefully constructed with himself as its protagonist—had been corrupted. Its symbolism had been turned upside down. The All-American Boy, a televised icon of righteousness and redemption, now engendered conversations of money and murder.

On Sunday, November 14, the day he returned to Youngstown, Ray called his sweetheart.

"Is Gina there?"

"No. Gina's not here."

Ray called back Monday, Tuesday, Wednesday, and Thursday. And for five straight days, the whereabouts of an aspiring Miss America remained unknown.

Finally, on Friday—the day Ray's handlers announced that his next fight, a supposedly easy payday in Italy, had been postponed— she came to the phone.

"Gina," said Ray. "Where you been?"

She had been busy on the pageant circuit, she explained.

He asked if she had seen the fight.

"Raymond," she said, "my parents think it's best if we don't see each other anymore."

That hurt as much as anything Duk Koo hit him with. For all Ray knew of subjects as various as women and car bombs, he was still an innocent. He hadn't known how cruel people could be, or the evils they could acquire from their own parents.

A week or two after returning to Youngstown, Ray finally got out of his apartment and went to his nephew's Pop Warner football game. Little Ellen's son, Jason, was eleven now. One of his teammates spotted Ray on the sidelines.

"Do you know who I am?" asked the boy.

Ray didn't understand why the kid was laughing.

"I'm Duk Koo Kim's son," he said.

For all the heartlessness, Ray didn't lack for sympathy, either. Expressions of condolence, more than a thousand, some simply addressed to "Ray Mancini, Youngstown," kept arriving at 807 Cambridge Street. The local Wolves Club honored him as its Man of the Year, setting aside proceeds for the Raymond Mancini Scholarship Fund, an annual stipend bestowed upon a deserving Cardinal Mooney student. In Washington, Congressmen Lyle Williams of Ohio and Silvio Conte of Massachusetts hosted a reception in recognition of the way he had faced "adversity without hesitation and without complaint."

As Conte's man put it, "The kid has kind of been down in the dumps."

Chuck Tanner understood. The Pittsburgh Pirates manager, from nearby New Castle, Pennsylvania, drove to Youngstown one morning and promptly informed Ray that they were going to spend a day in the therapeutic state of not giving a shit. They stopped for breakfast at a pancake house, played a leisurely round of golf at the Youngstown Country Club, and enjoyed a hearty dinner at Sandolini's in Meadville.

"I didn't talk much," said Tanner, whose exceptionally close '79 World Series team was known for its theme song, Sister Sledge's "We Are Family." "A kid like that, you let him do all the talking. You just want him to know he has a friend. Hell, he didn't mean to hurt anybody."

A few days later, Ray went to Atlantic City to watch Gonzalo Montellano lose a unanimous decision to Kenny Bogner, now being mentioned as a prospective opponent for the champion's comeback. It was a test, said Ray. He winced at punches thrown in the early rounds, but soon found himself bobbing and weaving in his ringside seat. By the end of the fight, he said, he couldn't wait for a shot at Bogner.

"I knew the fire was still there," he told UPI.

Those around him were less sure. Big Ellen sought counsel from Kae Bae Chun, her tae kwon do instructor at the YMCA. A former bodyguard to the South Korean prime minister, Chun inquired of his contacts in Seoul on behalf of the family. Ray wanted to go to Korea to pay his respects, but Chun advised against it, saying the grief was still too raw.

Master Chun, as his students called him, also had a message for Ray. "The Korean people do not hold anything against you," he told him. "They wish you well, and believe Duk Koo's spirit lives through you."

The sentiments were a source of great relief and some pride for Ray. The idea of this spirit still troubled his mother, who met again with Master Chun in the cafeteria at the YMCA. Was there a way, she asked, to make peace with it?

"Write a letter," Master Chun told her. "From one mother to another."

Chun, who got Sun-Nyo's address with a single phone call, felt a special sympathy for Duk Koo's mother. He understood the stigma, as his own mother raised four children alone after their father died from a hunting accident.

"Write what you feel for her," he said.

Big Ellen spent several days composing a three-page letter. She told Sun-Nyo that she had been praying for her, for God to restore, as Chun recalls, "her sense of harmony and joy." She wanted to know if there were anything Sun-Nyo needed. She asked Duk Koo's mother to consider Ray as her own son, the Mancinis as her family, and ended with an invitation to come to Youngstown.

"The last words of the letter were 'I want you to live with us,'" says Chun, who wept while translating pages already blotted with Big Ellen's tears.

On January 13, 1983, exactly two months after the Kim fight, at a press conference announcing his return to the ring, Ray proclaimed himself healed: "I have no mental blocks . . . I have buried the memory of all that."

He had resumed workouts at the Times Square Gym, where he ran into none other than Emile Griffith: "Emile came up to me and he says: 'Welcome back.' That's all he said. I said to myself, 'That's it. That does it for me.'"

Where Emile couldn't help, George Feeney would. Feeney held the British lightweight title. That didn't mean much in the States, where the presumption against British fighters went back to the 1920s, when "Phainting Phil" Scott became the first in a long line of his majesty's "horizontal heavyweights." However, Feeney, from Hartlepool, England, was just what Ray needed at this delicate juncture. At 16–7, with only seven knockouts to his credit, Feeney's fights usually went the distance. In other words, he could take a punch without being particularly dangerous.

"It was an especially good time for a nontitle fight," said Dave Wolf, who was looking for signs "of any subconscious masochistic tendency" in his fighter, a subliminal desire to do "penance by getting bashed."

As concerned as he was with Ray's psychiatric state, Wolf and Bob Arum had to restore his commercial appeal, too. By now, CBS was out. Mort Sharnik's bosses at the Tiffany network had been stung by the criticism. "The perception was that they had put on a mismatch and gotten a guy killed," says Arum. "They were out of the Ray Mancini business."

Hence, the Feeney fight went to NBC, which would televise it live from the Palazzo Dello Sport in St. Vincent, Italy. A ten-round, nontitle bout, it was a glorified exhibition. "My title's not at risk," said Ray, "but my marketability is."

As it regarded Kim's death, Ray was much quicker to acknowledge the financial implications than the emotional ones. Then again, still just twenty-one, self-examination was not yet his strong suit. This was a kid, street-smart but unworldly, who had just shown up for the press conference with *Penthouse* Pet Linda Kenton—his new "sparring partner," reported the *New York Post's* Page Six—while telling everybody how much he was looking forward to meeting Pope John Paul.

He also wanted to say, for the record, that he was against most of the so-called reforms being bandied about in Washington and elsewhere. Sure, he wanted fighters to receive more vigilant medical examinations. But proposals for headgear and twelve-round title fights—"the true championship distance is fifteen rounds," he said—were anathema to Ray. They would only diminish the sport that made his father a hero.

Still, the reporters wanted to know about Kim. "We acknowledged each other," said Ray. "All fighters do that. You can look into each other's eyes and tell what kind of man he is . . . He brought out the best in me."

Even as Ray waited for someone to change the subject, the newly healed fighter had begun to well up with tears.

Not long after touching down in Italy, Ray attended mass as an honored guest of the Turin Football Club. Then he took in a soccer game, where he was introduced to a stadium of delighted fans before traveling the final ninety kilometers to the Grand Hotel Billia, in the Alpine resort town of St. Vincent.

Italians considered him one of their own, a favorite son. He signed autographs with the salutation *a mio amico*. An elderly contessa wrapped his hands before sparring sessions. Drivers honked as they passed him doing his roadwork. A sizable contingent from Ray's ancestral Sicilian home of Bagheria would make the day-long journey by train. They would camp in the Grand Hotel's lobby, playing accordions and chanting "Boom Boom" in robust accents.

Perhaps Ray, or someone in his camp, should have noticed when the newspapers quoted him on the plane crash that killed the entire Turin soccer team in 1949. Ray had never heard of the plane crash. Then it was reported that Dave Wolf had won $359,000 at the local casino. Wolf, who didn't own a tie required for admittance to the casino, was sleeping at the time, recovering from the transatlantic flight.

The truth was, Ray didn't really care what was in the local papers. He was happy to be far from his usual fight venues, relieved for the respite, grateful not to be talking of death and Duk Koo Kim.

It would have pained him more to know what was going on in Seoul. Not only had the settling of Kim's affairs created more than a schism between the fighter's family and Young Mee's. It had poisoned Duk Koo's own blood relations, too.

The value of his estate, according to an exclusive in the Korean daily, *Joon-Ang Ilbo*, came to $158,108 and included the proceeds of the WBA's $100,000 insurance policy. Young Mee would receive sixty percent, Sun-Nyo and her husband the remaining forty.

Duk Koo's mother had told Hyun-Chi Kim that she didn't want any money for the death of her son. Nevertheless, as he recalls, the old woman "was portrayed as a greedy person living in splendor" on the insurance money.

"Things got complicated," says Kun Sik Kim, Duk Koo's eldest stepbrother. Under Korea's old family registration system, mothers were listed under the names of their first-born sons. That was a problem for Sun-Nyo, as she had three previous husbands, sons, and stepsons.

"She not only had to meet her first son again, but her whole family history was exposed," says Kun Sik. "None of us on this side of the family had known about her past, and none from that side knew about Duk Koo. But once they found out about Duk Koo, they came here several times."

"I asked the lawyer to hurry up and wrap up the issue before it went to the press," says Kun Yeung Kim, the stepson who had accompanied Sun-Nyo to America. "All these people with all sorts of surnames—Baek, Lee, Kim—whom I had never met before, now appeared and sued to get a share of the money." Among them, Kun Yeung thought, was a now-grown boy who first showed up with Duk Koo in Banam. "Then people started whispering, 'How many more children are there?'"

Then, a week before Mancini's return to the ring in Italy, Sun-Nyo Yang took her life. She drank a bottle of pesticide. The real cause of death, however, unmentioned in any autopsy, was insurmountable grief and shame.

Kae Bae Chun, the former bodyguard from Youngstown by way of Seoul, inquired as to the fate of Ellen's tear-stained missive. It hadn't yet arrived, he was told.

"That letter," he says, "could have saved a mother's life."

Within hours, reporters descended on the Grand Hotel Billia. Though Ray declined to speak about the suicide, press agent Irving Rudd issued a brief statement expressing his "deepest sympathies and profound sorrow." Then, trying to keep to his prefight routine, Ray had his regular Sunday night dinner: filet of sole, spaghetti, and vegetables. He took an apple and a banana back to his room for dessert.

Still, Italy's national sports papers—*La Gazzetta dello Sport* and *Corriere dello Sport*—claimed Ray was too grief-stricken to eat. They said he cloistered himself in his hotel room and prayed. They invented quotes from him, saying he would travel to Korea as soon as possible and pray at the graves of Duk Koo and Sun-Nyo. *La Gazzetta* also ran a picture of Ray taking communion. It had been taken two weeks before, at the church in Turin.

"One paper said I was so distraught I went to a local cemetery and prayed over a grave because I was thinking of Kim," says Ray. "Absolute lie. They didn't care. They just made shit up."

Finally, Ray confronted a reporter who had been so friendly upon his arrival. "Giovanni," he asked, "why did you do this?"

"Ray, you must understand," he said. "We are journalists. It makes a good story."

"That's all they wanted to talk about," says Chuck Fagan. "Kim, Kim, Kim."

"It wouldn't go away," says Tank.

And Ray was just beginning to understand that it probably never would.

As it happened, Sun-Nyo was found at home by her husband, and pronounced dead forty minutes later at a local hospital. But, as Ray told the *New York Times*'s Dave Anderson, he was trying not to know the details.

"God forbid, I got to fight in a few days," he said. "I thought I was getting Kim's death out of my mind. I know it's human nature to bring it up to me again now that Kim's mother is dead. No matter how much is past, I guess it's never past. I'm trying to be the best champion I can but it seems like I'm going to be forever linked to Kim's death. Is this what people are going to remember about me? Or are they going to remember me as a good champion?"

The hours preceding the Feeney fight were harried ones. Ray attended mass in an eleventh-century church with relatives from Bagheria. Then, back at the hotel, he greeted still-arriving contingents from Sicily and Youngstown, including his parents, while refusing suggestions that he take a nap.

Also in the lobby was Dave Wolf, pacing, agitated, and threatening to cancel the fight on account of the substandard, slack-roped ring. At this point, Wolf's tactics seemed just another prefight ritual. The bout went off as scheduled, live, at three in the afternoon, eastern standard time, on NBC's *Sportsworld*.

Though the British journeyman proved an unexpectedly difficult test, Wolf was quick to proclaim a larger victory. "If it had been an easy fight, we'd still have all those questions," he said. "We're right back on course."

Wolf had to know better. In the seventh, Feeney opened a gash over Ray's left eye. In the eighth, he shook Mancini with a series of rights. The Englishman would recall contemplating "a sensational upset in that moment."

The fight was typical Mancini, in that it wanted for neither blood nor action. But there was no knockout, just a surprisingly close ten-round decision. Two judges scored it 98–96, another had it 98–95. It was unanimous for Ray. Just the same, it did nothing to restore his reputation as a champion.

"I needed a tough fight," Ray told reporters.

For all his protestations, he knew something was wrong. Years later, he speaks of that night as if confessing: "That was the only fight I can remember not caring if I won or lost. People just didn't understand. I was so mentally and emotionally drained, I didn't give a shit. I just wanted to get it over with."

Bob Arum had been in New York, drinking vodka at the St. Regis Hotel when he seized upon an inspired idea.

"We'll call it: the Chairman and the Champs," he said.

"C'mon," said Mickey Rudin, Sinatra's longtime lawyer. "Never."

"Just run it by him," implored Sol Kerzner, owner of the Sun City resort in the South African Republic of Bophuthatswana.

"Frank will never go for it," said Rudin.

About an hour later, Arum got a call to meet at Kerzner's suite, where Sinatra's attorney was already waiting.

"I don't believe it," said Rudin, whose other clients included Elizabeth Taylor, the Aga Khan, and Warner Bros. "He had no interest until I mentioned Mancini. Then, soon as I did, Frank says, 'I'm in.'"

The promotion in Bophuthatswana, "a place only about four people in the world can spell," said the *Los Angeles Times*'s Jim

Murray, would feature two championship bouts. The first would be a junior middleweight title bout featuring Roberto Duran. In the second, Kenny "Bang Bang" Bogner, 18–1–1, with a loss to somebody named Livingstone Bramble, would challenge Mancini for the WBA title.

The key, of course, was Sinatra, who would do a thirty-minute concert in the ring before Mancini's entrance. Sinatra was more than the most famous entertainer in the world; it was his imprimatur that made the show respectable. Though the ostensibly enlightened and allegedly integrated Republic of Bophuthatswana had been a state since 1977, it remained under the control of South Africa, whose apartheid laws were the cause of a worldwide boycott. South Africans could not compete in the Olympics, the World Cup, the Davis Cup, or Wimbledon. "Landing Frank Sinatra is worth its weight in Krugerrands," wrote Murray. "Sinatra is a performer whose record on race relations in unassailable, and who sent his personal attorney, Milton (Mickey) Rudin, to personally check out Bophuthatswana for any symptoms of segregation or applications of apartheid."

"I found none," reported Rudin.

The card was scheduled for May 27, 1983, three in the morning local time, to be broadcast around the world on closed-circuit, pay-per-view, and subscription television. Arum predicted gross revenues between $20 and $25 million. This would be Ray's first million-dollar purse, double Duran's and five times what Bogner, another lightly regarded challenger, was getting. For Ray, the time had come to start cashing in.

He arrived in Johannesburg six weeks before the fight and by April 28, had already sparred thirty-one rounds. That's when a sparring partner named Teddy "Hookin'" Hatfield hit him in the right shoulder, causing Ray to drop his hand and wince in pain.

"It felt like something snapped," he said. "I knew it was bad."

Ray tried to continue, but Murphy Griffith called off the session without hesitation. Griff had seen Ray wade through some hellacious beatings, in the gym and under the lights, only to give better than he got. The single exception would be Arguello.

Hookin' Hatfield was no Arguello. Still, X-rays revealed a broken collarbone.

"In twenty years of sports medicine, I've never seen this kind of injury caused by a blow to the shoulder," said Dr. Clive Noble, an orthopedic surgeon who examined Ray on behalf of the South African Boxing Board of Control.

The WBA's lightweight champ would need at least eighteen weeks of complete rest. "I apologize for not being able to go on," he told the press, close to tears.

Meanwhile, Arum called Sinatra. "Frank, we'll get another guy," he said, wondering where the hell he was going to find another Italian fighter as good as Ray.

But Sinatra was adamant. "If the kid ain't fighting," he said, "I'm not singing."

Sinatra wasn't the only A-lister still enamored with Ray. Four months after the Kim fight, it was announced that Sylvester Stallone had finally purchased Ray's life rights for a TV movie. There was now talk of Maureen Stapleton playing Big Ellen, but Ray still wanted to star as Ray. In anticipation of his screen test—the first of many, he supposed—he signed with William Morris. "Sly is a great guy," he said in an interview, "and he told me I don't really need acting lessons . . . It's important to be natural. Geez, that's not hard for me to play myself."

The movie would end with Ray's redemption of his father, winning a title that, as far as the Nielsen audience was concerned, had been lost on a battlefield in Metz. It's not that Duk Koo Kim was written out of the script. He had never been part of it.

As Gina Andriolo told the *Washington Post*'s David Remnick, "We think an 'up' kind of story has more appeal."

Then again, even as the months passed, it was difficult, if not impossible, for anyone to forget about the Kim fight. Irving Rudd employed his best old-school press agentry. He had Ray compete in a Sambuca-sponsored bocci tournament. He had him inducted as an honorary member of Teamsters Local 966 and Longshoreman's Local 1814. There was a public workout at the Fulton Fish Market in lower Manhattan (with Ray skipping rope to "Eye of the Tiger," of course). And there was an apparently endless supply of *Penthouse* Pets willing to escort the champ to his public appearances. As Rudd knew full well, delectably carnal centerfolds were not only ideal props for securing a mention in the New York gossip columns, but for making a prima facie case that Ray was over what his own people referred to as "the Kim thing."

While it remained unclear whether Ray could move on, it was now certain that the rest of the world could not. The Congressional hearings convened in the wake of the Kim fight went nowhere, very loudly. What began with such fanfare, with Howard Cosell being sworn in as a witness on Capitol Hill, ended with the House killing a modest $880,000 proposal to create a federal Advisory Board on Boxing. The measure went down by a vote of 167–254, inspiring an editorial in the *New York Post*. "How many more Duk Koo Kim's," it asked, "won't wake up before our national conscience does?"

The answer wasn't finite. But one way or another, every dead fighter seemed to point back at Ray. For example, the eighth to die that year, according to *The Ring*, would be Isidro "Gino" Perez, of West New York, New Jersey, by way of Juarez, Mexico. Perez made two thousand dollars for his final bout, a lightweight pairing against Juan Ramon Cruz at Madison Square Garden's theater-style arena, the Felt Forum. Perez had been ahead when he was knocked out in the seventh round and lapsed into a coma. He passed away six days later. Though his record, 13–1–1 (or was it 17–1–1?), was the subject of some confusion, the source of his notoriety was not. At the time of his death, Perez was still best known for his fight with Freddy Bowman two years earlier. Bowman, who took months to die of the injuries inflicted that night in Atlantic City, had been Ray's nemesis as an amateur back in Youngstown.

To Ray and those around him, the news was a relentless conspiracy of circumstance. Over the Fourth of July weekend, referee Richard Green was found in his North Las Vegas home, dead of a single gunshot wound to the chest. Green's work in the ring was universally well regarded. He was as good at the Silver Slipper as he was officiating championship bouts at Caesars. At forty-six, Green had been the third man in the ring for Larry Holmes's destruction of Muhammad Ali, for Duran's loss to Wilfred Benitez and for two of Ray's title fights against Frias and of course, Kim, a fight that earned him kudos for acting with decisive mercy. There was no suggestion that the fatal bout had left him impaired in any way. Green continued to referee and just the night before his death worked an ESPN card at the Showboat Hotel.

"Friends said he did not seem despondent but appeared in good spirits," according to the *Las Vegas Review-Journal*.

From the *Las Vegas Sun*: "Police said Green was found lying in bed with a revolver by his side. Three shots had been fired—one in the ceiling and one in the wall. No suicide note was found."

To satisfy his own curiosity, Ralph Wiley met with the daughter of Green's first marriage. Her name was Regina, and she was convinced her father's death was the result of a professional hit.

"My father had too much to live for," she told the writer. "Everybody liked him . . . I was one of the first ones who found him . . . I live three minutes away . . . Every door in his house was closed, including the bedroom door. I know he never closes those doors. I know my father's routine. And his car door was unlocked. I know if he never locks no other door, he locks that one. You know, I swear it's got something to do with boxing . . ."

Not long after the body was found, Regina began receiving calls at home, a male voice telling her, "Your daddy killed himself."

Green's second wife, a security guard at the MGM Grand, told Regina she had received similar calls.

Two weeks later, Mancini appeared at Madison Square Garden for a press conference announcing his fight there against Orlando Romero of Peru, another in a long line of the WBA's obscure number-one contenders. It had always been his dream, Ray said, to fight in "the mecca of boxing," where his father had faced

Marty Servo before 19,000 fans on a Henry Armstrong undercard. Ray had already instructed his personal seamstress, Dorothy Bagnoli, to make black shorts with red trim, as those were the colors his father took into battle in the very same ring when Boom made his Garden debut January 24, 1940. Still, the questions inevitably reverted to November 13, 1982, and the never-ending fallout from Kim's death.

"I don't entertain questions like that," said Ray.

That didn't stop them from being asked. Ray left the Garden in a limo, joined by Malcolm Moran of the *New York Times*. Moran gently inquired why he had decided to continue fighting.

"There was no decision to be made."

Ray repeated himself, though his voice was barely audible. Then he motioned at the notebook on which Moran was scribbling down his words.

"Please," said Ray, "I don't want any more about that."

Chapter 12 | The Ballad of Bobby Chacon

Now more than ever, Ray was the most sought-after opponent in boxing. Hector Camacho, of Spanish Harlem, tried to bait him into a title shot, his manager calling Mancini "a middle-class sissy." Representatives for Olympic gold medalist Howard Davis practically campaigned for a chance. And Bobby Chacon would get gleamy-eyed at the subject of Mancini. "That's the one I want more than any of them," he said.

"I can make all of them a lot of money," said Ray.

But the prospective superfight remained Aaron Pryor. "Pryor–Mancini would be a war," wrote the *Daily News*'s Dick Young. "Also a gold mine. Conservatively, promoters figure it to be worth $4 million to each man."

"Megabucks," said Ray. "Aaron Pryor and myself is a match everyone will want to see. Our styles fit each other. We're both from Ohio. And let's face it: It's black and white, and that's what sells."

Problem was neither Ray's manager nor his promoter knew what was left of their fighter. Arum hadn't traveled to the Feeney fight, but he had heard from his Italian partner, Rodolfo Sabbatini. "Sabbatini told me the kid didn't have it anymore," says Arum. "He put him in with a bum and Ray struggled."

And nothing in the seven months since—the layoff, the Kim questions, the broken collarbone, even Ray's emergency tonsillectomy in July—had done anything to lessen these doubts, either.

Enter Romero, another southpaw, who had never fought outside his native Peru.

"Romero is the lightweight champion of Peru," wrote Dick Young. "This means he has beaten a truckload of guys named Luis and six llamas."

Even at 30–0–1, he only had twelve knockouts. "Another mandatory, but not dangerous," said Arum. "A bum from a country that had hardly had a professional fighter."

Romero's purse was reportedly $80,000. Ray figured to gross about $750,000, with $600,000 guaranteed for the scheduled fifteen-round championship bout. Then he would fight the thirty-one-year-old Chacon, a big name, big money fight, but not nearly the risk posed by Pryor.

Ray's vintage training sessions with Griff, conducted once again at Grossinger's Hotel and the Times Square Gym, generated a new flurry of favorable coverage. He rolled seventy-five-pound logs up a steep hill. He ran with ninety-pound sandbags, then he put the sandbags on his back and pumped out sets of push-ups. He waded into shoulder-deep water and threw punches at half-hour intervals. All told, he sparred 125 rounds in preparation for Romero.

But it was easier to fool the fourth estate than his own cornermen. Ray never had a surplus of talent; rather his genius was an ability to train at full physical and emotional capacity, and fight in a ferocious state that seemed to gladly exceed normal human limitations. If training was his devotion, Ray had been a happy monk, his body and brain hermetically sealed from distraction and doubt.

"He had to be mentally and physically 100 percent to win his fights," says Tank. "He couldn't have one without the other. But now the worst thing that could come into his mind, kept coming in."

It started with Kim. Yes, Ray thought, it could have been him.

Then came the great national debate on the ethics and efficacy of boxing. It cost him his standing as an All-American boy, his legitimacy as a suitor for both Miss Ohio and Coca-Cola.

Next, the bottle of pesticide. And the revolver found at Richard Green's side. What began as Ray's redemptive narrative was now awash in grief and ghosts.

"No matter what he did, he couldn't get away from it," says Chuck Fagan. "That's all anybody wanted to talk about. Ray had to defend himself anytime a reporter wanted to do a story. Being the champ wasn't as much fun. It became a job instead of a passion. And after a while, it took away his innocence."

Ray would still run the hills, roll the logs, and whack the tires with a sledgehammer. His routine *looked* the same as ever. He was in great shape, but in another way, he was also a mess. If doubt is the enemy of orthodoxy, then Ray had become blasphemous.

"For the first time," says Tank, "he started questioning things."

The mere sight of the Catskill mountains—terrain he once ran as a conquering hero—now offended him.

Do we have to?

Again?

Who needs this shit?

Joy became drudgery. What's more, Ray's obliviousness to the sport's corruptions evaporated. Perhaps this realization shouldn't have come as such an epiphany, certainly not for the son of a one-eyed fighter who couldn't get a title shot. But quite suddenly, Ray knew he was in a dirty business.

"I fought for love of the game," he says. "I fought to win the world title for my father. I fought for righteous reasons. But after the Kim fight, there was nothing righteous about it anymore."

For his part, Boom cared less about his own redemption than his son's retirement, the prospect of which, said Ray, would likely make his old man "the happiest person in the world." The subject of retirement came up with increasing frequency now. Ray had Stallone in his corner. He had William Morris. He had options.

"I'm twenty-two now," he said. "I want to be gone at twenty-three."

Dick Young, New York's most popular and irascible columnist, was rooting hard for it to be so. A month from his sixty-sixth birthday, Young had been covering boxing since the forties. Wanting to see a fighter retire with his hard-earned fortune, his sense, and his good looks still intact, he recalled the previous champ who tried to walk away: "Bobby Chacon, walking on the wild side, quit at age twenty-three, after he had blown the featherweight title out of his nose. He thought he was going to be a big movie star."

Instead, there he was ringside for the Romero fight, one in a crowd of 10,000 attending the Garden's first lightweight championship bout since Duran TKO'd Ken Buchanan eleven years earlier. Having already survived bouts with alcohol and cocaine, not to mention the suicide of his ex-wife, Chacon had mounted an epic comeback. Now, after his thrilling win over Cornelius Boza-Edwards earlier that year, he was looking forward to the biggest payday of his career with Mancini.

Unfortunately, watching Romero match Ray shot for shot, Chacon's first million-dollar score now seemed in peril. After eight rounds, the fight was reported to be even on the judges' cards. The swelling above Ray's left brow had finally broken open—"exploded," in the account of one ringside writer—with the application of a right hand from Romero. There was also an inch-long laceration under Mancini's eye, and a mouse under his right.

"There goes the mortgage," Chacon told himself.

"Perhaps he was rusty," Ralph Wiley, always a Mancini fan, wrote in *Sports Illustrated*. "Sketchy," said the *Post*'s Bob Drury. "Listless, dull and immobile" was Michael Katz's description in the *Times*.

Finally, and quite unexpectedly, Ray connected with a left hook to Romero's chin. "A perfect punch," said Ray. "A lucky punch," said the Peruvian pugilist, who nevertheless was counted out at 1:56 of the ninth round.

Ray didn't like what he saw in the mirror on his dressing room wall. "Oh, God. I don't want this," he said. "I'm not a pretty boy, but I don't want to end up like a lot of guys. You can't buy a face."

He was taken by limousine to Lenox Hill Hospital, stitched up, then returned to his suite at the St. Moritz, where he spent almost half an hour under a hot shower. Ray still couldn't get over the condition of his slit and lumpy mug. This wasn't mere vanity. He would need this face for his next vocation. Only now, four years into his pro career, Ray was just beginning to understand: It was easier to play a champ than to be one.

"You see my father's right eye?" he said. "I don't want that."

For the first time, Ray didn't want to be like his dad.

As tragic figures go, Bobby Chacon seemed a happy one, and universally respected by his peers. From Pacoima, California, and a decade older than Ray, Chacon traced the source of his rage to a taunting uncle who'd slap him around on a regular basis. A small kid, Bobby didn't have the size for football or baseball, but being angry and good with his hands made him an outstanding gang member. It didn't hurt, either, that he kept a blackjack stashed in his lunchbox.

Then, at sixteen, still a nominal student at San Fernando High School, Bobby met Valorie, the love of his life. "There was a beauty about Valorie," he once told Ralph Wiley, "that only I could see."

They had been watching the fights on television, live from the Olympic Auditorium in Los Angeles, when she suggested, somewhat insistently, his vocational calling. "You can do that, Bobby," said Valorie.

By twenty-three, he was featherweight champ of the world, a distinction he earned at the very same Olympic Auditorium. And though Chacon's vices were conventional—booze, women, and cocaine—his lust for them was especially severe. Within a year or so, he had blown it all: the Bentley, the swimming pool, and of course, the title.

Chacon would spend the next seven years shedding blood, most of it his own, to restore his standing and reclaim a title. In doing so, he earned a reputation for putting on epic shows against equally game fighters, among them Ruben Olivares, Alexis Arguello, Cornelius Boza-Edwards, and Rafael "Bazooka" Limon. None of his opponents, however, fared worse than Valorie, now his wife and mother of their three kids.

For years, she had been begging him to quit, both boxing and screwing around. Bobby and Valorie had each taken too many beatings. He would always promise to leave the life, but he never did. He needed the money, the action, and the pussy. Chacon also needed to fight. And by 1982, the accumulated weight of Bobby's broken promises broke his beloved. Valorie became psychiatrically unmoored, losing weight and often speaking of suicide. In March, with Bobby in Sacramento just days before his fight with Salvador Ugalde, they spoke on the phone.

"She said that we could move away," Chacon would recall. "I asked her to where, where could we move away from it . . . ? I wanted to stop. I did . . . I burned up the engine in a borrowed car getting back . . ." Too late. Valorie used a .22-caliber rifle. "I couldn't believe how much blood. So much blood. I turned her over. I saw the hole . . . She looked as beautiful as ever to me. All that foolishness I did. That killed Valorie."

The next night, with Valorie's father and brother working his corner, Chacon knocked out Ugalde in the third round. His purse was $6,000. But he would've done it for free.

"I tried to kill Ugalde," he said.

Within nine months, Chacon would be a champion again. His fifteen-round decision over Bazooka Limon—their fourth fight going back to '75—won him not only the WBC superfeatherweight title, but recognition as the victor in *The Ring*'s "Fight of the Year." In his very next fight, May 15, 1983, he overcame an early knockdown and severe cuts over each eye to earn a unanimous decision over Boza-Edwards. Once again, it was *The Ring*'s "Fight of the Year."

"He still smiled a sweet, chilling smile at the sight of blood," wrote Wiley. "It was his own blood he laughed at now."

At thirty-two, Chacon was bigger than ever. He was glib, gallant, and self-deprecating in a way that made even fighters— especially fighters—into fans.

"He has been my idol," said Ray.

What could be better, then, than a fight between men now mythologized for their capacities to hemorrhage heroically? The match was agreed to weeks before Mancini–Romero, and formally announced just a few days later, with Ray still wearing sunglasses to cover the laceration over his eyes.

The promoter was an upstart named Bob Andreoli of Providence, Rhode Island. Having made his fortune in real estate and costume jewelry, Andreoli now had big designs on boxing. He had already signed heavyweight champion Larry Holmes for a couple of fights. Now he outbid Arum, who already feared Ray was shot, for Mancini and Chacon. Ray would get $2 million, more than the sum of his purses since winning the title from Frias. Chacon's fee, reported to be $1 million, was actually about $650,000—not that he was complaining. Fighting Mancini would still make him $200,000 more than his previous biggest payday, the $450,000 he just earned for defending his title against Boza-Edwards.

Although the bout figured to happen sometime in November, the site was still unknown. The Carrier Dome, with a seating capacity of almost sixty thousand, on the campus of Syracuse University, was a possibility. So were Madison Square Garden, Caesars Palace, and Houston's Astrodome. Andreoli, reported the *New York Post*, "is so confident, he has announced the fight without having a site date or TV deal set."

In retrospect, Andreoli's belief in the commercial leverage bestowed by his two epic bleeders seems a bit naïve. With November already crowded for big fights, including a middleweight championship between Marvin Hagler and Roberto Duran, Mancini–Chacon was postponed to January. In the meantime, Ray would fight a tune-up on another Andreoli promotion, a Vegas card headlined by a bout between Holmes and Marvis Frazier.

Ray was matched with Johnny Torres, a Florida club fighter, for $200,000 on little more than a week's notice. The promotion, televised on NBC, would be recalled as a night of shameful mismatches. Frazier, son of former heavyweight champ Joe Frazier, lasted until 2:57 of the first round. Torres, who butted open a small cut above Ray's left eye, managed to survive until 2:58. A natural junior welterweight, Torres was conscious when taken to Desert Springs Hospital, but had no memory of the fight.

Ray needed the work, but not the aggravation that followed. "Holmes–Frazier and Mancini–Torres never should have happened," wrote *New York Post* sports editor Jerry Lisker. "Why the unranked and outclassed Torres, instead of a top-rated contender like Hector Camacho, Howard Davis or Edwin Rosario?"

The perception of Boom Boom Mancini, at least in the media, had changed. The toll of the Kim fight no longer engendered any sympathy. Perhaps this was inevitable, given the trajectory of a star's life, that the All-American boy would become testy and feel persecuted by his erstwhile boosters in the fourth estate. Ray and Dave Wolf went so far as to accuse NBC's excellent play-by-play man Marv Albert of being unduly critical, going back to the Feeney fight.

"I can understand him not liking my boxing work," responded Albert, drawing little distinction between the fighter and his manager, "because he isn't able to write my script."

Albert wasn't alone, of course. The same fight writers who once argued that young Ray had been fed to Arguello like a lamb to the slaughter, now saw him as boxing's golden calf, protected, but easily bloodied.

Then again, that was a big part of the attraction to any Mancini–Chacon pairing. "My corner's going to measure my bleeding by the pint," laughed Chacon. "And Ray, well, I figure Ray should start bleeding just about when they hit the high notes of the National Anthem."

"It is not one for the squeamish," advised the *New York Times*. "Viewer discretion is advised."

In due course, Andreoli found a date, a site, and a television outlet: January 14, 1984, live from the Lawlor Events Center in downtown Reno, Nevada. It would be broadcast live by Home Box Office, an increasingly popular cable channel with designs on the networks' boxing business. "If we were going to be the home of big event boxing," recalls Ross Greenburg, then a young HBO producer, "we needed to have Ray Mancini on our roster."

A 4–1 underdog, Chacon was almost a decade older than the champion, and was coming up in weight to meet him at 135 pounds. Still, judging from some of the coverage, the prefight presumptions ran against Ray. The *New York Times*'s Mike Katz considered the fight Mancini's toughest challenge since winning the title, and an opportunity to answer his detractors, of whom Katz was now one. The *Times*'s man wasn't impressed by what he was seeing of Mancini in Reno. "He was constantly nailed by sparring partners who had been pressured against the ropes," wrote Katz, pointing out that "Chacon does his best fighting off the ropes now."

Mancini, on the other hand, couldn't recall being more confident going into a big fight. "I remember watching tapes of Bobby, how he liked to be slick and play off the ropes," says Ray. "That's where he wanted to be. But that's where I wanted him to be, too. I'm bigger. I'm stronger, and I'm younger. I'm twenty-three. He's thirty-two. OK, we'll fight on the ropes, but we'll fight at my twenty-three-year-old pace."

All true. Unfortunately, fought at that speed, the bout would satisfy nothing but a minor bloodlust. With Chacon's back to the ropes, Mancini pounded him for two-plus rounds. It was the kind of performance, Katz allowed, that should "mute many of his critics." Finally, at 1:17 of the third round, referee Richard Steele intervened to stop it.

Though the aged challenger's face was described as "a mask of blood," Ray's was uncharacteristically unmarked. Perhaps that accounted for the fans' frustration. And for a time, it seemed as if all 11,104 of them were chanting "Bull-shit!" Then came the rain of beer cans and ice cubes, forcing the HBO announcers to finish their broadcast from under the press table.

At the postfight press conference, Chacon would complain, in his good-natured way, that Steele should have given him a little more respect. "Sure, there's been deaths in fighting," said Chacon, clearly referring to Kim. "But the referee stopped it just a little too soon."

Steele didn't want to stop the fight, but he couldn't wait on

Chacon to fire back, either. Having refereed the Boza-Edwards fight, he understood Chacon all too well, that the man observed no distinction between masochism and valor. "Boza-Edwards doesn't have the punching power of Boom Boom Mancini," he told the *Washington Post*'s David Remnick. "The crowd wanted Bobby to win, but they didn't care for his safety."

Chacon needed twenty-five stitches after Boza-Edwards.

He only needed ten after Ray.

As the years passed, Chacon would argue that his training had been interrupted—nay, cursed—by the irresistible vixens and witches of Reno.

What about me, Bobby?

In his mind's eye, they would hike up their skirts at the foot of their trailers.

I love you.

C'mere, Bobby.

"There were eight or nine of them," he says. "It was the dumbest thing I ever did. But how could I say no?"

That's the story he trained himself to tell. But with his back on the ropes and Ray's fists on his liver, his jaw, and his brow, he knew better. At the moment of mercy, just after Steele stopped the fight with almost two minutes remaining in the third, Bobby Chacon turned to the ref and whispered in his ear.

"Thank you, Richard," he said.

Chapter 13 | Cutman

Soon after the Chacon fight, Dave Wolf received a visitor from Cleveland. Don Elbaum had been keeping an eye on Ray since his amateur days in the Lake Erie Golden Gloves. Better yet, Elbaum was an advisor to the man who had vanquished Arguello, Aaron Pryor.

"I want to put on the biggest show this town's ever seen," said Elbaum, explaining that he had the blessing of Browns owner Art Modell and permission to use Cleveland Stadium, a massive structure that seated 81,000 for football.

"Let me think about it," said Wolf.

"Two and a half million, each fighter, guaranteed," said Elbaum. With the closed-circuit money, the purse could go up to $3 million, easy.

It was a good proposition, Wolf had to admit. But by the end of February, Wolf was boasting of "a firm $5 million offer" to fight Pryor. And based on all the chatter, there was even more money out there for Ray.

"Six million for Mancini and $5 million for Camacho," bragged Camacho's manager, Billy Giles, angling for a date at the Garden.

Talk of purses was all nonsense until the checks cleared. However, the numbers being thrown around were proof, even after Kim's death, of the public's enduring taste for violence inflicted and received by Ray Mancini. Elbaum kept calling.

"Let me think about it," said Wolf.

"Dave," said Elbaum, "what the fuck is there to think about?"

"Ray's the champion," said Wolf. "If we don't defend against Bramble, we'll be stripped of the title."

Bramble being Livingstone Bramble, of Passaic, New Jersey, by way of St. Croix.

"Don't take that fight," Elbaum pleaded. "You'll lose."

Bramble was merely the latest in the WBA's never-ending supply of number-one contenders. *Lose?* Wolf could barely stop snickering.

The mandatory defense was set for June 1, at Buffalo's Memorial Auditorium, with Ray getting a purse and a percentage of the syndicated TV revenues worth about $1.5 million altogether. The Greater Buffalo Chamber of Commerce had lobbied Arum's *Top Rank* for the date. But so had Ray, who wanted very much to fight in Nick Mancino's adopted hometown.

"Buffalo was like a second home to me," says Ray. "I'd been going there since I was a kid."

Uncle Vinnie and Aunt Becky and all the cousins still lived there. Although Boom's father had passed away some years before, Ray would dedicate the fight to Boom's father, Grandpa Nick. As far as Buffalonians were concerned, Ray was one of theirs. Then, on the eve of the fight, he signed on as the national campaign chairman for Cooley's anemia, also known as beta thalassemia, a hemoglobin defect most commonly found in persons of Mediterranean descent.

"Cooley's anemia is to Italian-Americans what sickle cell anemia is to blacks," said Wolf, explaining that Ray had already lined up Frankie Valli and Frankie Avalon for a benefit.

No one particularly minded, then, when word spread that Bramble—whose Rastafarian heritage was regarded as something of a novelty in 1984—would dedicate the fight to the Ethiopian soldiers who died defending Emperor Haile Selassie from Benito Mussolini's invading Italian hordes. Or that Bramble was casting a voodoo curse on Ray. As the WBA number-one contenders went, at least this one would have a little cachet. Besides, a little racial conflict never hurt the gate.

The tension was already palpable at the opening press conference in Buffalo, when Bramble asked Ray where he was from.

"Youngstown, Ohio," he said proudly.

"You should come from Cincinnati or Cleveland," said Bramble.

"Why is that?" asked Ray.

"Because they both got ball clubs and you could be the catcher," said Bramble, a 4–1 underdog. "That's what you're gonna be with me, my catcher."

The next day, the fighters appeared at Regine's in New York. Mancini was posing for pictures with Jeanine Giordano and Jennifer Oliveri, ten-year-old poster girls for Cooley's anemia, when he heard Bramble issue a stream of profane insults.

"Watch your language," said Mancini. "You have little girls over here."

Bramble responded by repeating himself, but more loudly. Then, for good measure, he cursed Ray's sister, mother, and father, too.

"Like waving a cape in front of a bull," noted one reporter.

Ray threw a right hand. There was some shoving. But the fighters were soon separated, Ray still heaving with rage.

"I will get you," he said.

Bramble laughed in his face. The press conference, as far as he was concerned, had been a resounding success. Bramble offered a stark contrast to Ray's best-known opponents: Arguello, with the manners of a Latin aristocrat, and Chacon, the cheerful bleeder. Bramble understood Sonny Liston's theorem, that most fights were cast as cowboy movies, as battles between the virtuous and the evil.

"I never had a choice, I was given the role," he says now. "But I played that role great."

Bramble had a litter of five pit bulls, one of whom he named "Snake," a python he called "Turtle," and a boa constrictor christened "Dog." He was a vegetarian (a dietary practice looked on suspiciously in places like Youngstown and Buffalo) who believed that Selassie was Jah's messenger on earth.

But what about the voodoo? one reporter asked.

"I'll tell you after the fight," he said.

Growing up in the Virgin Islands, the son of two working parents—his father at the Hess Oil refinery, his mother at a home for the aged—Bramble never believed in voodoo. But what better way to fuck with Ray than a system of belief to summon spirits of the dead? Ray had been trying to cope with his own animistic beliefs for a while now, with the ghosts of his brother and Kim and Kim's mother and Richard Green. Now Bramble had found a way, not only to unnerve Ray, but to exploit the sense of belief that made him a champion in the first place. Faux voodoo was perfect to piss off and confuse such a devoted Catholic as Ray.

"I made him think I had the voodoo," recalls Bramble. "I tried to put everything in his mind: pit bulls and snakes. I wanted him to think I was crazy. I wanted this man to *hate* my black ass."

Unlike so many of boxing's famous heels, Bramble didn't embrace his villain's role merely to enhance his prospects at the box office. Rather, his purpose—"to be the biggest jerk I could be"—was purely tactical. In fact, he regretted his behavior at the press conference. "It wasn't nice," he says. "His parents were there, and they were devastated. But I had to do my job."

He had been studying Mancini for several years now, anticipating that any lightweight's road to fame and fortune would go through the pride of Youngstown. The voodoo persona had two functions, the first being to merely distract. "I wanted him thinking about everything but how to beat my ass," says Bramble.

Second, but more important, was to keep Ray seething with anger. For Bramble, it wasn't enough that Mancini didn't take a backward step. He had to ensure that the champion kept coming forward. He couldn't stop waving the red cape.

"There was nothing special about me," says Bramble, recalling his education as a boxer. "I did the basic things over and over. I just knew how to protect myself."

At 20–1–1, Bramble's only loss was a decision to Anthony "Two

Guns" Fletcher, who had outpointed Ray twice as a novice back in '78. Bramble was a natural counterpuncher, with an astounding nine-inch reach advantage over Ray. He didn't have one-shot power, nor was he particularly fast. Rather, he had an awkward style that made opponents look bad while wearing them into submission. His defensive posture was disciplined, with those long arms bent at the elbow to form a gloved fortress protecting his torso and head.

"Ray had a much better jab than he got credit for," says Bramble. "The last thing I wanted him to do was box. I wanted him coming forward and swinging wildly. It wasn't going to be easy beating Mancini, but I had the master plan."

Ray had his own plans. Having angrily—and uncharacteristically—told Bramble "I'm going to cut you in half," he began his most rigorous fight camp ever. He would train seven weeks, as opposed to the usual six, at high altitude in Lake Tahoe.

"You run one mile here," Murphy Griffith told a visitor, "and it's like five miles anywhere else."

Still, the weight did not come off as easily as it usually did, and Ray remained sluggish through camp. Perhaps it was Tahoe's six-thousand-five-hundred-foot elevation. Also, his hemorrhoids were acting up. Nothing unusual there. Ever since the Feeney fight, they would begin to bleed at each camp. Made sense, Ray figured, as the higher caloric intake he needed while training meant more frequent trips to the bathroom. *You'll get an operation soon as you retire,* his doctor told him, *don't worry.*

Ray couldn't help but worry. He saw a crimson pool every time he flushed the toilet. The condition was clearly getting worse. There was only one thing to do. Or rather, one thing he knew how to do: work harder.

"I was an animal," he says, "running up those mountains."

In mid-May, the Mancini camp flew east for the fight. Ordinarily, a move to thick, oxygenated air at sea level—a drop of almost six thousand feet—would confer a substantial physical boost. "But by the time we got to Buffalo," recalls Ray, "I was spent. I had nothing."

• • •

More accurately, he had nothing but aggravation, as Dave Wolf bit hard on the rotten bait cast by the Bramble camp. Shortly before the fighters arrived in Buffalo, Bramble had been interviewed by the Warren *Tribune* and called Mancini a "murderer." "He killed Kim," said Bramble. "It doesn't matter if it happened in the ring. It's still murder."

Wolf's response, exactly what Bramble and his manager, Lou Duva, so desperately wanted, came in the form of a prepared statement: "His ethnic slurs . . . his vile remarks concerning Mancini and his family, his public profanity, his threats of prefight violence and his statement that Mancini is 'a murderer' have created a climate of dangerous hostility."

Still, Wolf wasn't done. A couple days later, during the first of Mancini's public workouts at the Buffalo Convention Center, he let loose with a diatribe calling Bramble "a subhuman wart hog."

"There's no longer any reason to treat him like anything other than the pig that he is," said Wolf, who then had a spectator ejected as a suspected spy for the Bramble-Duva camp.

Wolf was perfectly good writing for the page. But when it came to prefight stage management and low-brow production values, he was not Lou Duva's equal. A former trucker from Paterson, New Jersey, Duva got his start putting on fight cards at Ice World, a Totowa skating rink where he once billed a Teamster driver as a prince from Zaire. Duva, whose craggy, jowled mug resembled that of a damaged bulldog, had a good eye for boxing talent, but his real aptitude was for promotion. Going against a guy like Wolf, he would instantly morph into an old-school wrestling valet.

"He says Bramble is anti-white and anti-Italian," Duva noted delightedly. "What am I, an Egyptian?"

In fact, Duva admired Mancini, and had long regretted passing on him as an amateur. What's more, he knew the locals in Buffalo considered him a traitor. "I would've liked to be on the other side with Mancini," he says. "But what was I going to do? I had my fighter."

And as Bramble appeared for his first day of public workouts, the fighter informed the press that he was drinking a potion brewed from island herbs. "It lets me see right through Mancini," he said. "And by seeing through him, his strength leaves him."

Bramble's antics hadn't merely distracted Ray. By now, they'd rendered the champion doubtful and defensive. "I never said anything about this being a racial thing on his part," said Ray. "I think Dave got a little carried away." Nor did Mancini appreciate his manager's reference to Bramble calling him a murderer. Of all people, Wolf should have known better.

"It's irrelevant to this fight," insisted Ray. "It hurts me to see that word. I don't want my mom and dad to see it. I don't like the way it sounds or the way it looks."

Too late. Wolf's reaction guaranteed that the murderer angle would remain in play and be much discussed at the final press conference.

It was scheduled for the Convention Center two days before the fight, but that very morning Ray found himself unable to get out of bed. In short order, Dave summoned a physician, who surmised that the champion was suffering from a viral infection.

"He can't fight," said the doctor.

"I'm calling it off," said Wolf.

"No, you're not," said Ray.

Buffalo was expecting a sellout. An outfit named Katz Sports had syndicated the television rights, selling the fight as a prime-time broadcast to 115 stations, covering 80 to 85 percent of the country. Ray had a million-dollar purse (as opposed to Bramble's $150,000) at stake. There were the charter busses coming from Youngstown.

"I'll beat him no matter what I got," said Ray.

With that decided, the entourage set out for their last prefight appearance with Bramble. It already felt like a somber occasion when Ray turned to Tank.

"Just don't let him touch me," he said. "Don't let him get near me."

• • •

To commune with spirits real and imagined, a reputed witch doctor attended the press conference. Bramble and Duva called him "Dr. Doo," and claimed he had been imported from St. Croix to cast a spell on Mancini. Never mind that the alleged shaman had been Bramble's basketball coach as a kid in St. Croix. Duva had him outfitted with an English bowler and a dashiki, and gave him an old medical textbook to use as a prop.

"It was a dirty trick to play on Ray," says Duva, "but it really did spook him."

Did you call him a murderer? reporters asked Bramble.

"I can't recall," he said.

You don't remember?

No, said Bramble. "But the evil that men do lives after them."

The line was written by Shakespeare for Mark Antony. And it made Bramble happy to think that neither Mancini nor most of the reporters could identify its origins (Act 3, scene ii of *Julius Caesar*). Still, everybody got the general idea, as the words were no less subtle than Dr. Doo's phony incantations: a curse upon the House of Mancini.

Fight night at the War Memorial Auditorium saw Lou Duva get just the raucous reception he anticipated. "Those Italians in Buffalo booed the hell out of me," he says. "And rightfully so."

Attendance was just under fifteen thousand, with most fans cheering wildly as Ray made his entrance, an Italian flag stitched to the back of his white silk robe. Still, none of them were rooting as hard for Mancini as the fighters sitting at ringside. They included Hector Camacho; Aaron Pryor, whose advisor, Elbaum, was carrying a quarter-million-dollar check made out to Mancini as a deposit on their next fight; and Harry Arroyo, Ray's stablemate from the Navy Reserve back in Youngstown, who now held the International Boxing Federation's version of the lightweight title.

"The line that used to stand in front of Sugar Ray Leonard now stands in front of Mancini," Dick Young had written. "With Sugar gone, Mancini is the glamorpuss who can produce the golden gates."

How despondent they would have been to know the truth, that

Ray's chances were less than the officially proclaimed 4–1 odds. Wolf and Duva had spent the better part of the previous day arguing over Marty Denkin, the WBA's referee. But, by now, those close to Ray had to wonder if the choice of ref would even matter. For the first time, their man couldn't even make weight, needing an extra early-morning run on the day of the weigh-in. Even after shedding his jockstrap and gold chain, Ray was two ounces too heavy. Finally, after a trip to the bathroom, he got down to the 135 pound limit.

As he watched Ray shake out in the ring, Mike Cefalde couldn't help but think of the night before. He had been in Mancini's suite, listening as Griff tried to lighten the mood with a joke. Everyone tried to laugh but Ray.

"He was white," says Cefalde. "I mean, white like a piece of paper."

And now, even as he blew kisses to the crowd, Ray felt as if he were hiding a terrible secret. "That's a scary feeling," he says. "You got a guy who wants to rip your head off, and you know you got nothing."

Though Bramble claimed to have been "practicing" his head-butting technique, the clash of heads that opened Ray's right eyelid was accidental. It came just 2:40 into the first round. Within moments Ray looked like something out of a slasher flick.

"It's a terrible cut," said broadcaster Al Bernstein.

The eyelid, he noted, was about the worst place to sustain such a gash. The thin folds of skin and subcutaneous tissue made for a drippy wound that could blind a fighter with his own blood.

If Ray was now desperate, he didn't fight that way. Rather, he moved in behind an impressive jab and began to whale away in customary fashion at Bramble's midsection. Bramble received the incoming blows with clenched arms before returning fire with straight punches and a curiously effective right uppercut.

It soon became clear that cutman Paul Percifield's solutions of thrombin and adrenaline, sealed with a thick layer of petroleum jelly, had been expertly applied. The flow of blood slowed through the next couple of rounds, as Ray appeared to be boxing and brawling as well as he ever had. Bramble was correct to have been concerned about the jab, which suddenly seemed like a new, or perhaps underused, element in Ray's arsenal. What's more, those rights to the body evoked the vintage Mancini, round but precisely intended to murder a man's will.

"This fight is a war," said Bernstein. "Bramble is landing his shots, but Mancini just a little quicker."

The third round began as more of the same. "Bing, bing, bing," Ray recalls. "I'm slapping the hell out of him."

But as these rhythms became predictable, Bramble peered at Ray from behind his gloves. His expression as articulate as language, as if to say: *You're shitting me. That all you got?*

"He looks at me, like, he *knows*," says Ray. "I was hitting him with a lot of punches. But I couldn't hurt him."

Toward the end of the third round, Bramble changed to a southpaw stance. He had been known to do this, but never to such effect. Kim and Orlando Romero, both of whom gave Mancini more trouble than anticipated, were southpaws. "Watching the Romero fight, seeing Ray get hit with that right hook, that's when I knew," says Bramble. "I planned for Ray as a southpaw. I worked on my right hook to make it perfect for the Mancini fight."

The right uppercut wasn't bad, either. But Bramble, in a move that confused even his own corner, went back to a conventional stance through the fourth, fifth, and sixth rounds. Finally, in the seventh, he turned southpaw again and caught Ray with a right hook.

Mancini, his nose bleeding profusely, was still ahead on all the judges' cards. Bernstein, the announcer, had him up by three points, going into the seventh. But now, as Bramble connected on yet another hook, the first of a series that left Ray staggered, the fight had changed.

"Ray is in trouble," said Bernstein.

Still, he refused to move, preferring to trade punches in his weakened state than to preserve his lead from a distance.

"I wonder whether it is a matter of macho with Ray," asked

Bernstein's partner, Bill Mazer. "Because he dislikes this man so much that he won't move."

"A valid argument," responded Bernstein. "Or maybe Ray is just too tired to move."

Either way, Mancini ignored Griff's exhortations until he caught Bramble in the middle of the ring. The flurry began with a left hook, and by the round's end, it was Bramble who was holding on. Ray's former self, which is to say, the fighter he was before Kim, would have finished Bramble right there. But tonight, it was all he could do to wobble the man.

In the ninth, with Bramble fighting southpaw again, he opened a cut over Ray's left eye. Still, Ray stayed right in front of him. "Psychologically, what Bramble did before the fight — getting Mancini as angry as he did — may have been effective," said Mazer. "Mancini will not listen to his corner."

By the twelfth, with Ray still holding a conceivable edge on the judges' cards, Griff was screaming: "Move, move, move!"

"Griff," Mancini whispered back in his corner, "I got no legs."

He had no arms, either. By now, he was pushing his punches. They lacked any snap or power.

"He can't hurt Bramble," said Bernstein, who noticed that Ray's right was finding its target, but to no effect. "It has no impact."

"You look at the face of Mancini, and it looks like he's been through a meat grinder," said Mazer. "There is not a mark on Bramble's face."

Ray would throw 1,408 punches that night — an extraordinary number, especially compared to the 880 tallied by Bramble — but only connected on 338. Perhaps even more astonishing: Two of the three WBA judges still had Mancini ahead going into the fourteenth. But fifty-three seconds into the round, with Ray on the ropes, his arms limp at his side, and Wolf ready to throw in the towel, Marty Denkin stopped the fight. "Good guy," Ray says of the ref. "He gave me every chance."

"Somebody beat me to him," said Hector Camacho.

"A quarter million dollars in my pocket," recalls Elbaum. "And I can't *give* it away."

"I'm sorry for Ray," said Aaron Pryor, who had slimmed down to 135 pounds in anticipation of their fight. "That's a tough way to go out."

"You could see something in Ray's eyes," noticed Duva's son, Dan, who ran the family's promotional business. "What it said was, 'I don't want to be here. . . . In my opinion, Mancini is not going to fight again."

"If Dave Wolf lets Ray fight again, I'll strangle him," said Bob Arum. "Ray doesn't need this anymore. He's been taking too many punches."

Ray spent the night at Millard Fillmore Hospital, where he was treated for exhaustion. He was given a sedative and eight stitches to each eyelid.

"You get me the rematch yet?" he asked Wolf.

"It's there when you want it."

"Okay," said Ray. "Then I can sleep."

Chuck Fagan was married in Youngstown the following week. Then the wedding party set out for Maui, where a despondent Ray tried to get a little R&R, broke up with a girlfriend named Shawnee, and returned to the mainland with a familiar, if renewed, sense of ambition. He wanted Bramble, and he wanted his title back.

By now, Ray attributed his loss to the extra week in Lake Tahoe. "Overtraining," he called it. Still, cause seemed less important than effect, the facts less seductive than the potential for another parable.

"The story's already been written for me by Stallone," he said. "He's a genius. He wrote *Rocky III* about me before it even happened."

That movie, in which Rocky Balboa took back his title from a strange and menacing black fighter played by Mr. T, who had disrespected Rocky's loved ones, grossed $125 million. Its theme song was the number-one hit of 1982. Ray didn't care that Mr. T was a cartoon, while Bramble was real, resourceful, and adept at the practice of pugilistic psychiatry. He wanted what he wanted.

Toward that end, Wolf enlisted a team of five physicians to examine Mancini and sanction his return to the ring. Sure, there was scar tissue around his eyes, but his reflexes were undiminished, and his vital signs, as measured by a CAT scan, an EKG, and an EEG, remained vital. In the meantime, with Bramble already signed to face his mandatory WBA challenger, Edwin Curet, Mancini again agreed to fight Kenny "Bang Bang" Bogner. The date was set for September in New Orleans.

Wolf figured the quickest way back to Bramble was for Ray to show well in "a good, hard fight" against another ranked opponent. Nevertheless, Ray's decision mystified a generation of old-timers, guys who fought not to starve. *Sport* magazine ranked Ray as the second highest-paid athlete of 1984, grossing $3.2 million, behind only middleweight champ Marvin Hagler at $3.3 million. The anticipated streams of endorsement income may have dried up after the Kim fight, but Ray remained considerably more flush than the highest-paid performers in other sports (the Phillies' Mike Schmidt, for example, at $2.1 million; basketball's only $2 million player, Kareem Abdul-Jabbar; or running back Herschel Walker, slated to make $1.5 million with the USFL's New Jersey Generals).

Over a lunch with Ray, Rocky Graziano, and the *Daily News's* Bill Gallo, Lenny Mancini recalled that his biggest purse was $2,500 for Baby Sims after the war. Yes, times had changed, but time itself remained a lurking treachery for fighters. Only guys like Stallone got better with age.

Graziano, now working as a celebrity spokesman for Lee Myles Transmissions, waited until father and son were out of earshot before confiding in the newspaperman. "I thought one time he was a real good fighter who took a punch pretty good," the real Rocky said of Ray. "But now I would advise him to stop. The kid's got plenty of money . . . He could be a good actor. Like me."

Training camp convened later that summer at Villa Roma, the Catskills' token Italian joint. As had been their custom, Ray and Chuck went out early each morning to run the rolling hills. But now, for the first time, not only did Chuck pass him, but Ray stopped running.

"Goddammit," said Chuck, "if you don't want to fight no more, just retire."

"It's not that," said Ray, trying to catch his breath.

"You don't have to do this."

"No," said Ray. "Something's wrong."

He was bleeding again. Soon as training had begun, his hemorrhoids started acting up. Still, he slogged through camp, sustaining an inch-long cut over his left eye while sparring two weeks before the fight. It wasn't a problem, the reporters were told.

"Not worried at all," said Ray, who appeared for a public workout in New Orleans with bandages over the cut.

That was September 5. On September 6, two days before he was to face Bogner live on ABC, Ray was examined by his personal physician, who advised him to cancel the fight.

"Any light hit is going to open this cut right away," said Dr. Jeffrey Schwartz. "It looks like a dotted line."

Wolf ordered the Mancini camp to clear out, and disregarded a Louisiana court's order for Mancini to be examined by a local doctor. The state's Boxing and Wrestling Commission announced it was suspending Mancini for sixty days.

"It's like revoking my Romanian citizenship," scoffed Wolf, whose sarcasm nevertheless obscured an uncomfortable truth.

"The cut wasn't bad enough to stop that fight," says Fagan. "We made it look a little worse than it was. Ray was going to get beat. He had nothing. Absolutely. Fucking. Nothing."

A week or so later, Chuck was listening to Ray explain the symptoms of his lethargy to a doctor at the Cleveland Clinic.

"Go ahead," said Chuck. "Tell him."

"Nah," said Ray. "It's nothing."

"Tell him."

"What?" protested Ray. "It's a harmless condition."

"Doc, don't let him tell you that. Happens every time he goes to the bathroom. This kid's bleeding like a sonofabitch."

The ensuing tests revealed the hemoglobin levels in Ray's now-thin blood to be about half the normal level. "There's two ways to look at this," the doctor informed him. "You're half dead. Or half alive."

Either way, he should never have been fighting. Fortunately, the condition had a relatively easy short-term solution. The hemorrhoids were cauterized. Ray was put on a high-iron diet, and his body was given time to fully heal. It would be December before he even set foot in a ring. By then, he had the only thing he still wanted out of boxing: a rematch with Bramble.

The fight would air live from Reno on HBO, which paid more than $1 million for the rights, and rebroadcast a week later on CBS. It was unusual for both champion and challenger to receive an equal purse, to wit: $750,000. But Mancini's allure was still the bank against which everyone borrowed. Bramble's promoter even came up with $150,000 for the number-one contender Tyrone Crawley to step aside and wait for the winner.

The Duvas paid the sum without hesitation. America knew Ray had redeemed his father, but could he avenge his own loss? Who wouldn't want to see that?

Actually, the sole dissenter was Sylvester Stallone. By now, production for his CBS movie, less than subtly titled *Heart of a Champion: The Ray Mancini Story*, would begin in a matter of weeks and conclude two days before the Bramble fight. Robert Blake, best known as the wisecracking detective on the hit series *Baretta*, had been cast as Boom. Stallone still figured the key was getting Ray to play Ray.

Even after news of the rematch broke, Stallone kept asking him to reconsider and pull out. "We'll make something up," he said. "You'll come back a movie star."

Ray was still considering an array of plausible excuses when a janitor put down his mop to greet him in the lobby of the New York Hilton.

"You got to beat this Bramble," he said. "You got to get the title back."

The janitor was a black guy, maybe ten years older than Ray, who thanked him and explained that he was on his way to the press conference.

"I got a son," the janitor volunteered. "I want him to be like you."

If the exchange seems trite in retrospect, it also forced Ray to clarify his thoughts, to distinguish between his now-conflicted senses of obligation and ambition, strategy and duty. It was better to go out as a fighter than come back as a movie star. Ray sat through the session at Gallagher's steakhouse, listening to Bramble complain about the food and predict his demise by knockout. The fighters refused to be photographed together, much less shake hands.

Once in Reno, Bramble would traipse through the MGM Grand with his pet boa constrictor, Dog. Casino security guards weren't the only ones agitated by a sunglass-wearing Rastafarian with a large serpent wrapped around his upper body. On at least one occasion, the hotel's caged mascot, one in a long line of MGM lions, picked up Dog's scent and began to roar mightily.

Bramble's strategy hadn't changed. Persona remained part of the plan. "First I beat him dead with my mind," he said of Mancini. "Then I beat him dead with my fists."

Bramble kept talking of death. He'd chosen to wear trunks embroidered with a skull and crossbones, though only after Duva drew the line and prohibited him from having Kim's name stitched to his shorts. He even "sparred" with a chicken, a session that reportedly ended with the fowl's untimely demise. Again, Bramble's purpose was to antagonize and distract, to elicit misgivings Ray didn't have before the Kim fight. Mancini was most dangerous fighting on instinct. Bramble wanted him thinking. To think was to doubt.

By now, even Ray was worried about his own propensity to

bleed. Would bleeding cause him mere anxiety? Or fatigue? Or would it become an excuse?

Ray was changed in every way—mentally, emotionally, and physically—from his former self, the kid who won the title. "The press-kit photos of Mancini all dated from the Frias bout," noted the writer Bill Barich, "so it was disconcerting to see how much his face had changed since then. He wasn't unmarked anymore. His nose was broader, more splayed, and the skin was stretched tight over his cheekbones, as if it had no give left in it. Around his eyes, the flesh was pearly and shone under the lights."

"There are thick humps of bone and flesh over each eye," wrote John Ed Bradley of the *Washington Post*.

A friend from Youngstown, now trying to make it as an actor, thought the color and contour of Ray's eyebrows suggested Terry Malloy, the noble ex-pug in *On the Waterfront*. Marlon Brando made Malloy iconic, but the sad ridges constructed of makeup and spirit gum didn't hurt either.

If only Ray could disappear the damage with baby wipes and cold cream. The sutured skin was tougher than ever, but the flesh around those old wounds was now pulled even thinner. Below the skin, the subcutaneous tissue was so tender that it would cut whenever Ray sparred. "By the time an actual fight rolled around, the cuts were primed to burst to the surface," Barich wrote after speaking with Mancini's physician.

It had happened against Romero at the Garden. It happened against Bramble in Buffalo. It happened in the Catskills training for Bogner. And with every expectation that it would happen again in Reno, Lou Duva purchased a doll from the MGM hotel gift shop.

The figurine didn't look much like Ray. But the needle Bramble used to impale it was sufficiently representational for reporters attending the prefight press conference.

"That doll's you," bellowed Duva. "It came straight from the Virgin Islands. Take a good look at it, Ray. Look at those eyes."

"How your eyes feeling now?" taunted Bramble, probing with

the needle. "You think you can see me, Ray? You think you can look me in the eyes?"

Mancini's attempt at a chuckle came out a sneer, as he fingered the so-called gift Bramble had given him moments earlier: a ceramic skull. It was Valentine's Day, the fourth anniversary of Lenny's death.

Except for the odds, which now claimed Bramble as a 5–2 favorite, it began not unlike their first fight. Once again, Ray tipped the scales a quarter pound too heavy and had to drop his drawers to make weight. With 11,758 in attendance (including Camacho, outfitted in a gold lamé suit with rhinestone-studded sunglasses), the fight produced a live gate in excess of $800,000, making for the biggest sporting event in Reno history and another resoundingly pro-Mancini crowd.

The challenger entered the ring to a mighty cheer, attired in a hooded robe with red silk, as if he were pugilism's great cardinal. As promised, Bramble wore the skull and crossbones stitched to his trunks. His arrival was lustily booed.

Then the fighters quickly resumed their customary positions from their first match, both of them in the center of the ring. Ray was more busy; Bramble, going early to the southpaw stance, was more deliberate. With their toes inches apart, and their heads often touching, neither yielded any territory. The ferocity and the pace now seemed familiar, but the action itself was better. No longer anemic, Ray was more crisp, flinging his hooks to the body. Still, no one was surprised when, after just one round, he returned to his corner with a cut over his left eye.

"I tried to work that left eye a lot," said Bramble. "After a while, though, I just quit, because it seemed to no avail."

His apparent futility was Paul Percifield's doing. The cutman from Texas, in Mancini's corner since the sixth round against Johnny Summerhays back at the Packard Music Hall, was never better. Soon enough, Bramble opened a second cut over the left eye. But Percifield kept the bleeding and swelling under control.

He had three two-ounce bottles of adrenaline hydrochloride, a solution used to reduce blood flow, and a vial of milky coagulant he mixed from sterilized water and thrombin powder. He also had the *enswell*, a cold piece of metal used as an iron to press down the swelling and in severe cases, Percifield says, "to mash the blood out of a wound."

In the fifth round of a very close fight, Bramble opened another inch-long gash near the corner of Mancini's right eye. It began to flow immediately.

"As if he'd been slashed with a razor," wrote Barich.

Gruesome as they were, the red streaks running down Mancini's cheek and staining his chest and arms didn't impair his vision. Rather, the more perilous lesions, the ones that could end the fight, were on the left side. At one point, HBO commentator Larry Merchant declared: "I'm ready to give the Nobel Prize for medicine to Ray's corner."

However, there were limits to what medical science or Paul Percifield could do. He could impede the bleeding, but the swelling was another matter. By the seventh, Mancini's left eyelid looked as if it had been stuffed with plump red grapes.

"My eye is closing," Ray complained in between rounds. "I can't see them shots."

In the eighth, with Bramble jabbing away at the cuts, referee Mills Lane called time and asked Nevada's ringside physician, Charles Filippini, for an opinion. The doctor, wrote Barich, "leaned over the ropes and pried open Mancini's closed eye with his fingers, and peered into the bloody socket, determining that Mancini's eyelids weren't split and that his retinas were not detatched." The fight would go on, at least a little longer.

"I want to destroy him for good," Bramble had said. "I want to make him look stupid."

And now, who could doubt it would turn out like that? Another fighter's inevitably tragic coda had begun. This is how it would end: with Ray shuffling after his opponent and pawing at his face to wipe away the blood. The blue canvas speckled with red, most of the droplets having leaked from Ray's right eye.

"He had as bad cuts as I've ever worked on," says Percifield. "I never did stop the right one because I ran out of medicine working on the left." Three bottles of Adrenalin and a vial of thrombin were gone, and with them, one would surmise, Ray's chances. The HBO crew was already framing Ray's demise.

"His corner has about run out of miracles," said Barry Tompkins, the blow-by-blow man.

"I think this is it," said Sugar Ray Leonard.

"This could be the last round of Ray Mancini's career," said Merchant, a decorated former newspaperman.

But, soon enough, Ray had Bramble against the ropes. By the ninth, Tompkins noted that "Bramble seems to me the more tired fighter."

"Ray would just *take* punishment," recalls Bramble. "It's like he was saying 'give me more, more.' He had more stamina than anyone I ever knew."

Mancini was "so sliced up," as Bramble puts it, he was half-expecting Mills Lane to stop the fight. Percifield wouldn't have been surprised, either, as he was down to used swabs and cotton balls, figuring that the residue of Adrenalin and thrombin was better than nothing at all. But on into the championship rounds, it became clear that Lane didn't want to disrupt what the audience saw as a hero's narrative. The more Ray bled, the more he was cheered.

The battering continued, with Ray mounting another comeback in the fourteenth. The crowd roared as Bramble finally backed up.

At the beginning of the fifteenth round, Merchant prepared his viewers for a justifiable improbability. "Ray Mancini may be stealing this fight," he said.

"All of a sudden," recalls Chuck Fagan, "Bramble is starting to shit himself."

But then, fifty seconds into the round, Lane suspended the action and the momentum for Dr. Filippini to take another look at the right eye.

"I wanted to choke the sonofabitch," says Fagan.

"I see good, I see good," Ray pleaded. "Please. Please."

The fight went the distance without further incident. To the dismay of a packed house, Bramble was declared the winner by unanimous decision, a single point on each of the judges' scorecards. The crowd began to chant "bull-shit," but Ray had no beef. Not only was Bramble the champion, but also, the first to acknowledge his predecessor.

"I love you, Ray," said Bramble, who later apologized to Ellen and Boom "for any discriminations that I may have made against them."

Next, it was Merchant's turn to sign off on the broadcast: "I don't think I've ever seen an athlete get more out of his talent."

He wasn't alone in anticipating Ray's retirement. "It's his decision," Boom said of his son's future. "But if it were up to me, I'd tell him to forget about it."

Ray himself didn't know if he wanted to fight again, but found himself longing for domestic tranquility at the postfight press conference. "I wish I had a wife," he said.

Only now did the full extent of his cuts become evident. There were four, two above each eye, their length less disturbing than their width. "As if he had red slugs sucking away at the corners of his eyes," noted John Ed Bradley.

After speaking to reporters, Ray was taken to the hospital. "The doctors were at it for a while," he remembers. "They had to stitch over and behind each eyelid."

Then Ray returned to the El Dorado Hotel, where he had a big dish of chocolate ice cream and a party in his suite. Chucky and Tank were still swearing that he won the fight. But the ex-champ didn't seem to care. He was in a pretty good mood for a guy who had just received seventy-five stitches. He had his respect again. Bramble could keep the belt.

"I couldn't take the pounding I gave him, no way," says Livingstone Bramble. "If my name was Ray Mancini, I'd have left that damn ring a long time ago. I would never try to measure my heart with his, never."

While Ray was getting sutured, Bramble went back to his room and drew a bath for himself. It was a nice, big Jacuzzi. But as he slid in, the water began to change color, as if infused like a pot of tea. First, threads of crimson, then the water turned to something like rust. Finally, Bramble soaked in a pool the color of new brick.

He hadn't realized how it had covered him. It was all over his chest, his back, his calves. It had run down his arms and soaked the inside of his gloves. It was in his cuticles and fingernails.

And the smell. He kept scrubbing, but it stayed with him. "That's the worst," says Livingstone Bramble. "The smell of blood."

Chapter 14 | Show Biz

There were dissenters from the ringside consensus, the most prominent among them being Dick Young. "I had it even after 12 and gave Mancini the last three rounds when Bramble stopped fighting," he wrote. "I don't subtract points for blood."

Ray didn't need a sportswriter's opinion to fortify his own. Nor did he take much comfort in learning that his opponent tested positive for a banned stimulant, ephedrine, apparently contained in the Chi Power supplements Bramble had been taking. The Nevada State Athletic Commission fined Bramble $15,000 and Duva $5,000, but did not vacate the title. No matter. If this were the end of his career, Ray was content.

It was the rest of the world that seemed to have a problem. Shortly after the fight, PBS's respected *Frontline* series posed the question: Should boxing be banned? "Down for the Count," as the hour-long piece was called, featured the typically outspoken testimony of Howard Cosell, now a zealot railing against the sport that had helped to make him famous. The program's press release used the Mancini–Kim fight as the central image to illustrate boxing's fundamental inhumanity.

Next, with *The Heart of a Champion* finally ready to air, the American Medical Association launched a preemptive strike against the CBS movie of the week. "For a film to be made about a person whose principal fame was killing another fighter in the ring and not even to acknowledge that is at the very least unbalanced," said Dr. George Lundberg, editor of the *Journal of the American Medical Association*.

Even the director, Richard Michaels, who saw his first fight in preparation for filming, sided with those who would ban the sport. "I went to my first fight at the Olympic Auditorium, and I'll never go back," he told the *New York Times*. "It was very animal."

However one saw the second Bramble fight, Ray had acquitted himself well, even heroically. But again, in the aftermath, such valor seemed for naught. During a poolside interview at the Sahara Hotel in Las Vegas, the normally eager-to-please Mancini became angry when asked about Kim. "There's no need to discuss it," he said icily. "Today's today and yesterday's yesterday. It's in the past and I just don't think about it."

"I understood he was there to promote something, but there was no way I could interview him and *not* ask him about it," recalls the Associated Press's Tim Dahlberg, who had covered the Kim fight. "It's a question that has to be asked, and once I did, all of a sudden he regarded me as the enemy. He started to give these short, terse answers. Finally, I said goodbye. But I was taken aback by his response because it clearly showed that he hadn't come to grips with what had happened in the most infamous moment of his life. If you ask me, the wound was still pretty raw."

Reporters weren't alone in thinking that Mancini had been unable to cope with the fallout from Kim. "The old Ray wouldn't have had any trouble with Bramble," says Arum. "It wasn't a question of styles. The Livingstone Brambles of this world couldn't beat the pre-Kim Ray on their best days. You can't tell in training; you can only tell in the fights. His heart wasn't in it anymore. When you kill a man in the ring, it must always be in the back of your mind that it could happen again."

Despite every intention to the contrary, Ray had become a kind of patron saint to those afflicted with ghosts.

Later that year, in a hallway at Sharpsville High School, just twenty-five miles from Youngstown, seventeen-year-old Jack Peterson got into an altercation with his best friend, Bob Knapp. The boys had been hanging out at a friend's house over the weekend, and Knapp remembers Jack teasing him for drinking. On Monday, as they returned to class from the lunchroom, the teasing led to a fight. The school nurse recalls that Knapp may have had his friend in a headlock, perhaps even landed a punch. Still, as high school rows go, this wasn't particularly vicious or violent. "Friendly horseplay," said the school superintendent. It would've been quickly forgotten if Jack hadn't suddenly collapsed, unable to breathe.

"It was a freak thing," says Janet Fryman, the nurse who arrived moments after a phys. ed. teacher administered CPR. "It turned out that Jack had heart disease."

The boy was taken to Sharpsville General Hospital, then airlifted to Mercy General in Pittsburgh, where he died six days later. The cause of death was attributed to asphyxiation, reportedly due to food particles or fluid in his lungs.

"It was my best friend," says Knapp. "Nobody knew what to say to me, so they just kind of didn't say anything."

With Knapp depressed, withdrawn, and ridden with guilt, a friend of the family got in touch with Father O'Neill, who had become something of a local celebrity as Boom Boom's priest. It was suggested that an audience with the former champ might prove therapeutic.

"I never met somebody who was famous," says Knapp. "I was just a kid. Having him come to the house just made me feel good." They spoke for a couple of hours, then Ray left him with a copy of the best-selling paperback by Harold S. Kushner, *When Bad Things Happen to Good People*. It was inscribed:

To my friend Bob,
You are truly a good person, believe it!!
Stay strong, God Bless You
Ray "Boom Boom" Mancini

The specter of Jack Peterson would haunt those closest to him. "The family fell apart after that," says Fryman.

Jack's parents moved. His brother eventually took his own life. Meanwhile, Bob withdrew, finding it difficult to make friends. "It's a little harder for me to get close to people," he says.

But, through it all, he'd recall Mancini's visit as a mission of mercy: "He made me feel like I wasn't the only one."

• • •

Never had a champion risen from such idyllic circumstances as those depicted in *Heart of a Champion: The Ray Mancini Story.* Even an unemployed steelworker, noted one critic, "looks like an associate professor." The real traumas in the life of the protagonist (played by Doug McKeon, a young actor best known for playing Henry Fonda's surrogate grandson in the Academy Award–winning *On Golden Pond*) were obscured or unmentioned. As played by Robert Blake, Boom didn't need his son's help to get home from the bar. Lenny's death was portrayed as an unspecified accident. The *CBS Wednesday Night Movie* for May 1, 1985, concluded with Ray winning the title against Frias, six months before Americans ever heard of Duk Koo Kim.

That omission, argued the *Washington Post*'s Tom Shales, transformed a typically bad TV movie into something "heedlessly deceitful" and "morally indefensible." "If we can't get a punch-drunk Congress to ban professional boxing, as Howard Cosell among others has urged, maybe we can get someone to ban lousy boxing movies," he wrote, identifying the film's maxim—"Believe in yourself"—as an unpardonable offense.

"I wonder if Duk Koo Kim believed in himself," asked Shales.

Even more hurtful than the critics was the appraisal of Ray's own father, who watched the movie with family and friends at the VIP Lounge in Niles. Chuck Fagan could see Boom's face slacken each time Blake came on screen. A former child actor, Blake had steadfastly refused to meet with him in preparation for the role. Now Boom watched himself depicted as a dese, dem, and dose caricature with a porkpie hat (as opposed to the snap-brim fedoras he favored in real life).

In one scene, Blake-as-Boom admonished Ray to "just go in there and knock the bum out."

Now the father's expression changed from mere disappointment to mortification. Blake had libeled him.

"What's the matter, Boom?" asked Chuck.

"I never called another fighter a bum," he said. "Never in my life."

By the time they were in the parking lot, people were telling Ray what a good job McKeon had done. The kid was a good actor, sure. But it was plain to see that he couldn't even fight a little. Stallone had been right. If there were a sequel, Ray vowed, he'd play himself.

After getting cut by the Pittsburgh Steelers in the summer of 1969, Ed O'Neill returned to his hometown of Youngstown, where he enjoyed a reputation as a football player and street fighter of some renown. He spent the next ten years bouncing from job to job: working in a mill, teaching school, tending bar. Finally, at the age of thirty-one, he decided to become an actor. By the time Big Ellen ran into him at the YMCA, he had appeared as a cop in an Al Pacino movie, *Cruising*, and a mercenary in another picture, *Dogs of War*. O'Neill had even done a little Broadway, playing a heavyweight contender in *Knockout*, starring Danny Aiello, at the Helen Hayes Theater. Still, the bulk of his experience had been limited to beer commercials and regional theater.

"Do you know my son, Raymond?" asked Big Ellen.

"Not personally," said O'Neill, who had first seen Ray and Lenny on an amateur card at the Struthers Field House. "But I'm a big fan."

"I want you to talk to him," she said. "He's interested in acting."

"I don't know, Mrs. Mancini," he said. "I'm kind of just starting out myself."

"Please," she insisted. "This boxing isn't going to last forever."

The very next day, they all met in the cafeteria at the Y. It was before Bramble, O'Neill recollects, and Ray was still the champ, a fact made clear by the way he carried himself.

"Raymond," said Big Ellen, "this is Ed."

O'Neill thrust out his hand, to which Ray responded with his fingertips, forming a kind of limp beak. It was an unmistakable act of disrespect, an indication that Ray was only doing this to placate his mother.

This fucking guy, thought O'Neill. *What's he go, a buck forty?*

Ray, with his mullet haircut, was dripping in gold: the bracelet, the rings, the "Boom Boom" breastplate hanging from his neck. "Like an Italian Mr. T," as the actor describes him.

"So," said Ellen, "Ed is a very successful actor."

The ensuing conversation, such as it was, went back and forth between the actor and the mother who kept nudging her son.

"Are you listening, Raymond?" said Big Ellen, concerned that he wasn't preparing to act the way he prepared to fight. "Doesn't he need to study?"

O'Neill, then immersing himself in the works of Shaw, Ibsen, Arthur Miller, and Constantin Stanislavski, spared Ray the required reading list. But he did suggest, somewhat hesitantly, the value of vocal training. The vocal chords were just like any other muscles. Plus, as O'Neill knew from experience, unless you were being cast as a dockworker or a gangster, the Youngstown accent wasn't necessarily an asset. Reciting poetry also helped with elocution, said O'Neill.

Now Ray looked right at him. *Poetry?*

"It helps," he said.

Ray checked out of the discussion for good. Looking back, O'Neill can't blame him. He was twenty-two, and he was the champ. He didn't want to read Eugène Ionesco. He wanted to stay famous without getting stitches. Still, the actor would always remember the look on Mancini's face: *Who is this guy, anyway? I know movie stars.*

In June 1985, four months after losing the rematch with Bramble, Ray moved to Los Angeles, anticipating his own second act. He was acting on the advice of his William Morris agents, who, in no time at all, had him shooting an aerobics video. "My Knockout Workout" featured four headband-wearing, spandex-clad cuties demonstrating how to "Boxercise your way to fitness." Ray bought a condo—two bedrooms and a pool, in Brentwood—and started having his hair cut in Beverly Hills. It was the stylist, Giuseppe Franco, who introduced him to another client, a big fan of Ray's.

Mickey Rourke had a quality Hollywood respected even more

than talent. He was hot. Having already starred in *Diner* and *The Pope of Greenwich Village*, he was primed to be a new generation's leading man. But there was another role Rourke wanted even more.

"What you do is honorable," he would tell Ray. "What I do is not."

The all-but-ex-fighter didn't know what to say to that.

"It's a shit business," Rourke told him.

Again, Ray didn't understand. Rourke had just shot a picture with Kim Basinger, who acceded to his character's every sexual desire. What was so shitty about that?

"If it's so bad," asked Ray, "then why don't you get out?"

"I don't know how to do anything else," said Rourke, who explained that he had boxed as a kid in Miami.

They would have lunch or espresso at Café Roma in Beverly Hills. Ray would tell Mickey he wanted to become an actor. "You know how many people out there would give anything to be you?" he said.

"I'd give anything to be you," said Rourke, who impressed Ray by knowing all the old fighters.

Ray got a kick out of Mickey's workouts. The movie star built a gym in his loft in a busted-out section of Hollywood. He'd move around with a sparring partner for a couple of rounds, then he'd take some calls. Then he'd box another round, and break for an espresso, or maybe a smoke.

"Mickey," Ray asked, "is this *method* boxing?"

In truth, Ray's method wasn't working anymore. For years, he had lived by rigorous, Spartan routines. Now the prospect of another training camp seemed like going off to jail. Except for the jewelry, Ray had been careful with the $6 million he earned in purse money. Why abstain from food and women? he asked himself. Why bleed? He had redeemed his father. He was rich. And as a result of these victories, his desire was diminished. Ray was working out at Mickey's place, trying to, anyway, when he finally had an epiphany; he was done. He dialed Dave Wolf and told him to call a press conference.

• • •

The retirement, Wolf announced, came despite a $3 million offer to fight Pryor and a promise from Camacho's promoter to top that figure. But Ray's decision, rumored and prematurely reported for months, was now official.

"It's time to move on to something new," he said.

At the Sporting Club in Lower Manhattan, Ray assured reporters he had gotten everything he ever wanted from the fight game: a title for his father and treasure for his unborn heirs. This wasn't about his eyes, as had been reported. And it certainly wasn't about Kim, whom he purposely did not mention. It wasn't that he couldn't win back the title, either. It's that he didn't have to.

"I didn't want to pay the dues," he said, promising to avoid the fate that had befallen so many would-be ex-fighters. "I have used boxing . . . I am not going to let boxing use me."

Mancini was twenty-four years old, with a record of 29–3. His retirement was big enough news to warrant mention in Johnny Carson's monologue. Asked what he would do now, Ray said he was already up for a big role.

"A sort of TV Rambo," he said.

In the early 1980s, after Robert De Niro won an Oscar for his portrayal of her ex-husband, Vikki LaMotta had a fling with Ray. She was more than twice his age, but at fifty-one, had recently appeared in a phenomenally successful *Playboy* pictorial. Still, her agelessness surprised Ray less than the reaction of her ex. He'd run into Jake LaMotta at joints all over New York: a nightclub, a press conference, anywhere fighters still went on the arm. If Jake's was a familiar face, so was his combination of suspicion and rage familiar to anyone who had seen *Raging Bull*.

"You fuck my wife, Ray?" he'd ask, seething. "You fuck Vikki?"

"No, Jake," Ray lied. "Never."

Not only was the lightweight champ afraid of a crazy man forty years his senior, it was impossible to tell the difference between

De Niro's Jake and Jake's Jake. Life imitated art, sure. But fighters imitated actors imitating fighters. The lines of demarcation between the real life and the role became impossibly obscure.

Legions of ex-champs had tried their luck at show business: Jack Dempsey, Max Baer, Sugar Ray Robinson, Rocky Graziano, and of course, LaMotta, just to name a few. But they had all played versions of themselves. So why shouldn't Ray play Ray? What was the difference between the person and the persona?

In his first year after retiring, Ray landed bit parts in two episodes of *Who's the Boss?* starring another friend of his, Tony Danza, an undistinguished boxer who became hugely successful in sitcoms. He appeared once as a soldier in a Steven Spielberg show, *Amazing Stories,* and as an ex-con in a CBS movie, *Oceans of Fire.*

But the Rambolike series never panned out. Action heroes, Ray soon found out, were easily conceived at meetings with agents and producers, but the actual roles were exceedingly rare. Perhaps he should've known. After all, Ray had been a TV action hero almost from the time he turned pro.

And, soon enough, he found himself grieving for that life. Sipping espresso in Café Roma with Mickey Rourke was great fun. But it wasn't a substitute for what he had been.

"I was in a bad state of depression," he told a reporter.

This wasn't the normal sense of loss brought on by an athlete's retirement. Rather, it was an acknowledgment, at only twenty-four years old, that he had already played the role of a lifetime. It was an existential dilemma, a question of mortality. And, as such, he called Father O'Neill. "You accomplished your lifelong dream at a very young age," the priest told him. "Everything else from here on will be anticlimactic."

Ray understood. It was something he'd have to live with: "Nothing ever will give me that same feeling."

In January 1987, Ed O'Neill reintroduced himself to Ray at a Santa Monica restaurant. Il Forno, as it was called, had opened the previous year with a crew of cooks and waiters from Café

Roma. It offered neighborhood Italian food, as good as you'd get back East, in a Southern California strip mall.

Ray was happy to have found another expatriate Youngstowner, not to mention an actor, but had no recollection of their meeting at the YMCA. O'Neill was in town to shoot a pilot. It was another family sitcom, he explained, but it wasn't another TV family, which was to say, it wouldn't be the Cosbys or the Cleavers. The Bundys would be as fucked up as everyone else, just funnier. The daughter was dumb and slutty. The son was awkward and hapless. The wife was always asking for something her husband no longer cared to give. Al Bundy, as played by O'Neill, was a former high school football star who knocked up his then-girlfriend and sold women's shoes in a mall.

A screwed-up family on a start-up network, something called FOX? Ray didn't know quite what to make of that. But by now, the name of the show was sounding good to him: *Married . . . with Children.*

If Ray seemed slightly humbled (a natural consequence of any actor's maiden voyage through Hollywood), it surely had nothing to do with the girl on his arm. Ed couldn't help but notice how she sparkled: a beauty, yes, but not of the starlet or playmate phyla native to regions of West Los Angeles.

Her name was Carmen Vazquez. Her father had fled Cuba in 1966, and earned a comfortable living with his brother as co-owners of a sausage-making business. Carmen grew up in Miami, where her parents spoke only Spanish, and graduated from high school in June 1986. That's when she met Ray, on a cruise to celebrate her freshly minted diploma. Carmen was a month shy of her eighteenth birthday, an age at which she still thought his mullet was kind of cute.

Ray bumped into her as she was taking the luggage from her aunt's car. He wore a blue silk shirt with baggy blue pants. Very *Miami Vice*, she thought. His belt, shoes, and feather-laced fedora were all white.

Ray excused himself, smiling flirtatiously, and Carmen, as she recalls, probably blushed. Then she turned to her friend. "*Dios mio,*" she said. "I hope he's on my ship."

"Who?" asked her friend. "That little one?"

Her parents, Eloy and Silvia, would have been mortified. Carmen had told them that the nuns and priests from the school would be accompanying them as chaperones. But as Mrs. Vazquez waved from a dock at the disembarking ship, there were no clergy to be seen.

"When my mother realized," says Carmen, "she almost had a heart attack."

The SS *Norway* would tour various Bahamian ports for a little more than a week. Among the cruise's attractions was Boom Boom Mancini, on the arm as a celebrity guest to regale fellow passengers with tales of his reign as lightweight champion of the world.

That's what Carmen found him doing in the lounge, telling his stories. He smiled at her as she passed. Then she made a habit of passing, and smiling back. Ray was with his mother and father, and maybe some friends.

Finally, she asked someone who he was. A famous boxer, she was told. Carmen didn't recognize the name, but surely her brothers would. They followed *el boxeo.*

"Mr. Mancini," she asked sweetly, "can I take a picture of you for my brothers?"

They got to talking, and soon enough found their way to Singles Night, where they danced until the band reached its finale with a version of Celine Dion's "The Power of Love." Then, with the musicians dismantling the instruments and the amps, Ray asked her to spend the night in his cabin.

Carmen was frightened of the man she was already falling for, and the one about whom her parents had warned her. They could be the same guy for all she knew. Carmen was seventeen. Ray was twenty-five. She had never been out of her Cuban neighborhood. He had been all over the world.

"I'm not going to have sex with you," she said.

"I'm not going to even try," he said.

And he didn't. They kissed, and he held her all night. He was good to his word. "He didn't take anything off," she remembers. "And he could have."

It went on like that for the duration of the cruise. A month later, on the occasion of her eighteenth birthday, Ray sent her flowers and a card. "This is the one I've been waiting for," he wrote.

Soon, Ray flew to Miami, where the Vazquezes held a big family dinner. Carmen's mother, who produced a giant platter of *arroz con pollo*, loved him. Her aunt Consuelo loved him. Her brothers loved him. But her father, Carmen recalls, "thought he might be full of shit."

As Eloy Eladio Vazquez spoke no English, Ray looked him in the eye and instructed Carmen. "Tell him he can ask me," said Ray, reciting a line that seemed straight out of *The Godfather*.

"Ask you what?" said Carmen.

"Ask me what my intentions are."

With his would-be lover acting as his translator, Ray assured her father that his purpose was honorable and asked permission for the courtship to begin.

Permission was granted. Then, the next night, Carmen fell asleep in Ray's hotel room. At about five in the morning, she bolted awake, threw on her clothes, and jumped in the car. Her father was standing in the driveway when she got home.

"I don't give a shit who he is," said Eloy Eladio Vazquez. "You are never seeing that man again."

Enter Aunt Consuelo. The father had a soft spot for his sister, as she had been stricken with polio as a child in Cuba. But she was also blessed with an ability to cry on cue.

"Please, please, I beg you," said Consuelo. "I was never able to walk. Let the girl enjoy her life."

Eventually, the father relented, and with his surrender, the real wooing could begin. Even as the romance shifted venues—Los Angeles, Las Vegas, Miami, New York, Ohio, wherever Ray had occasion to be—the pattern did not. "I would lie to my dad," says Carmen, "and my Aunt Consuelo would cover up for me."

Ray had a sense of inevitability about Carmen. From the beginning, he knew this was the story he would tell, that of falling in love with the virginal bride on the cruise ship, of asking for her father's blessing, and the passionate, tender weekends that followed.

The families met the following spring in Miami. Silvia Vazquez presented the Mancinis with an elaborate tropical fruit platter upon their entrance to the family home. "I've never seen such a beautiful papaya," exclaimed Big Ellen, not knowing that *papaya* was a Cuban expression for the female genitalia. Meanwhile, Mrs. Vazquez couldn't get over the way Boom would kiss Carmen on the lips. "Mom," she said through gritted teeth, "that's how they do it."

On the Mancini side, there was unanimity on the subject of Ray's girl. They all loved her, friends and family, but none more than Boom. "He forgot everything and he'd ask you the same question a million times," says Carmen. "But what a sweet, sweet old man. Everytime he saw me and Ray together he'd go 'Look at huggy bear and kissy face.' He loved me."

Apart from her obvious charms, however, Carmen possessed the attribute most desirable in any prospective mate. In the Youngstown vernacular, she was a stand-up girl. As months passed into seasons, Ray gave up his other girlfriends, finally entering a state that could be described as committed, if occasionally flirtatious. It wasn't just women. Ray sought approbation, recognition of who he was and what he had meant, especially to the people of Youngstown. As the city settled into a state of perennial recession, its two most recognizable sons were Jim Traficant, the former sheriff elected to Congress after a mind-boggling acquittal in his mafia bribery case, and Ray. Traficant was fundamentally corrupt, and Ray fundamentally virtuous, but each in his own way was a politician. Nourished by adulation, they knew how to work a room.

When in Youngstown, Carmen noticed how Ray would purposely take the long way around the bar, collecting all manner of compliments, backslaps, I-knew-you-whens, and autograph requests, before settling into his booth for dinner. Then he'd receive well-wishers throughout the meal. Carmen was still just a kid. She didn't mind, except for the girls. Were they former sweethearts or one-night stands? She wondered.

And what of the one that night at The Boathouse, the girl who mouthed the words "Call me." Even from across the room, she acted as if Carmen weren't there. Worse still was Ray's response: holding an imaginary phone by his ear and pretending to dial.

Carmen said nothing.

Finally, after they left, Ray asked if she was okay.

"I'm fine."

"Well, you don't look happy."

"I know you haven't been home for a while," she said. "And I know everybody loves you. That's okay."

"But?"

"You're an asshole, Raymond."

He winced. Nick Mancino wouldn't have stood for that. Or his old man. Or Michael Corleone. This wasn't in the script. A woman calling him an asshole? This wasn't a regular woman, though. "You're right," he conceded. "I'm sorry."

On August 29, 1987, Virgin Records released Warren Zevon's *Sentimental Hygiene*. His first album since weaning himself from drugs and alcohol, it seemed to confirm his status as a darling of the troubadour classes. Among those contributing to various tracks were Bob Dylan, Don Henley, George Clinton, Flea, Brian Setzer, Michael Stipe, and Neil Young. Zevon's great gift was for sardonic lyrics. But the second song after the title cut lacked any of his typically seditious sensibility. "Boom Boom Mancini," as he called it, was straight ahead, no irony, no humor, no sarcasm. Like most of middle America, the rocker admired why Mancini fought—"like father like son"—and how—"if you can't take the punches it don't mean a thing." Zevon also thought he got a bum rap for Kim's death:

> *They made hypocrite judgments after the fact*
> *But the name of the game is be hit and hit back*

Then, the chorus:

Hurry home early—hurry on home
Boom Boom Mancini's fighting Bobby Chacon

Chacon was still fighting, of course. Just a couple months before *Sentimental Hygiene* hit the stores, he had been knocked down three times at a Holiday Inn in Tucson. He came back to win that one, knocking out Martin Guevara in the third round. But now, after a six-month sentence for violating probation, Chacon's notion of victory was relative. He'd been fighting for money since 1972, but money was what he still needed.

Kinder fates awaited Ray. That much was clear on a summer night when Carmen gathered the Vazquez family in front of the television to watch *Late Night with David Letterman*. Ray didn't know until he got a call in Brentwood. Warren Zevon was singing his song.

Ray was honored. He was in love. He had every reason to be happy. Still, taking the long way around the bar like a casino greeter just wasn't the answer. He was still a young man. But at twenty-six, his fame had grown old.

"I was in the light," he told a reporter, "but the light moved."

By 1988, Mickey Rourke had cast Boom in a bit part as an old trainer in a busted-out gym. The movie was called *Homeboy*, a kind of vanity project for Rourke, who apparently saw something sublime in the role of an obstinate, alcoholic pug.

Ray would've loved a part in a Mickey Rourke picture, but he was off filming *The Dirty Dozen: The Fatal Mission*. It was another forgettable TV movie, but it would be his only screen credit of the year. Then again, if his acting career hadn't yet blossomed, Ray had to take part of the blame.

"I remember telling him to take some acting lessons," says Ed O'Neill. "But he had this idea that it would screw him up, that it would ruin his spontaneity, his natural street thing."

By now, they were frequent dining companions at Il Forno, and Ed a full-blown star. *Married . . . with Children* was the hottest property FOX owned, and a couple of seasons in the TV business left Ed ideally suited to diagnose Ray's problem. It wasn't just a lack of formal training. It was his very nature. What served Ray so well as a fighter worked to his detriment in Hollywood.

"Coming straight forward doesn't help in a town where everyone's coming at angles," says O'Neill. "Once Ray shows how much he wants something, he's exposed. That's the way it works out here. Once they sense your desire, they fuck you."

Fame was perishable. But *hotness*, the real coin of the realm in Hollywood, was ephemeral. As Ray himself explained to the *Boston Globe*'s Ron Borges, "Producers and agents told me if I fought, I could be hot again."

No, he told them. *No chance.*

Then it was *maybe*.

Next, *who?*

And, finally, *how much?*

The Comeback Fight was a staple for fans in the eighties. They could be epic; Ray Leonard came back after three years to win a split decision over middleweight champ Marvin Hagler. Or they could be disastrous humiliations, as Larry Holmes discovered when Mike Tyson knocked him down three times in a round. They were, however, always lucrative, and usually personal, the product of accumulated insults and unresolved rivalries.

So it would be for Ray, who couldn't stand that little prick who paraded around in skirts calling himself the Macho Man. He had disliked Camacho ever since they were both CBS darlings, but now these sentiments gave him the justification he needed to come out of retirement.

The idea was broached publicly in May 1987, when Camacho still held the WBC lightweight title. It was to be a fifteen-round nontitle bout. The news moved the prospective combatants to begin slurring each other in earnest.

Camacho, for his part, would vow on national television to "give the All-American boy an All-American beating."

"He runs like a dog and holds you like a woman," said Ray.

By February 1988, with Camacho out on bail for assault and cocaine charges, they finally signed a deal: fifteen rounds at 140 pounds. The New York papers were outraged.

"It's sick," wrote Mike Katz, now with the *Daily News*.

"A horrid mismatch," said the *Post*'s Michael Marley.

Perhaps it was fortunate, then, that the bout was cancelled when the promoter couldn't secure a venue. Still, Hector and Ray kept at it, a mating ritual peculiar to fighters. Ray had been retired almost four years. Camacho had wasted almost as much time keeping very late nights. They needed each other; they just had a funny way of showing it.

"If this becomes like the Duk Koo Kim fight, then it's okay," Camacho told Marley. "I wouldn't celebrate killing Mancini but I wouldn't go into retirement, either. I would go to his funeral. That's no hype. I hate this guy."

Finally, with the aid of promoters Lou Falcigno and Joe Gagliardi, a date was set for March 6, 1989, in Reno, where Ray was a guaranteed draw. By then, the trend begun in the wake of Kim's death had become the accepted convention. Ray would only have twelve rounds to catch up with Camacho.

What's more, he'd be without Dave Wolf, whose contract he'd let lapse. It was just one fight. Ray had been doing this long enough. Besides, he'd be bringing along one of his guys from William Morris. "What do I need a manager for?" he asked.

With the fight just a day away, the answer should've been self-evident. The Camacho camp wanted to weigh in at eight thirty the night before. Mancini wanted to weigh in at eight thirty the next morning. Frustrated members of the Nevada State Athletic Commission split the difference and ordered the fighters to step on the scales at two thirty in the morning.

When the Mancini entourage got back to the suite, Chucky asked, "Would Wolf ever allow this to happen?"

"No," Ray conceded. "He wouldn't."

To make matters worse, the ring was impossibly large, almost twenty-one by twenty-one feet. "If it was up to me," says Fagan, "I'd have pulled a Dave Wolf, and told them to play a movie."

It wasn't up to Chuck, though. It was all Ray's call. Yet again, boxing would imitate show business. Ray had made his desire plain, and he got fucked for it.

Ray didn't seem to care, though. Neither the ring, nor the prohibitive odds against him, nor the four-year layoff really worried him. He saw only good fortune coming to him. The fight was being sold on pay per view at $19.95 a pop, a portion of the proceeds going toward his $1.4 million purse. The Lawlor Events Center again would be packed in his honor. Some fighters lost heart making that agonizingly lonely walk from the dressing room to the ring, but Ray anticipated a charge of ecstatic fortification. "I feed off the public," he said. "That's where I draw my courage." He wanted the crowd. He wanted Camacho. And he wanted his girlfriend to know exactly what kind of star he had been.

Carmen, for her part, was enthralled. Even the presence of Ray's ex-girlfriend didn't bother her too much. She was a striking Asian beauty, apparently unaware that Ray was no longer available. But Carmen believed him when he told her not to worry— about the girl or the fight or what the reporters were saying about him getting all cut up. Camacho couldn't hurt him. Everything would be fine, better than fine. He said this all as if making a vow.

Meanwhile, Mickey Rourke and Giuseppe Franco had flown into town to support their man from ringside. Everybody loved Raymond, and Carmen would recall the week as a big party that ended with twelve thousand fans screaming her boyfriend's name as he entered the ring.

He wore the name LENNY stitched to the waist of his trunks, a tribute to his brother. Camacho's ensemble, on the other hand, celebrated his own sense of whimsical vanity. He entered in a blinding matador's outfit, before stripping down to a sequined loincloth.

As it happened, the widely anticipated mismatch never materialized. The southpaw Camacho would stick and run, then run some more. Ray was relentless in pursuit. But when he got too close for Camacho's comfort, the matador would grab and hold. There were occasional skirmishes of note: a Camacho flurry (impressive looking, but to no effect) in the eighth, Mancini's straight right in the ninth, his looping left hook to the chin in the tenth.

"Mancini made the fight," said the admiring referee, Mills Lane, who took the additional liberty of calling Camacho "a crybaby."

Actually, it wasn't much of a fight, certainly not by Mancini's standards. The fans cheered Boom Boom, and booed his opponent's incessant retreat, but nothing could even the advantage conferred upon Camacho by the twenty-one-foot ring. The announcement of Camacho's split decision victory was greeted with a hail of cups and coins from the audience, many of whom had bet Mancini.

Some weeks later, and somewhat apologetically, a veteran Vegas wise guy tried to explain the judges' decision. "You were a three-to-one dog," the gangster reminded Ray. "We couldn't let that happen. The town would've gone bust."

Did they give me the business? Ray wondered. Then: *Did it really matter anymore?* Truth was, his desires had been satiated, at least for now. He had gotten his dose of the bright light. He had made a score, in defiance of every prognostication, and emerged uncut and unmarked. Now it was time to bet a sure thing.

He married Carmen six weeks later at St. Dominic's in Youngstown. A wonderful reception followed at Mr. Anthony's Banquet Center on South Avenue. It was official, Ray was done fighting. The marriage license listed his occupation as *entertainer.*

Chapter 15 | Body and Soul

Eventually, Ray relented and sat in on a couple of acting classes. That's not to say he ever saw the value in pretending to be a pear. "Who is gonna hire me to play that?" he asked.

What he especially disliked, however, was the instructor lacing into an aspiring actress, his relentless inquiry into the marrow of the girl's troubled relationship with her father, the way he made her cry in front of the other students. Sister Gregory back in Youngstown couldn't have been so mean.

"This wasn't school," remarked Ray. "This was therapy."

So Ray found another drama teacher, Howard Fine. Ray could understand what Howard was trying to accomplish with him. The lessons were one on one. They worked on the clock, an hour at a time, rehearsing specific scenes. "Like he was my trainer," said Ray.

It didn't hurt, either, that Fine had come recommended by Mickey Rourke. "I love Raymond," Rourke told an interviewer. "We're like brothers."

By now, Mickey was hell-bent on a career as a prizefighter, and wanted Ray to work his corner. Ray, on the other hand, wanted to enlist Mickey in his various projects, as he'd begun to call them. Ray knew enough about fighting to respect Mickey as an actor. Mickey, for his part, admired the man who'd been champ. Like brothers, perhaps, but brothers on divergent paths. Mickey had already begun to wreck his career as a movie star. Ray, with perfect attendance at Lamaze class, was about to become a father.

Carmenina, known as Nina, was born February 6, 1990. She

had an abundance of dark hair, with greenish eyes and a preternaturally pouty mouth. Giuseppe Franco and his stylists always celebrated her arrival at his Beverly Hills salon. A baby seemed a novelty among the Mancinis' Hollywood friends, notes Carmen, who recalls Mickey and his girlfriend dropping by their new apartment in Santa Monica to meet the infant.

Mickey held her, and seemed to rejoice in doing so. His girlfriend, a model/actress named Carré Otis, did not. "She was so tall and so beautiful it seemed like she wasn't part of the human race," says Carmen. "But you could see there was something off about her, something not *there*. Both of them, her and Mickey, two beautiful, damaged people."

By the time Mickey made his pro debut—outpointing a thirty-three-year-old mechanic in Fort Lauderdale—Otis would be struggling with a heroin addiction. Ray and Carmen, meanwhile, were very happy as homebodies.

"Once in a while, we would go out with them, but it was very Hollywoodish," says Carmen. "By midnight, Ray would want to go home. He never wanted to be apart from Nina. He adored that child. It was the beginning of a great time in our lives."

By September 1991, Carmen was two trimesters into her second pregnancy and Ray had left William Morris. His new rep, Robbie Kass at Innovative Artists, wasted little time before calling his brother.

Sam Henry Kass still lived in an apartment in the building where they'd grown up, on Orange Street in Brooklyn Heights. He had attended about five high schools before embarking on a brief, itinerant career as a sportswriter. Finally, in Owensboro, Kentucky, he realized that covering high school football was his manner of avoidance, that he was meant, or perhaps cursed, for a career in the family business, which was the theater. Sam then returned to Brooklyn and began writing plays, all of which were critiqued with a ruthless kind of love by his father.

Peter Kass was a protégé of the great playwright Clifford Odets, and regarded, in the words of one colleague, as a "holy madman of the theater." He had been a writer and director, a Broadway performer and master acting teacher at Boston University and New York University. His students included Faye Dunaway, Olympia Dukakis, John Cazale, Maureen Stapleton, and Val Kilmer.

"Don't worry," he'd tell his son. "You'll finally be liberated the day I die."

Was he kidding? Not really, thought Sam, whose first off-Broadway production, *Side Street Scenes* (directed by none other than his old man), was deemed "an engaging comedy" by the *New York Times*. The *Times* cited another effort, *Lusting after Pipino's Wife*, for its "sharp and witty" dialogue. At the time of his brother's call, he was casting another of his off-Broadway shows, *Siddown!!! Conversations with the Mob*.

"You want to try something interesting?" asked Robbie. "How about Ray 'Boom Boom' Mancini?"

Sam was certainly intrigued. He recalled the beats of Ray's career as did millions of Americans, filtered through the prism of television: Bramble, Chacon, Kim, Frias, Arguello, kissing his old man on the lips. "I wish I could've done that," he says. "I wish I could've made my father that proud of me—even in defeat. I wish I could have failed on that large a stage."

There was, however, another question. "Can he act?" Sam asked his brother.

"Just give him a call."

"When do you want me there?" asked Ray, already so excited at the idea of playing a *mafioso* on stage that he put Sam on speaker-phone so he could start banging out push-ups and sit-ups.

"Well, let's not get ahead of ourselves," said Sam, who had not yet offered the role.

"Okay, so tell me about the show."

It was three one-act plays, Sam explained, and would run Thursday, Friday, and Saturday nights for seven weeks beginning November 1. The Trocadero Theater was located in the basement of an Italian restaurant at the corner of Charles and Bleecker Streets in the Village. The parts of two of the aspiring gangsters had already been filled by promising young actors: Holt McCallany and Nick Turturro. Sam was looking for the third.

"So," said Ray, "when do you want me there?"

Another week or so would pass before Sam could convince a neighbor to temporarily abandon his apartment for the Mancinis: Nina, the very pregnant Carmen, and Ray, who arrived with five impossibly heavy suitcases filled with dumbbells, barbells, and other assorted exercise equipment. Apparently, Ray would train for the stage much as he trained for the ring.

It wasn't easy for him, though, sixty pages of dialogue with just three actors. "He had to work very hard to get his lines down," says Kass. "I attributed that to inexperience, nerves, and quite possibly, Livingstone Bramble. But there wasn't a phony bone in his body."

Backstage, Ray would shadowbox before the curtain went up. Even the more practiced actors found it a difficult room to work: noisy, with waiters who kept pushing drinks and patrons from Mulberry Street (many of them Ray's guests) who thought they were part of the show and liked talking back to the cast.

On opening night, Ray forgot his lines. Turturro, freshly praised for his scenes in Spike Lee's *Jungle Fever*, gave Ray his cue again. Nothing. And again. Nothing. Finally, not knowing what else to do, he slapped Ray across the face.

"Not exactly the Stanislavski method," recalls Kass. "But it worked."

Turturro remained in character. Mancini picked up the dialogue.

The next morning, Ray had breakfast with the *New York Times*'s Robert Lipsyte. He told the columnist he was trying to "make my bones as a working actor." He spoke quite candidly of Mickey Rourke's pro debut as a kind of desecration. "He's a friend of mine," Ray explained. "He wanted me in his corner, but that was a freak show. It was wrong."

The conversation began with Ray asking, in the manner of an actor hoping for praise, what the columnist had thought of his performance.

"You act the way you used to fight," said Lipsyte. "Not a lot of finesse, but a lot of energy. Straight ahead. Fun to watch. I was surprised how good you were."

"This is what I got to hear," said Ray. "Last night, for the first time in my life, I felt like I could call myself an actor."

Ray was still so charged he hadn't slept. He had plans, projects, ambitions. Still, he had to admit, he'd put them all on hold for another shot at Camacho. "Make that match and I'll be there in a New York minute."

As it happened, it wasn't Camacho, but a fighter named Greg Haugen who'd lure him back into the ring. Haugen had already done three stints as a lightweight titleholder. In 1991, he became the first man to beat a still-elusive, if over-the-hill, Camacho. Haugen wore a permanent scowl, a squinty-eyed warning to the legions of doubters who had disrespected him along the way. Even his own father called him Mutt.

Mancini saw no reason to respect him, either. Haugen was a game and competent counterpuncher. But there was nothing brilliant about him, and thus, nothing to fear.

"I don't know, Raymond," Ed told him one night at Il Forno. "I've seen him on TV. The kid fights all the time."

Ray had fought once since 1985. Why would he want to return against a guy who was still hungry and with a lot to prove?

"What?" asked Ray, a little offended.

"I'm just saying," said Ed. "Guy's got an educated jab. And he takes a punch."

"I'll walk right through him," said Ray.

"I hope you do," said Ed.

When news of the fight broke, Ray would speak of the challenge, of wanting to know whether he could still compete at a world-class level. That was only part of his motivation, however. He had enjoyed his off-Broadway apprenticeship. But even as it nourished something in him, it also left him famished. He had played bigger stages, after all, much bigger. Besides, off Broadway didn't pay.

He was a father again, too. Just after Thanksgiving, Carmen gave birth to a son. It was a troubled pregnancy that ended with Carmen hemorrhaging, slipping into unconsciousness after the delivery. She spent a week in ICU, after which she recalls Big Ellen standing over the baby and weeping with joy.

"Oh my God," she said. "He looks just like Lenny."

His name was Leonardo, and along with the now-toddling Nina, he became the object of great affection during a white Christmas spent in Youngstown. Then, not long after that, Ray left to train. Carmen accepted him at his word, all that stuff about him wanting the challenge. Still, money had something to do with it, too. Ray had now doubled down on his responsibilities as a provider. The purse for Haugen was $500,000, and the winner would get a shot at the great lightweight champion Julio Cesar Chavez. That could be worth millions.

"I have a wife and kids and an obligation to support them," as he explained to a reporter. "The opportunity won't be there forever. And I can make more from this fight than all my movies together."

Ray called Tank. "Get ready," he said. "We're fighting Haugen."

"*Greg* Haugen?"

"Yeah."

"Who's our tune-up fight?"

"There is no tune-up," said Ray. "I got to do this in a big way."

A *big way*. Tank understood what that meant. Off Broadway was fine and all, but Ray wanted to resurrect his starring role, Boom Boom. He wasn't alone, either, judging from the reception he received during the press conference at Mickey Mantle's restaurant in Manhattan. The reporters and TV guys treated him like a long-lost pal, asking about his wife and his kids and most of all, his father.

"The whole press conference was about Ray," remembers Sam Kass. "He was back in his glory. The words were flying. Then I look over at Haugen, who's sitting off to the side with his wife.

They looked like they both just escaped from the trailer park. No one wanted to talk to them. And Haugen's seething. *Seething.*"

Outside, after the press conference broke up, Haugen began taunting Ray. If Ray was so sure of himself, why didn't they make a side bet? Of the million-dollar pot, the winner would get $550,000, the loser $450,000.

"Ray is not a betting man," says Kass. "But Haugen goaded him into it."

That night, they returned to the apartment on Orange Street in Brooklyn Heights. On the back of an old grocery list—milk, eggs, bread, and various items—Ray calculated what would be left of his purse after paying Murphy Griffith, taking care of his mom and dad, and paying training expenses and taxes. Then he put down the pencil and left the room. As soon as he did, Sam checked Ray's math, shocked and dismayed to see that the basis for his subtraction was $450,000.

Camp was in Reno, and Griff made Ray work the mitts as he never had before. But it was plain to see his timing was off. "I kept waiting for something to kick in with Ray," says Chuck Fagan. "It never did."

Haugen kept talking. "I want to punish him before I knock him out," he said. But neither the words nor the side bet seemed to energize Mancini, who went into a depression, away for the first time from his wife, his daughter, and as Carmen put it, the baby boy he wanted so badly.

Every time he heard Eric Clapton's "Tears in Heaven"—a huge hit about the death of the guitarist's four-year-old son, Conor—Ray would start bawling. "I remember him looking in the mirror," says Tank, "asking, 'What did I get myself into?'"

Carmen and the kids arrived about a week before the fight. At first, Ray wanted them to stay in his room. Then he thought better of it, and put them in an adjoining part of his suite.

"The kids would start crying and Ray would break training to sit and play with them," says Sam Kass.

He especially liked watching *Barney* with Nina, rolling around on the carpet and singing along with the purple dinosaur:

I love you
You love me
We're a happy fa-mil-y

Now even Carmen had to wonder: "How can he win this fight when he's been humming the *Barney* song all day long?"

The Mancinis attended an especially somber mass before the fight. It wasn't until Ray stepped into the ring, however, that he fully understood the consequences of his vanity. It was another packed house in Reno. Telly Savalas and James Caan had come to cheer their fellow star. Ray was certainly the better looking fighter: broader, more muscular, and with a great Giuseppe Franco haircut, suitably coiffed for an MTV video.

But Haugen seemed an evil elf: spry on the balls of his feet, with angry slits for eyes, sneering and smirking at Ray as Mills Lane gave them instructions at the center of the ring. For the first time in his career, Ray averted his gaze. "I always looked at a guy's belly," he says. "But this time I looked down. I knew. I'm thinking, 'I got no business here.'"

For half a round, he seemed good enough. But now, without headgear, he began to paw at the fashionably long locks now dangling in front of his face. Still, hair was the least of his problems. His timing was irretrievably lost. By the second round, a clash of heads all but closed Ray's left eye. He couldn't see the right hands from Haugen, who doled them out in a steady, unhurried cadence.

True to his word, Haugen would make Ray suffer. He began taunting between flurries, and when that was no longer enough, he looked out over the ropes directing his smiling derision at Carmen, Boom, and Big Ellen at ringside. Haugen's grin, noted Showtime's Al Bernstein, was "positively demonic."

"Every punch, I felt it," says Carmen. "Then I felt very hot, like I couldn't breathe." A few seats away, Ray's nephew—Lenny's son, Anthony, now almost twelve—started to vomit.

Ray managed to make the fourth and fifth rounds respectable. However, by the sixth, with the packed house chanting "Boom! Boom!" there was nothing on his punches. Still pawing at his hair, it was clear he had crossed an invisible line. He wasn't a fighter anymore. Rather, he was like his friend Mickey, an actor playing a fighter.

The seventh saw Haugen counter Ray's looping right hand with a right of his own. It landed flush on the chin, as Ray tumbled forward. The Reno-Sparks Convention Center went suddenly silent.

"I remember Carmen's scream piercing through the arena," says Sam Kass, who looked over and saw old man Boom, stoic and expressionless, and Big Ellen, looking down as if to pray.

Ray's lapse in consciousness was momentary. Then he found himself trapped in the ropes, struggling like a bug in a web. He got to his feet, yes. That was no acting. But Mills Lane embraced him while waving off Haugen.

"No, son," he said. "That's enough."

Haugen leaned over the ropes, leering and pointing, taunting the Mancinis one last time. Then he was off to celebrate the biggest purse of his career. Another moment passed before Haugen's wife and mother appeared in front of Carmen, presenting her with a bouquet of flowers, as if to apologize.

Carmen would receive yet another apology, this one from her husband at the press conference. He was sorry to have put her through it all, which was to say, sorry for acting like a fighter. She forgave him, of course. And once she understood that the lacerated cheek and swollen ear would heal, she felt a relief akin to joy.

"It was finally, fucking over," says Carmen. "It was done."

The story of Ray "Boom Boom" Mancini, the fighter, had finally reached its denouement. And as far as Carmen was concerned, it would be a surprisingly happy ending. The man she loved, the father of her children, was free to play the roles of his fancy, but no longer to con himself. No pugilistic imposter would ever again come between the Mancinis of Santa Monica and their domestic tranquillity.

In fact, it would be several years before Ray stepped into another ring, and only then at the advice of his dentist. "Guy I know's a big fan of yours," said the dentist. "Even got his own gym."

Didn't smell like a gym. That was the first thing Ray noticed. It was clean and carpeted and absurdly well-appointed, like an old-school fight club reimagined by designing teams from Equinox and the House of Blues. There were vintage fight posters and autographed memorabilia (posters from Larry Bird and Magic Johnson, gloves from Muhammad Ali, all inscribed "To Bob"), and the portrait of a forgotten Hebraic battler painted in oil some seventy years before. The building's other tenant was a reform synagogue.

Ray's big fan was getting his hands wrapped. Then he began to shadowbox. For an old guy, thought Ray, he knew what he was doing. They shook hands, with Ray explaining how honored he was. The man spoke lyrically, in an American accent of undetermined origin.

"Would you like to move around some?"

Ray did his best to accommodate his host without hurting him.

"You can hit me," said the man.

Ray kept taking it easy. When they were done, the old man removed his headgear and started gingerly touching his jaw. "Ray," he said. "Can you lay off those head shots?"

"You okay?" asked Ray, suddenly concerned.

"Yes," said Bob Dylan, smiling wryly, "but I think I have a few more songs left in there."

The young couple bought a white stucco home their children would forever call the happy house. It was just blocks from Il Forno, and when Ray wasn't holding court at the restaurant, Carmen was cooking: steaming hot plates of black beans, plaintains, *arroz con pollo, ropa vieja,* and lasagna. A salad always accompanied dinner. For dessert: chocolate Haagen Dazs or Hershey's Kisses.

The only holiday they didn't celebrate was Valentine's Day, because of Ray's brother, Lenny. Still, the couple more than made up for it with their Friday date nights. If it wasn't Il Forno, it was Chaya on Main Street, or Hal's in Venice. Then maybe a movie or a concert. They still felt like newlyweds.

Ray had his projects—bit parts, paid appearances, and most notably, a role in an impressively cast independent film written by Sam Kass, *The Search for One-Eye Jimmy*. Carmen, meanwhile, enrolled at the Fashion Institute of Design and Marketing in downtown Los Angeles. She wanted a career in fashion, maybe as a buyer, and Ray was all for it, anything she wanted.

"As long as you still cook," he said.

Of the three bedrooms in that house, only one was used regularly. The Mancinis slept as a family, a human tangle on a big bed in the master suite. It was a water bed until the night Leonardo accidentally punctured the lining with the metal braces he wore as a corrective for severely pigeon-toed feet. "We almost drowned," Carmen says, amusedly. Like most episodes associated with the happy house, the deluge is recalled happily.

There were puppies and trips to Lake Tahoe. And if something happened to Nina in school—an argument or hurt feelings— she knew she could always call her dad. She would wait defiantly in the principal's office until he arrived. Then they would go for lunch at Subway. Nina would order a turkey sandwich and SunChips, and her dad would talk until she felt better.

Christmases were spent in Youngstown, where Nina would recall Big Ellen's voice: *Boom . . . Booomeeeee?* By now, her grandfather wore an eye patch. In his guayabera shirts and feathered fedoras, she thought he was dapper, occasionally confused, and smelled "like old man and patchouli."

Boom would hold Carmen's hand as they watched television on the old couch, his good eye surveying the background.

"Who's that old lady?" he would ask. "Why's she always watching us?"

"She's your wife, Boom," Carmen said patiently.

"It's not your mother?"

"Your wife," said Carmen. "Ellen. Ellen?"

"Oh," said Boom, clasping her hand a little tighter.

• • •

Early in 1996, the Mancinis left the happy house and moved to Indianapolis Street, near the Santa Monica Airport. A bigger home, it was purchased in anticipation of a bigger family. Ray Jr.—known as Ray-Ray—was born on March 26.

Boom seemed especially infatuated with his grandson, though not quite in the way he thought. Once, Carmen drove to Orange County with her parents and Ray-Ray in the back and Boom in the passenger seat. They were on the 405 Freeway when the old man reached for her hand.

"Tell your parents I don't care that he's not my son," said Boom. "I'll care for him. I'll put a roof over his head. I'll raise him like he was my own."

"Boom, he's your grandson."

"What?"

"Ray-Ray. Your grandson."

"Carm? I'm sorry."

They didn't pass another exit before Boom was telling her again, "I don't care if he's not mine. You're the love of my life."

"*Ay dios mio,*" Carmen's mother said in Spanish. "The old man thinks you're his woman. Tell Ray to get him to the doctor."

The diagnosis was Alzheimer's, which, horrible as it was, sounded better to Ray than the other word. "Ray just couldn't accept that his dad had dementia," says Carmen. "It was just really difficult for him."

Alzheimer's was an old person's disease. *Pugilistic dementia* was brought on by a youth misspent with too many Billy Marquarts. Whatever the case, Carmen reasoned that Boom's affliction was a natural progression in the life of a fighter. She made herself promise to always love Ray. Even if he forgot her name.

"What's it like?"

These fucking guys, Ray thought. Every once in a while, they'd still sidle up to him: at a bar, a country club, an autograph show, maybe the Marriott in Phoenix. Ray never could decide what was worse, the question itself, or the smiling presumption with which it was said, like something that passed between old friends.

"I mean, with your hands?"

Ray would break out the old ring stare, but that didn't always work. The drunks especially, they had a hard time taking a hint.

"What's it like to kill a guy?"

At that point, Ray usually chuckled in disbelief. "You're shitting me, right?"

"No—"

"Yes. You are."

Carmen was less polite, like the time they were in Vegas for a big fight at the MGM Grand. She was walking back to their seats when the announcer introduced her husband at ringside: "Ladies and gentleman, the former lightweight champion of the world, Ray 'Boom Boom' Mancini!"

"Whoo-hoo!" she heard a man say, "let's hear it for the murderer."

Carmen wheeled around and looked him in his eyes. "Would you like to say it to his face?"

He didn't understand.

"The *murderer*," she said. "He's sitting right over there. You want to tell him to his face?"

"No. I'm—"

"How dare you," said Carmen. "He's the father of my children. He's a kind man."

"Sorry."

The guy got up to apologize.

"Fuck you," said Carmen, pushing him back into his seat.

By now, she understood that the outside world was most comfortable casting her husband as either the murderer or the haunted penitent. They were roles, no more true than the ones he played as an actor. What pissed her off most, however, was the idea that their family could be perennially prosecuted for something that wasn't even a topic of conversation in their daily lives.

"We really didn't talk much about it," says Carmen. "It was

something that was there. We knew it, and we knew we'd have to find a way to explain it to the kids."

Nina was at a third-grade basketball practice when a boy told her that her father killed a man.

"That's not true," said Nina. "You should watch your mouth."

Carmen and Ray hadn't planned on explaining it this soon. Nina was eight that day when she came home crying. Ray calmed her down, and told her to have a seat on the couch. Then, not knowing what else to do, he put a tape of the Kim fight into the VCR.

She was brave to watch as she did, without tears.

"You see?" Carmen said. "It was an accident."

"You didn't mean to do that, Popi," said Nina. "It was just something that happened."

Something that happened.

The words made more sense and granted more comfort than any benediction that came Ray's way in a confessional. Still, beyond his family and close friends, no one accepted that the truth—his version, at least—was more nuanced. He needed his daughter's understanding, sure, but not her forgiveness.

"He never mentioned a word about it for years," says Ray's sister, Ellen. "Once he made his—I won't say 'peace'—but once he dealt with it, it didn't come up. It was just an understanding. He didn't want to talk about it. We weren't going to bring it up."

In fact, as it pertained to Kim, Ray would achieve something very close to peace. As his belief in spirits remained devout, Ray communicated with Kim in the same way he communicated with his brother from time to time. Like Lenny, Kim occasionally appeared in his deepest sleep.

"There have been times that Kim came to me in my dreams," he says. "I can't always remember what was said or what was done . . . I don't know if I apologize to him or we just kind of looked at each other . . . In one of the dreams, I remember, we shook hands, embraced, and he left. It was like, no words . . . I don't know . . . There are people who know more about dreams than I do. I don't know if it was me doing it for myself, thinking about him so much that he finally came to me . . . or if in actuality he somehow did come to me and put it to rest."

Psychology or theology? Did it matter? Like the priest once said, *just be*.

On the seventeenth anniversary of the fight, Ray finally broke his public silence on the matter and spoke at length with the New York *Daily News*. He described Kim in almost fraternal terms, saying he knew the fighter "better than his mother."

"I knew him better than anybody in the world because I knew what he was inside," said Ray. "It's almost like a spiritual thing. You learn a lot about a person in the ring, something crosses over. He learned what I was about. I learned what he was about. . . . Maybe there's times you can have too much heart."

Perhaps he had come to realize that the newspapermen weren't so different from the actors, writers, and directors he knew. Everybody wanted a good story, Ray most of all. Only now, he'd been in show business long enough to understand that good stories weren't necessarily happy ones.

Besides, at the cusp of a new millennium, with his fortieth birthday in sight, he had other things to worry about. The flavored cigar business—vanilla, chocolate, amaretto, and mint, just to name a few—would prove less than the Baskin-Robbins–type windfall he envisioned. He was still playing bit parts. If there had been a kind of resolution with Kim, then the question now before him was, in its own way, no less existential. If the role of Boom Boom was no longer available, then what could he play?

Actually, he knew the answer, and had for quite some time. As a producer of Hollywood blockbusters once told him, "Son, you shouldn't have to convince the audience. Sometimes you just got to hit 'em with the obvious."

In other words, no Shakespeare in the Park. If the part of Boom Boom was no longer available, then it had to be Charley Davis.

Ray's infatuation with John Garfield had only intensified since men of Mort Sharnik's generation first told him he resembled the star of *Body and Soul*. It was a classic noir film about a fighter who got, as Ray's father would call it, the business. Then again, the

business was an eternal hazard, afflicting fighters across generations. Hence, the movie's themes—ambition and corruption, as
configured by boxing and the mob—remained as relevant as they
were when it became a hit in 1947. Ray figured he was the perfect
guy to reprise the role. He was retro before there was retro. But,
more than that, who better to play a disillusioned champ than a
disillusioned champ?

"Mule," he said, using his nickname for Sam Kass (abridged
from "Samuel," and intended to note what Ray considered to be
his writer-friend's invincible obstinacy), "I want to play the John
Garfield role, and I want you to write it."

"Write it?" said Kass. "You don't even know who owns the rights."

"The rights?" Ray paused. "Let me worry about that. Mule, I'm
gonna get this made."

Truth was, Kass wanted an excuse not to write it. After the Haugen fight, Ray had contributed $35,000 toward the production
of Kass's script, *The Search for One-Eye Jimmy*. The sum made
him the project's biggest single investor, ensured that shooting
would proceed in Red Hook, Brooklyn, and also, that Harvey Keitel would be turned down for the part of Lefty.

"You mean Boom Boom Mancini beat me out for a role?" a
disbelieving Keitel told Kass. "Don't ever fucking call me again."

Even without Keitel, though, the movie had an excellent cast
of ascending actors: Holt McCallany and Nick Turturro (who
found his sartorial inspiration for the part from Hector Camacho),
Nick's brother, John (who played Disco Bean, the self-proclaimed
Baryshnikov of Brooklyn), Steve Buscemi, Michael Badalucco,
Jennifer Beals, and Samuel L. Jackson.

"Ray held his own," says Kass, whose oddball, pleasantly vulgar,
and often hilarious movie led to a pilot deal in Hollywood and
a gig on the writing staff of *Seinfeld*. Still, the writer's ambition
proved no match for the fighter's.

"Ray was consumed with *Body and Soul*," says Kass. "He
wouldn't stop calling me. I mean, relentless, day and night."

Finally, he prevailed upon Kass to accept $50,000 for a script
with the understanding that he would also direct the movie. Kass

figured it was easier, not to mention more loyal (Ray had, after all, helped him make *One-Eye Jimmy*), to take his friend's money than to volunteer an opinion that the film would never be remade.

About six weeks later, Kass delivered a first draft.

"I love it," said Ray.

"And what about the rights?"

"Don't worry, Mule. I'll get it."

The odds against him were daunting: not just obtaining the rights, but getting a studio to bless Ray Mancini as a second coming of John Garfield. Still, his passion for the task was commensurate with his need. Public adulation was his nourishment. Ray had been starving.

Those closest to him understood. Sam would recall traveling by subway from Brooklyn Heights to the Village, where they performed *Siddown*. It should've been a twenty-minute trip. But with Ray stopping to converse with every well-wisher, on every subway platform, in every car, at every corner, it could take hours. *He needs this*, thought Sam.

Ed O'Neill noticed it, too. By now, with the success of *Married . . . with Children*, O'Neill was famous in his own right. Hell, he couldn't get off a plane in Africa without being recognized as Al Bundy. Now there were times at Il Forno when he had to ask autograph seekers to please let him finish his meal. But not Ray. The person who asked for Ray's signature was a friend for life. Ray and Ed would go to fights at the Forum in Inglewood, each of them being asked if he wanted the customary escort from the VIP lounge to the seats. Please, said Ed. No thanks, said Ray, who made his way down the aisle at a deliberate and leisurely clip, collecting handshakes, compliments, and pats on the back as if he had just won an election. From where Ed was sitting, the swarm around his friend suggested the flock of screaming gulls that appears near the end of *Moby Dick*. Still, there was no denying that Ray was in his glory.

Then there was the night Carmen came home to find him in the den, watching VCR tapes of his fights with a perfect stranger. Turned out they had met at Il Forno. "He's a fan," Ray explained.

Body and Soul would cure his need to collect other people's remembrances of Boom Boom Mancini. This would be his next story, literally and metaphorically, born of an entity incorporated as Boom Boom Productions, the story to sustain him through middle age. Again, he told Sam not to worry, that he would do what he had to do, and he did.

It took some years and a small cadre of attorneys to navigate through the studios and the estate of John Garfield. But eventually, Ray obtained the rights, a writer-director (Sam, of course), a $2.5 million budget (most of it from MGM, which would retain video and overseas rights), and a commitment from Showtime Networks Inc. to air the movie on cable. The budget allowed for another impressive cast with Oscar-winner Rod Steiger as the trainer, Joe Mantegna as the deviously underhanded promoter, Michael Chiklis (star of *The Commish* on ABC) as Charley Davis's best pal, Jennifer Beals, and Tahnee Welch as the ingénue. By now, Kass understood that Ray produced movies as he fought: head first.

"You're the only guy who could've put together a movie starring you," said Sam.

"This is my title shot," explained Ray.

If his pursuit of the belt was a classical quest, his movie-making brio was its Faustian flip side. "I could just feel it," says Sam. "Bad shit was going to happen."

The problems began even before the commencement of principal photography, which was set for April 1998 in Reno, where Ray was still more famous than any of his co-stars. Sam's high-powered agents at Endeavor were furious to learn that he was directing a TV movie for Showtime when he should've been at the filming of a pilot he had written, and they had negotiated, for FOX. The series was to star the profane comic Artie Lange as a doorman.

Showtime executives said there would be no *Body and Soul* if Kass wasn't there to direct Ray.

"I'm not doing it without you, Mule," Ray told him.

Sam instructed his wife to cease and desist from the purchase of all nonessential items. After his agents spent the better part of an hour screaming at him, he anticipated that Endeavor would drop him if he directed the movie, which, as it happened, had been over budget almost from the time he landed in Reno.

Filming went on fifteen, sixteen hours a day, six days a week. Starring in a movie, Ray soon found out, was different than training for a title shot. Actors became fatigued, too. They just couldn't show it. Sam wouldn't allow his scenes to run past six o'clock.

"He'd be really, really tired by then," recalls Sam. "His words would start to get slurred."

Meanwhile, Carmen noticed another change in her husband. She would visit on the weekends or Ray would fly home to be with the family Sundays. But, as the shooting wore on, Ray began to wonder if her time wasn't better spent at home. Worse still, he became infatuated with his co-star.

Tahnee Welch was the daughter of sex symbol Raquel Welch. She received the bulk of her formal education in Europe, and made her American film debut in the blockbuster *Cocoon*. Her other credits included a *Playboy* pictorial and a role in the prime-time soap *Falcon Crest*.

"She just melts the screen," Ray would say.

I know I'm your best friend, Carmen thought, *but I'm also your wife.*

Carmen never minded the flirting. She had no doubts as to his fidelity. She understood her husband's need for adulation, and still, to that point, considered herself the luckiest woman she knew. She had three kids and a marriage that remained romantic even after nine years. But finally, over a dinner in Reno, she knew something was wrong when he introduced her with Tahnee as "my two leading ladies."

The next Sunday, as Carmen recalls, Ray came home for a family day. They went to mass at St. Monica's. Nina had a softball game. Then she went to Whole Foods to get what she needed for chicken a la checca. Upon her return home, Ray said he was going to have coffee with Lenny, an actor friend of Mickey's. He said he'd be home before dinner, but that wasn't like him to miss any family time on a Sunday.

Ray excused himself and went upstairs to make a call. Carmen listened outside the door. He wasn't talking to Lenny. He was using his quiet voice.

She stopped him as he said good-bye. "Are you sure this is what you want to do?" she asked. "Are you sure you want to have coffee with Lenny?"

"You're not my mother, Carmen."

"I'm your wife," she said. "And that's why I'm asking if you're sure."

"I'm just going to talk to Lenny," he said. "I'm excited about the project."

As soon as he left, she went upstairs and hit redial on the phone. Caller ID came up with a number listed to Raquel Welch. *That motherfucker*, thought Carmen, already dialing another number. It was Lenny's, whose voice mail now informed her that he was out of town filming in Louisiana.

Carmen went downstairs, turned off the stove, and asked a neighbor to watch the kids. Then she drove to Barrington, parking the Blazer in an alley. She knew where he'd be, too, sitting outside at the place next to Coffee Bean.

Not only was he there with Tahnee, he was *eating*. It was like watching a movie, Carmen would recall. She went over to their table and stared down at him, interrupting as he tried to speak.

"You lying piece of shit."

Now she felt embarrassed, cursing in front of all these white American people in Brentwood. She turned back to the Blazer, Ray calling after her. Then she felt him on her arm. Carmen wheeled around, punching him as hard as she could on the chin.

Ray grabbed her, tried to hold her. But a thin man in running clothes broke up the clinch. "Sir," said the jogger, "please let go."

It made some sense, at least in retrospect. Ray's real vice wasn't women, but a weakness for adoration. And what could be more adoring than the affections of an ingénue?

Still, as Sam already understood, they were screwed. Ray's marriage was in more trouble than he could even acknowledge. And while Sam was justifiably proud for being a stand-up friend, he had committed career suicide. Endeavor had dropped him. The *Doorman* pilot went nowhere. "Artie Lange went to rehab, and I went to Reno," says Sam. "I think he got the better deal."

Body and Soul finally aired in September 1999 on The Movie Channel. There was a rave in *The Hollywood Reporter,* with its television critic declaring that the Kass-Mancini vehicle "succeeds admirably." Other than that, the film attracted little notice. More than a year had passed since shooting had wrapped. Still, in anticipation of his good fortune, the new story of his new life, Ray stuffed a silk pocket square in his sports jacket.

"C'mon, Mule," he said, "we're going out."

"What?"

"Big things are coming, Mule. We gotta be *seen.*"

They went to Ago in West Hollywood, notable primarily because Robert De Niro was a part owner. The young model/hostess took almost half an hour before seating them next to the kitchen. Ray sat facing the loud, crowded room, the swinging kitchen doors bumping into his chair every couple of minutes. It felt like they were riding the subway again.

"Ray," said Sam. "I think we've been seen enough."

Chapter 16 | Modern Family

By the new millennium, Il Forno had an eclectic cast of regulars, including Ray and Ed; the playwright David Mamet; Bill Clark, a decorated former New York City detective now developing hit cop shows like *NYPD Blue*; the Brazilian jiu jitsu instructors who'd opened a studio down the block; and the occasional, if retired, mafia figure. Starting a new life was tough enough; getting good Italian food in LA was an even dicier proposition.

These patrons included Bill Bonnano Jr., whose father famously declared himself the Boss of Bosses, and Michael Franzese, whose father, Sonny, was esteemed (albeit, within the industry) as an underboss for the Colombo crime family. After serving time for his role in a massive gasoline bootlegging scheme, Franzese settled in Southern California, another born-again motivational speaker who coached Little League. Ray sent him a bottle of wine.

"You never send me a bottle of wine," said Ed, noting that Franzese had testified against his former associates. "Why him?"

"Whoa," said Ray, feigning hurt feelings, "respect."

Turned out that Sonny and Boom knew each other from way back, having served together in France. Still, Ed understood that Ray, like a good many Youngstowners, was really an organized crime buff. When it came to all the men-of-honor nonsense, Ray was a sucker, as evidenced by his experience with a man named Louis Eppolito.

An obese former detective from Brooklyn, Eppolito was as subtle as his arched, shoe-polish–black combover. Long suspected, but never charged as being complicit with the gangsters he seemed to know so well (an uncle and a cousin were both made men), Eppolito retired from the force and went west to seek his fortune as an actor and screenwriter.

"Nice, jovial guy," recalls Michael Giudice, who often waited on Ray at table twenty-four. "He'd put his arm around you. But something about him wasn't right."

Bill Clark also informed Ray of his misgivings. So did Ed. "Where did you find this guy?" he said.

"Whoa, he's a best-selling author," said Ray, referring to Eppolito's book, *Mafia Cop*. "And he wrote a screenplay."

Its eventual cast included ex-con Tony Sirico (best known as Paulie Walnuts on *The Sopranos*), Academy Award nominee Charles Durning, and Ray as a cop torn by his loyalty to the mobsters who once treated him like family. *Turn of Faith*, as it was titled, became Boom Boom Productions' second feature and the last helmed by Charles Jarrott, an aging British director best known for Elizabethan costume dramas and working with the likes of Richard Burton and Vanessa Redgrave in *Mary, Queen of Scots*. *Turn* was shot entirely in Youngstown, as Ray's enduring popularity back home eliminated the need for location fees and permits. With unemployment still almost triple the national average, the locals would've been happy to see any movie crew. A gangster movie, however, seemed especially apropos. Heavy industry never returned to the Mahoning Valley, but organized crime and political corruption remained as prevalent and blatant as ever. In 1996, for example, a newly elected prosecutor barely survived an assassination attempt sponsored by the local don. By 2000, Congressman Jim Traficant, who'd eventually do seven years for racketeering and bribery, found himself the target of yet another federal investigation. Finally, just as *Turn* wrapped, more than thirty-seven years since Youngstown was memorialized in the *Saturday Evening Post*, *The New Republic* published a next-generation postscript: "Crimetown, USA: The City that Fell in Love with the Mob."

Turn of Faith went straight to video, proof enough that there was no sense in merely imitating real life. A few years later, Eppolito and his partner-in-crime, another former detective named Stephen Caracappa, were indicted back in New York for extortion, narcotics, racketeering, murder, and conspiracy to commit murder. Ray not only predicted their acquittal one night at Il Forno, "the joint," as David Mamet had rechristened it, but even contributed to Eppolito's defense fund.

"Are you out of your mind?" said Bill Clark.

The resulting bet ("Everyone here is a witness," Clark said) would cost Ray $1,000, though curiously enough, not his supercharged capacity to believe. Eppolito was found guilty on all counts, including eight murders; his last known address was a federal prison outside Tucson, where he was serving a sentence of life plus 100 years. Still, the wager said less about Ray's judgment than his gloriously obstinate sense of self. Let the rest of the world dismiss Eppolito as a fat scumbag. To Ray, he was the possessor and teller of a great story. Now as ever, the story was sacrosanct to Ray. But something about his self-taught catechism, reciting copy from burnt orange newspaper clippings in his parents' basement, left him with blind faith in fables, unable to discern between the brilliance and the bullshit, even when it was his own.

Ray and Carmen tried their best, but the marriage had been doomed since she caught him with Tahnee. The arguments and recriminations escalated for years until they finally separated in May 2002. The single blessing in this was that Ray's parents never knew. Big Ellen died five months later, having been ill for quite some time. Boom passed away almost a year after that, in his sleep, with the television on.

"I think he died of loneliness," says Carmen. "He didn't have anyone he recognized any more."

In many respects, the death of Ray's parents was easier than the impending divorce. "It brought out the worst in him and it brought out the worst in me," says Carmen, recalling how Ray insisted on keeping the house at all cost. "He said he never wanted another man to step into that house, that it was sacred, our family home."

If so, its hallowedness would be violated in other ways. "My mom and dad would argue," says Ray-Ray, the youngest of the three children. "One night, I don't know, it just escalated. My mom ran out crying and my dad was just bawling, bawling, bawling. Me and my sister were there, trying to comfort him. That was the first time I'd ever seen him cry."

Not the last, though. "I remember some teary moments at table twenty-four," says Giudice, the waiter who became like an uncle to the kids, helping them with their homework and going to their games.

By now, it was clear that each child possessed a distinct nature. "Each one got a different part of Ray," says Carmen. It was the pretty one, however — the *girl* — who was biologically ordained the fighter, a reckless, pugnacious spirit the family had not seen since her uncle Lenny. Nina was an unafraid, enthusiastic combatant, seeking both offense and revenge. She scored her first TKO in the seventh grade on Santa Monica's Third Street Promenade.

"I think the girl threw a soda at me," recalls Nina, readily acknowledging that, on the verge of adolescence, she sought only the measliest excuse for provocation. "I could not wait for it to happen."

"Of all the kids," says Carmen, referring to the divorce, "the one who suffered the most was Nina."

"It really did not affect me the way a lot of people thought it did," counters Nina, still somewhat oblivious to the timing. She was the oldest, and therefore knew most about the loud and discordant state of affairs between her parents. Within a year of Carmen filing for divorce, she was getting high, hanging out with thugs, and periodically trying to run away.

After Nina's final attempt, Carmen and Ray called the cops. They filled out the missing person forms, even supplied dental records. By then, Ray had already put word out on the street. There was money for anyone who called with Nina's whereabouts. It was probably one of her hoodlum friends who gave her up. Twenty minutes later, Ray arrived at a Santa Monica apartment with the Brazilian jiu jitsu instructors, Renato and Ricardo, yelling at everyone to get down on the floor.

"My dad grabbed me," says Nina. "They took me to the police station, and the police said I would have to go to the hospital. . . . Then they took me to the psych ward at UCLA. I was fourteen."

It was there, some weeks later, that Nina was woken in the middle of the night by a short-haired woman and a large Polynesian man. They told her she could come of her own volition, or in handcuffs, which would entail a twelve-hour drive. "It was probably the scariest day I had in my life," recalls Nina.

But still not nearly enough to scare her straight. Upon her arrival at the Heritage School in Provo, Utah—part treatment center, part boot camp—Nina was strip-searched and informed that she would not be allowed to call her parents for a couple of weeks.

"This is some kind of mistake," she said.

No mistake, responded the supervisor, who, recognizing that Nina was about to hit her, called in a resource team. After being restrained, Nina feigned calm just long enough to get a poke at one of the guards. "I turn around and smack her right across the face," she says.

All told, Nina would spend the better part of three years in Utah. She learned to hate the therapist, who reminded her of actress Alfre Woodard, and to spend Christmases and birthdays in the visiting room. It did not cure her, but it almost killed her parents.

"It was the hardest decision we ever had to make," says Carmen, referring to Nina's forced matriculation at the Heritage School.

The divorcing couple would travel to and from Provo in the midst of contentious negotiations. There, they met with Nina and her various teachers and counselors. For all the guilt, shame, and of course, anger, Ray remained tender, optimistic, and uncharacteristically calm in these sessions, especially in front of Nina.

"Another man," Carmen concedes, "wouldn't have been able to do it."

Ray couldn't eat, and periodically found himself hyperventilating. In his own way, however, he kept coming forward. He would still show up at Il Forno. He would raise a glass, stare at his plate, and try to swap stories. The regulars were impressed with his straight-ahead stoicism, as if his daughter's demons were opponents, and Utah just another training camp, something hellish to be endured, not spoken of.

Still, it was plain to see; he wasn't there. Real gangsters—as opposed to actors—never looked as Ray now did, with the eyes of a condemned man.

As a child, Leonardo would wait for his parents to leave the house before sifting through his father's collection of VCR tapes. He studied them all, except for Haugen, which he had no desire to see. "I just wanted to know how my dad fought," says Leonardo, recalling his surprise at how CBS played the father-son angle. "I didn't know how big that storyline was."

Nardo, as Ray called him, was a terrific athlete, with an aptitude for anything he felt like playing: football, basketball, baseball, even soccer. But not boxing. When it came to boxing, he was a fan only. Nardo never read Joyce Carol Oates, but he'd understand her theorem nonetheless. "One doesn't play boxing," she wrote.

"My dad won a championship," he would tell himself. "What's the point of me fighting?"

Ray cheered vigorously at Nardo's schoolboy games. It filled him with pride and hope to think his scion was such a promising athlete. However, Nardo wasn't comfortable with the pressure that came with being the champ's son.

The boy mourned the boundaries of his former family life. "We had dinner at the table," he says. "We had bedtimes. We had dogs. We had a fence." Now, instead of staying at what had been the family home, he slept at Carmen's apartment. The normal Oedipal conflicts were intensified by the divorce. Not only did he believe that his mother needed him more, but the arguments with his father often degenerated into wars.

"I was hitting puberty," says Leonardo, "and I was angry with him."

As ninth grade approached, his parents were still paying lawyers to determine custody of the house. With their highest aspirations focused on their first-born son, they agreed to have him apply to St. Monica's High School. The admissions interview was set for a spring morning in 2006. As Carmen had already left for work—by now, she had a master's in education from Pepperdine, and a job at the local middle school—Ray arrived to pick him up.

"I'm not going," said Leonardo, still wearing shorts and a tee shirt.

"I want you to have options," said Ray.

"You can't tell me where I'm going."

"I am fucking telling you," said Ray, his fury barely contained as he told Leonardo to change into a clean shirt and his new pants.

"But these are *new* shorts," Leonardo protested.

It was all Ray could do to get him to change shirts.

Shortly thereafter, a nun received them in her office. The applicant's slouch conveyed a disinterest bordering on disrespect. The nun explained that there were many more applicants than openings, and asked why he wanted to attend St. Monica's.

"I don't," he said. "*He* does."

All his friends, Nardo explained, were going to the public high school. The public school had better sports teams. And he didn't care what his parents said, he wouldn't be attending St. Monica's. The interview ended not long after that, his application doomed.

As they walked to lunch, Nardo turned to his father. "I told you I wasn't going to go," he said.

Carmen joined them at the restaurant. She began to cry as Ray gave the blow by blow. Then she excused herself and went to the bathroom.

"Why is Mommy tripping?" asked Leonardo.

"She's tripping because we want what's best for you."

Now lunch was over. Nardo followed his father to the parking structure—both of them yapping as they went—to get his backpack. "Watch your mouth," said Ray. "I don't want to hear you no more."

"Don't tell me you don't want to hear me no more. I don't want to hear *you*."

"Keep your mouth shut."

"Don't tell me to keep my mouth shut."

Leonardo recalls his father bumping him, in the way that fighters do, and allows that he bumped back.

Ray remembers a shove. *Did that really just happen*, he thought, *a son putting his hands on his father?* Then came a flash of rage that seemed to acknowledge his semi-incarcerated daughter, his newly dating wife, their lawyers, his straight-to-video acting career, and now, the fresh humiliation brought on by an encounter with the nun principal.

By then, Leonardo's bouts of recalcitrance and disrespect made him accustomed to the occasional open-handed slap, but this was something different. "Left hook to the liver," says Leonardo, who ignored the pain well enough to retrieve his backpack. "It actually did hurt."

"Body shot . . . in the rib cage," says Ray. "I tapped him."

Kid didn't know how lucky he was, thought Ray. The good son himself still remembered that day during his sophomore year: telling Boom he didn't know what he was talking about, calling him an old man, finally *pushing* his father.

POW!

Next thing Ray knew, he was sliding down the wall. "It was just like the cartoons," he says. "Little Tweety Birds started flying around my head."

By Ray's standards, he hadn't done anything wrong with Nardo, certainly not given the offense. He was merely restoring order. Corporal punishment had been a part of Mancino family life for generations.

But that was ancient history. Those rules no longer applied. This wasn't Youngstown. This was Santa Monica. This was the new millennium.

The next morning a guidance counselor asked Leonardo how his interview went. My dad hit me, he said.

Eventually, it was decided that Ray would benefit from a course in anger management.

Anger-fucking-management?

His oldest son wasn't speaking to him.

His daughter was locked up in Utah.

His wife had a boyfriend.

He'd lost everything but the house. There he would rise and rule alone, all the while asking himself: "What the fuck happened to my life?"

In 2008, Carmen, known to her students as Mrs. Vazquez, received a second master's degree. This one, in educational administration from Loyola Marymount University, earned her an assistant principal's job. College Ready Academy High #4 was a charter school situated under a freeway in downtown Los Angeles. Two years later, more than 90 percent of the first graduating class were accepted at four-year universities, an astounding figure for a student body drawn from the city's roughest neighborhoods.

"I work with poor kids," says Carmen, "and a lot of them want to be fighters."

Her response, invariably, was to discourage them. There may be a fighting gene, a pugilistic predisposition carried in the blood, but boxers are both born and made. Carmen had seen enough to believe that which makes them fighters is tethered to a "pure dysfunction" somewhere in the family history. What's more, even worse than being a fighter, was being an ex-fighter.

"They go from being famous and adored to being nobodies," says Carmen. "Boxers, I think, have really sad lives."

Her father-in-law had been lucky, she thought. The bills didn't come due until late in Boom's life. But they always came due. The manifestations were varied: dementia, drugs, debt, detention. One way or another, those intimate with violence were corrupted or imperiled by it.

A cursory survey of Ray's opponents was proof enough. The roster started with Kim, of course, whose subdural hematoma made him an icon for the American Medical Association. But what of, say, Anthony Fletcher, a slick southpaw who twice outpointed Ray as an amateur? Two Guns, as he was known, was still a lightweight contender (not to mention a drug dealer) when he survived five gunshots while sitting in his BMW. He'd fight three more times before his arrest in another shooting, this one landing him on Pennsylvania's death row in 1993.

Hector Camacho was arrested on charges of drugs and domestic abuse and jailed for burglary in Mississippi. Still, he fought, losing his last bout by unanimous decision in the Kissimmee Convention Center. Camacho's too-long career didn't come as much of a surprise. Just days from his forty-eighth birthday, Camacho still seemed an ageless juvenile delinquent.

More shocking was the fate of Alexis Arguello, so admired for his great skill and patrician persona. He had political problems with the Sandinista government in his native Nicaragua, drug problems, and bouts of depression, but appeared to have overcome them all by 2008. That November, Arguello was elected the mayor of Managua. Eight months later, he was dead of a gunshot wound to the heart. It was ruled a suicide.

"I'd like to fight him again," Bobby Chacon says of Arguello.

Chacon is quite serious, although at fifty-nine, he tends to forget how old he is and where he lives: in his girlfriend's small, well-kept home in a working-class neighborhood just east of Los Angeles. Rose Legaspi met him at a church downtown, not far from the old Main Street Gym. He was often seen collecting cans in the neighborhood, a specter with a supermarket cart.

"They wrote a song about me," Chacon used to tell her.

Rose cleaned him up and, eventually, took him in. Now the Schoolboy looks good, but often needs her help to translate from the low, moaning language of dementia.

"I had a seven-bedroom house," says Chacon. "I had a pool. I had a Bentley. I had everything. And now what the fuck do I have?"

"Me," says Rose, still petite with dark, lustrous hair.

"What can I do for her?" he says. "What can I give her?"

"I don't need anything, Bobby," says Rose, explaining that "most of the time he's pretty content, but every so often, he starts thinking . . ."

"I love you, baby. I'm sorry. I killed you, baby. I'm sorry."

Now Bobby speaks of his first wife, Valorie, and her suicide. "With everything he put her through," says Rose, "he believes he drove her to it."

Sure enough, Chacon's dark mood passes as quickly as it came. If his stories are fragmented, other pleasures remain. He goes through his scrapbooks. He sneaks cookies after midnight. And every once in a while, Rose catches him humming along with the melody:

Hurry home early,
Hurry on home,
Boom Boom Mancini's fighting Bobby Chacon . . .

A few years back, Ray spoke at the Old Spaghetti Factory in Hollywood, an appearance occasioned by Chacon's induction into the California Boxing Hall of Fame. "Bobby," he said. "You were one of my heroes."

Still, with middle age upon him and his family irreparably fractured, Ray had begun to wonder about that kind of heroism. He would never be a nobody, the obscure ex-pug about whom Carmen had warned her students. No, Ray's kids had attended enough banquets and autograph shows over the years, listening to a host of celebrity spokesmen vouch for their old man's celebrity: Arnold Schwarzenegger, Sylvester Stallone, Magic Johnson. *Your dad was a great fighter,* they all said. Just the same, regarding his own children, Ray now had to wonder: Would he ever again be their hero?

Therapy.

The idea was anathema. "Like putting on a dress," Ray used to say. Not only would strangers tell him how to raise his kids, they would tell him how to *be* with them. Almost a century had passed since Nick Mancino came through Ellis Island, and now his American grandson, the famous fighter, had a shrink in Beverly Hills.

Actually, the woman with an office on Canon Drive was just

the beginning. She was to help him and Leonardo work though their issues. Then there was a shrink Ray saw for his own stuff. Why not? Nardo had his, and Carmen had hers, and Nina, who returned from Utah at seventeen, had hers. Then they would gather at the kitchen table every Wednesday afternoon in what had been the family home to work on the coming week's concerns and Nina's custody schedule. This required the expertise of yet another therapist and a parental advocate for both Ray and Carmen. These were often loud and fractious sessions, but the parents learned to agree for the first time in years. If Nina wouldn't always abide by their prohibition on tattoos, piercings, and certain parties, then at least they presented a united front.

Sometimes Ray would catch himself saying things like that. *A united front?*

What the fuck was that?

Success?

Assimilation?

Or emasculation?

This being America, everyone had an opinion. Nina found therapy "frustrating," and her father resistant to change. "He still thought he knew better than anyone else," she says, but grudgingly concedes that "it slowed down my path of self-destruction."

"I hated therapy," says Leonardo. "My shrink was an old guy with white hair and glasses. My dad's was a lady. I didn't see how an hour to talk about stuff would solve anything. But that whole thing made me and my dad closer. We started talking to each other. . . . He used to admit all the time he was in a bad place."

"Ray loves the stories," says Carmen. "Ray loves the story about his dad, and how he won the title for him. He loves the story of us: the virgin wife, the perfect family. But he doesn't like the dirtiness that went on."

To that point, Ray had been willfully oblivious to anything but the heroic possibilities in his own narrative arc. Now, with the blessing of modern psychiatry, the Mancinis were excavating an alternate family history. This was a darker interior thread, obscured by the sepia-toned evocations from Boom's scrapbooks:

A father leaving his son. Then Firpo smacking a boy not yet ten, but already man enough not to cry. Slick smacking Boom's mother. Boom sending Slick to the hospital. Little Ellen, toughest kid on the block, busting open a kid's nose. Ray seeing Tweety Birds. And Lenny the leg breaker. These were stories, too.

They weren't atypical in Youngstown, nor did they constitute, in the ambiguously clinical sense, *abuse*. Just the same, the time had come for a reckoning.

"Ray didn't do what the therapists asked him to do," says Carmen, who was still pissed off about losing the house. "He did ten times more. . . . This wasn't in his comfort zone. This wasn't like anything he knew, or anything his father knew. But he always showed up. Whether Ray wants to acknowledge it or not, he broke a pattern of violence that has been in his family for generations. Nobody recognizes that. Nobody celebrates it. But that takes a real man. That's what truly makes Ray a champion."

Being a parent, however, wasn't like getting a title shot. There were no press kits, no way to trick up the plot. The secret was no secret. You kept showing up. You took your shots, and kept coming forward. Ray's ability to absorb punishment, that which had ruined so many fighters, would remake him as a man.

The season for ecstatic, rapturous triumphs had long since passed. There would be no more championships. No star on the Hollywood Walk of Fame. It was enough, Ray finally realized, not to have been claimed by any of the fighter's fates. It was enough to *just be*.

His projects included a documentary, *Youngstown: Still Standing*, and a signature Cabernet Sauvignon. It was called Southpaw, made of California grapes blended to Ray's specifications by an Ohio winery, L'uva Bella.

"It's fruit forward," he liked to say. They kept plenty on hand at Il Forno and Alberini's Restaurant and Wine Shop back in Boardman, another of his favorite places.

Ray often went home, as he still called Ohio, to see his girlfriend. Tina Rozzi was fifteen, a kid with a crush, when she met Ray, and turned sixteen the day he won the title. But now that they were both divorced and in their forties, she made him feel like the young contender he once was. She didn't mind that he took the long way around the bar, either. "He needs that," says Tina. "It feeds him, brings him back to what was."

In California, Ray's mornings were spent rolling around with the jiu jitsu guys, or at the local yoga studio. On Tuesdays, he played paddle tennis with Sam Kass at Venice Beach, the asphalt gritty with sand. Inevitably, Sam got the court with the sun in his eyes.

Most days included a meal at the joint. Typically, Ray would stop by with Leonardo and Ray-Ray after one of their games. Nina's attendance was less frequent, as she had graduated from North Hills Prep (sans most of her piercings), got a waitressing job, and enrolled at Glendale Community College. Occasionally, they'd be joined by their cousin, Nicholas, a former Navy SEAL who worked for stretches as a contractor in Iraq and Afghanistan.

The product of Lenny's short-lived first marriage, Nicholas looked like his father, with an olive complexion and long hair. To Ray, he was yet more proof of an afterlife. On the morning of February 15, 1981, not yet three years old, Nicholas woke up and told his mother, "Daddy came to visit me last night."

"I believe that," says Ray. "God gave Lenny the chance to say good-bye to his son."

Dinners began with Michael Giudice announcing the specials. Nardo and Ray-Ray did their homework, argued over sports, and listened impassively as the grown-ups swapped their stories. Table twenty-four had a rotating cast: Ed O'Neill, David Mamet, Sam Kass, and the jiu jitsu guys. Occasionally, Carmen would stay for dinner after dropping off the kids. That seemed to put everyone in a good mood.

"You know, like it used to be," says Ed, now starring in another hit show, ABC's *Modern Family*.

Ray and Carmen had tried for an encore. But Carmen had a career. And in these modern times, with the *padrone* an endangered species, Ray seemed better suited for life as an ex than a husband. They counted themselves lucky to enjoy a functional divorce. Still, Carmen found herself worrying about the fate of her coparent, figuring that fighters were doomed to lose their stories with their memories.

"I know the end of his life will mimic the end of his father's," she says. "I loved him the first day I saw him. I loved him when I gave birth to the kids. I loved him the day I caught him with another woman. And I'll love him when he gets old. Just because he forgets who I am doesn't mean I won't be there for him."

Carmen wasn't alone in her concern. Sam Kass became uneasy. Ray started forgetting about their Tuesday morning paddle tennis. Funny thing, though: Ray never ever forgot one of his kids' games.

Unlike his own father, Ray didn't blend into a crowd. His was a ubiquitous, kinetic presence on the sidelines or in the stands, even when he tried not to be. He would sit alone in the right field stands at Ray-Ray's Little League games, the fumes from his cigar wafting into the dugout like a stinky incense.

"He goes to every single thing I've ever done," says Ray-Ray. "He's at every practice, every game."

He was the guy yelling at Ray-Ray to move his feet.

To take his man left.

Telling him, my grandmother's faster than you.

"He doesn't care what anybody thinks," says Ray-Ray. "You get used to it."

Was the ex-champ living through his sons? Or merely loving them? Let the shrinks handle that one, Ray figured. The boys and their games were the best thing he had.

Ray considered Leonardo the most promising athlete. "Special," he liked to say. Nardo played point guard and running back, football being his favorite sport. But in the summer of 2009, at a preseason varsity practice, a linebacker hit him helmet to helmet at the line of scrimmage.

"I was dazed," recalls Leonardo, "but I didn't fall." In fact, he dragged the linebacker with him for another five yards. As the whistle blew, though, his head was throbbing in pain.

The next morning, he collapsed in the shower. "Ma," he said. "I can't get up."

An MRI revealed bleeding on the brain, a speckled pattern similar to that which is seen after babies are shaken. It was Leonardo's second concussion in a matter of months, a cause of great grief for him and his father, and the end of his football career.

Leonardo withdrew. He changed, people said. But then, so did his brother. Ray-Ray was another version of the good son, the kind of kid who always wanted to please his parents. It was no coincidence then, certainly not in his father's mind, that he suddenly took up boxing.

At first, it was a way to stay in shape for the other sports. Then, as he began to spar, the other sports seemed to be metaphors for what boxing actually was. It was combat, sure. But more than that, it was the method by which three generations of Mancino's sought the paternal blessing.

"You don't have to do this," Ray told him. "Not for me."

Who was he kidding? If not Ray-Ray, then who?

The kid wouldn't need a scrapbook, either. He had YouTube, and the fight he kept watching was the rematch with Livingstone Bramble. "My dad didn't care about all those cuts—all he wanted to do is fight," says Ray-Ray. "I wondered if I could pull that same toughness out of myself."

At twelve years old and 130 pounds, the rhythms and postures of boxing felt natural to him, as if divined through ancient muscle memory. Wearing his father's hand-me-down equipment— red headgear, an Everlast cup, and Ray's old-school black boxing boots—Ray-Ray discovered a bloodlust that belied his normally sweet disposition. The only thing that felt better than hitting an opponent with a straight right hand was hitting him again. "If I get someone in the corner, I just start bombing," he says. "I don't want to stop."

He trained in the Bob Dylan gym, as he called it, and usually found himself paired with a slick southpaw called Junebug. A year older and already vastly more experienced, Junebug never wanted to be anything but a fighter. In addition to training both kids, Junebug's father trained Dylan and ran his gym.

Again, boxing wasn't like the other sports. It wasn't a game; it was an endeavor designed to test limits, to locate one's quitting point, usually in humiliating fashion. A bad day in the gym wasn't like a bad day on the field. "Sometimes," says Ray-Ray, "you just don't want to get hit anymore."

It wasn't the pain. It was a fatigue unlike any Ray-Ray would ever experience. Each blow became an obligation. "If a person hits you," he explains, "you got to hit them back."

The crowd, despite a five-dollar cover and several rows of folding chairs, was standing room only. This was January 17, 2009, and the gym had been packed in anticipation of a main event featuring David "Junebug" Mijares versus Ray "Little Boom" Mancini.

Ray-Ray wore red satin shorts with "Boom" embroidered on each leg, an Italian flag on the right, and "MANCINI" stitched to the waistband. In the dressing room, Ray held out his palms as mitts. Ray-Ray was nervous warming up, thinking how he had never been knocked down. There were lots of people out there, including all his brother's friends.

He asked his father to say a prayer like Griff. Ray prayed for no one to get hurt. Then he instructed his son's cornerman: "Trees" meant go for the head, "falls" meant the body.

Even as it began, Junebug stinging him with jabs, his chest suddenly heaving, Ray-Ray kept coming forward. Junebug's straight left hand loosened his headgear. Still, his father remained in the corner of his eye: the ex-champ gesticulating wildly, yelling "trees" and "falls."

In the second, Junebug snapped young Mancini's head back with another straight left. Then Ray-Ray charged, pushing the thirteen-year-old into the ropes. Junebug didn't stay there long; he was too good, too well-schooled. But Ray-Ray had acted on his obligation. In between rounds, Junebug's cornerman had to wipe the blood from his nose.

At the end, both boys were bloodied and arm-weary. The crowd rose as they embraced, the fight judged a draw.

"I'm proud of you," Ray told his son. "I think you won."

Ray-Ray could feel a peculiar fatigue begin to set in. "Like being supertired," he says.

The next few months saw him spend less and less time at the gym. Then, finally, none at all.

His forebears might not have understood. But this, at last, was the American way, and Ray-Ray didn't need a shrink to explain it. The boy now understood what made a man. It wasn't his past.

People still asked him about the rematch with Junebug.

But there wouldn't be a rematch. Now free from ancestral obligation, Ray-Ray didn't need it. He'd rather play basketball.

Epilogue | The Gift

June 23, 2011

Oblivious to the suburban serenade — chirping birds, a gentle wind rustling through the azaleas, the sound of children playing — Ray sits grim faced and nervous on his stoop. Finally, he snaps to attention as the white Escalade comes into view.

The young man who emerges from the Cadillac is nattily attired: light blue sports jacket, silk pocket square, button-down shirt, and khakis. At twenty-nine, Jiwan remains slender, his face still smooth and boyish. Those same features had troubled him as a child. Jiwan would turn to his mother and ask, "Why is my nose flat and not as high as yours?"

Because you're Duk Koo Kim's son, he would think.

Now the ex-fighter and the fighter's son exchange bows and a careful hug. "I wanted to meet you, and I'm very happy that you wanted to meet me," says Ray, then, pausing, concedes, "I don't know exactly what to say."

"Okay," says Jiwan. "I introduce my mother?"

"Yes, please."

Young Mee is flattered by the passing years. Her hair up, wearing a black cardigan with a print blouse, she's still dark-haired and glowy, even after the twelve-hour flight.

Ray bows again. "I hope this does for you what it does for me," he says, formally. "I can finally rest easy."

"You're happy?" asks Jiwan. "You can be."

"Could I introduce you to my children?"

Born seven months after his father's death, Jiwan always knew he was the son of a fighter. His grandfather had shown him a couple of newspaper clippings, but that didn't ease the boy's envy or his pain. Jiwan's friends all had fathers. What about him?

"Where is my father?" he would ask, usually before falling asleep next to his mother.

"He is in America," she would say. "Making money."

"When is he coming home to bring me toys and gifts?"

"Next year."

He believed her. He believed in *next year*, a season of gifts that would follow his father's return from the enchanted land of America.

Jiwan was nine when he overheard a friend's mother saying that he had no father. That night, Young Mee told him the truth, which he kept to himself. "I did not think that I should talk about it so lightly," explains Jiwan.

It hurt enough to have only a mother. But there was also the shame that came in the wake of Duk Koo's death: his grandmother's suicide and the portrayal of Young Mee as hoarding the insurance money. Besides, soon enough, the boy would have a stepfather with a factory job who took him to amusement parks.

"He treated me extremely well," says Jiwan.

At twenty-four, a junior in college, already finished with his compulsory military service, Jiwan was befriended by an American named Michael Owen. A baseball scout, Owen had been coming to Korea since '83. He was a missionary back then, when an old man in Incheon asked if he knew Ray Mancini.

"No," said Owen.

"Well, if you see him," said the old man, "tell him to keep to fighting."

More than two decades later, Owen gave Jiwan a DVD of his father's fight with Mancini. "When you're ready," he said.

Owen didn't know why he presumed to do this, and felt like an ass as soon as he did. However, Jiwan had no intention of watching it anyway. He'd seen enough fragments of the fight (though not the fatal one) on YouTube. "I felt good to know that I am the son of an admirable man," he says.

Watching his father die wasn't his idea of closure.

In 2002, Kim was mythologized in the Korean feature *Champion*. At the producer's behest, Ray traveled to Seoul for the premiere. But neither Jiwan nor Young Mee, who cooperated with the producers in return for a promise to preserve their anonymity, would attend. Still, the celebration of Duk Koo's bravery filled his son with great pride. "His will not to lose," says Jiwan, "was not for money or fame or power."

Rather, it was to ennoble the standing of a poor boy. It was for love.

In the years to come, Jiwan would pore through his father's journal. "I almost thought that I had written it myself," he says. "It reflects almost the same thoughts that I had, and it made me believe that if I were in his place, fighting that fight, I, too, would not have stepped back."

That's not to say Jiwan was without regret. The warrior's code — that admonition never to retreat — was something he regarded with ambivalence. Truth was, he wished his father had been less valorous.

"I wish he stepped back," says Jiwan. "I know how difficult it was for my mother."

Finally, in July 2010, Jiwan and Young Mee consented to be interviewed for Mancini's biography. It was difficult to reconcile the son of a dirt-poor fighter with the man he had become: studious, bespectacled, a second-year dental student in a polo shirt. Toward the end of the second session, Jiwan expressed interest in meeting Ray. "If he still happens to feel guilty about the fight of the past, if it still upsets him and makes him feel insecure, he no longer has to think that way," said Jiwan. "To his sons and daughter, I would say . . . I am sorry that you had to suffer. Your father is a good man and you do not need to feel pain because of the hurtful things that people say."

The following June, mother and son arrived in Los Angeles with a camera crew filming a documentary based on the biography. In preparation for the journey, Jiwan finally watched the DVD. He thought he was ready, but the viewing made him hate the man he was about to meet.

• • •

Ray begins by showing the photographs on his mantel: Ray with his kids, Ray with Ronald Reagan, Ray with JoeDiMaggio, and of course, the picture of his father after Billy Marquart.

"To me," Ray explains, "he's beautiful."

"Looks like you," says Jiwan.

"After the fight with your father, yes."

Now, Young Mee produces a sheaf of snapshots from her purse, moving back in time: Jiwan in his army uniform, smiling in his school blazer, a boy and his mother at a picnic, Jiwan as a plump baby, then, the engagement ceremony that preceded his birth by a year or so. The beaming groom and his resplendent bride sit before a great banquet table. Young Mee wears a spray of flowers in her hair, her mother-in-law, in a white silk robe, at her side.

"Your father's a good dresser," says Ray.

"How do you feel?" Jiwan asks, haltingly.

Ray looks him up and down, this young man with the silk pocket square. His own boys are in shorts and tee shirts. "You did well for yourself," he says.

The guest list for dinner includes Jiwan and Young Mee, Ed O'Neill (whom they recognize as Al Bundy), and the Mancini children. Nina is considering a career in restaurant management. The coming school year will see Leonardo enroll at Santa Barbara Community College, and Ray-Ray make varsity basketball as a high school sophomore. They dine al fresco, the table set with bottles of Southpaw.

"That's my wine," Ray says proudly, recommending the *linguini mare e monti* with baby lobster.

"I love pasta," says Jiwan.

Soon, Ray raises his glass. "I felt guilty about what happened for a long time," he says. "I felt guilty because of your mother. I felt guilty that you never met your father."

Young Mee dabs at her tears, but the confession continues even after the food arrives. "I didn't know they carried him out on a stretcher," says Ray. "It was a great fight, but after that there was nothing good about it. . . . I had no love for it anymore. I was already looking for a way out."

"It was better," says Jiwan. "For your health."

Jiwan has come with a confession of his own: "Now I can tell you that when I saw the fight the first time I felt some hatred to you."

But that, too, has passed.

"I think it was not your fault," he says. "You deserve. Maybe now your family will be more happy."

It has finally arrived, *next year*, that long-awaited time for gifts. But it's the children who bear them.

Ray lifts his glass a final time, addressing his ancestors as clearly as his guests.

"Thank you," he says. "Thank you for coming to America."

Acknowledgments

In 1999, I did a piece for my then-employer, the New York *Daily News*, on the anniversary of the Mancini–Kim fight. It was the first time Ray spoke extensively of the bout and its aftermath, but I conducted the interviews by phone.

We didn't meet until late 2007, at the suggestion of an outstanding ESPN producer, Craig Mortali. We dined at Il Forno, of course, where we were joined by Ed O'Neill. Our meal lasted until the waiters wheeled away the portable heaters, and for the first time since coming to California, I knew I was in the right place. I knew, also, that I should write Ray's story, or at least, my version of it.

Ray went home. Ed and I went for a nightcap at O'Brien's on Wilshire. There I told him, somewhat heatedly, of my ambition for a book about Ray and Kim and their ghosts.

Ed responded with a thin, amused smile. "Might be a little more to it than that," he deadpanned, mentioning something about "the old man," as he called Boom, and Ray's late brother, Lenny.

Ed would prove correct about most things pertaining to this project. Another couple of years passed before I could actually begin. I mapped out several other prospective biographies, each of them longer and, I think, more obvious than Mancini. But I kept coming back to the idea of Ray.

That I finally got this chance leaves me forever grateful to David Vigliano, for his tenacity and loyalty; to Dominick Anfuso and Martha Levin at Free Press, who flatter me with their faith; and to a great editor, Martin Beiser.

But mostly, I'm indebted to Ray. I told him he wouldn't make a penny off the book itself, that he'd have no control over the manuscript, and that the various inquiries—his brother's death, the Kim fight, even his divorce—were guaranteed to cause him pain. That said, when it came to fathers and sons, wounded fathers in particular, I thought I was the best guy for the job.

It's a perilous proposition, writing about a friend. Biography is an invasive process. But now, a couple of years later, I'm happy to report our friendship remains intact. That owes entirely to the subject's generosity of spirit.

As much of this book is about bravery, I'm heartened by Ray's children, Carmenina, Leonardo, and Ray-Ray, for telling their stories with such candor and courage.

They take after their mother, too. Carmen Vazquez enabled me to see a larger truth about Ray. His journey wasn't merely about redemption, she explained, it was about the sanctity of his stories.

Ray's sister, Ellen, added an intimacy to the history of the Mancinos in America. She granted access to decades of family photographs, her father's personal papers, and military records. What's more, with her husband, Tom, she made me feel like family at Christmas in Youngstown.

Also from Youngstown, Chuck Fagan and Tank DiCioccio. Ray was privileged to have them in his corner. So was I. Thanks to Father Tim O'Neill, Mike Cefalde, Dave Shaffer, Tony Congemi, Rick Rufh, Jim Cooney, Paul Gregory, Sherry Linkon (co-author of the immensely readable *Steeltown U.S.A.*), Pat Zill, and the lovely Tina Rozzi.

My gratitude to Todd Franko and the Youngstown *Vindicator*.

I greatly appreciate the help of Jack Gocala, police chief at Youngstown State University and an expert on organized crime in the Ohio Valley; the Youngstown Police Department; and especially Detective Bill Blanchard, who found archived crime statistics pertaining to Black Monday's aftermath and case no. 81–648, detailing the killing of Lenny Mancini.

For recollections of young Boom, I thank Benedict D'Amato, who provided a sixty-three-page manuscript tracing the D'Amato and Cannazzaro family histories; John "Ace" Congemi; George DeLost; and Vincent Mancino, Boom's brother in Buffalo.

In Pennsylvania: Thanks to the late, great Pirates manager Chuck Tanner, Janet Fryman, Robert Knapp, Sharon Danovich, the Perrys of Ellwood City, and my cousin, Ron Heiman, who turns out to be one hell of a reporter. I've now written three books that begin in steel country; each of them was fortified with superb research and dedicated assistance from Sam Allen.

In and around New York: Wallace Matthews, Joe Sexton, Adrian Wojnarowski, Jules Feiler, Scott Cooper, Don Cronson, Barry Weiss, Bill Francis (up in Cooperstown), and Leonard and Harriet Kriegel. I'm apparently unable to write a book without assistance from the father-daughter teams of Sal and Sam Marchiano or Alan and Stacey Siegel. Tim Bontemps of the New York Post was there whenever I needed anything. Toby Falk provided memories of Dave Wolf as a young man. Tom Hauser provided background on just about everything else. Gina Andriolo's recollections captured Ray's innocence upon his arrival in New York. Sydney Tanigawa was invaluable.

Aaron Cohen critiqued each chapter with diligence and a discerning eye. As Teddy Atlas might say, "He's a pro." Better still, a great friend.

I was lucky to have found a copy of The Times Square Gym, a book of ethereal photographs by John Goodman with text by Pete Hamill. Aside from my own father, Pete was the best teacher I've ever had.

From the boxing world: Bobby Chacon and Rose Legaspi are boxing's version of a romantic comedy, which is to say they can make you laugh and cry at the same time. Then there were Fred Sternburg, Angelo Dundee, Don Elbaum, Duane Bobick, Paul Percifield, Randy Stephens, Freddie Roach, Ed "Too Tall" Jones, the late Gil Clancy, Lou Duva, Joe Koizumi, and Major Lee Wonbek of the Korea Boxing Commission. I understand why Livingstone Bramble played the villain with Ray; just the same, no one is more willing or able to attest to Mancini's valor.

It's easy to see what Teddy Brenner saw in his protégé. Thank you, Bruce Trampler.

Bob Arum is one of the great promoters ever, but he showed me another side. Playing no angles, he was merely thoughtful, funny, compassionate, and exceedingly generous.

In Las Vegas: the public library and Dr. Lonnie Hammargren.

Thanks to Jerry Sullivan and the *Buffalo News*.

From the kingdom of television: Ray Stallone of HBO, Showtime's Chris DiBlasio. Chris LaPlaca took innumerable calls and made sure I had DVDs of Ray's fights on ESPN. Robin Brendle and Erik Ivan provided DVDs of Ray's CBS fights. Speaking of CBS, thanks to David Dinkins, Tim Ryan, and, especially, Mort Sharnik, whose storytelling sensibilities were honed in the press box.

"The Boss Scribes" (my favorite Don King-ism) provided a wealth of material. Royce Feour recalled the Vegas boxing scene in the early 1980s. Mike Rosenthal and Nigel Collins delivered crucial pieces from *The Ring*'s archive. I relied heavily on Michael Shapiro's fine 1987 *Sports Illustrated* story, "Remembering Duk Koo Kim." Then there are my debts to John Schulian, Tim Dahlberg, Mike Katz, Jerry Izenberg, John Ed Bradley, Bill Barich, Richard Hoffer, Dave Anderson, Michael Marley, Jon Saraceno, Larry Ringler, Bob Drury, Ron Borges, Al Bernstein, Hugh McIlvanney, the late Lester Bromberg, the late Bill Gallo, the late Dick Young, the late George Kimball, the late Harold Conrad, the late W. C. Heinz, the late Jim Murray, the late Ralph Wiley.

Bossest scribe of all: David Mamet.

For much needed encouragement at the outset of this project: Jim Rome, Rick Kot, Rob Fleder, and Ron Kurtz, whose detailed email touched me.

I'm often asked (mostly by New Yorkers) what's to like about LA. It's the stand-up people, of course: the aforementioned Ed O'Neill, Tim Brown, Jerry Steinberg, Phil Stutz, Chuck Shapiro, David Milch, Bobby Colomby, Lance Mayer, Alec and Leslie Sokolow, Richard Kantor, Larry Merchant, Evan Dick, Bill Clark, Patsy Bellah, Bill Plaschke, Michael Giudice, and the rest of the crew at Il Forno. Not only did Sam Henry Kass endure countless predawn phone calls, he's the rare writer who gladly parted with his best material.

Gigi Levangie: for inspiration, office space, and, as you call it, the paean to our love. I never had a fictional self, but he sounds good, even dead.

This book would not have been possible without the patience and understanding of Rick Jaffe and Steve Miller, my bosses at FOXSports.com.

For getting me to Korea: Michael Won of the *Korea Daily*, Grace Yoo, executive director of the Korean-American Foundation, and Steven Nam, who produced *Champion*. Nam introduced me to Chang Lae Kim. Chang—a director by trade and prince by nature—took care of everything else, from Seoul to Banam.

Thanks to Kae Bae Chun, Hyun-Chi Kim, Seo In Seong, Kun Sik Kim, Kun Yeung Kim, Kun Gu Kim, and Sang-Bong Lee, whom I know for a fact would rather cut off his pinky than fail a friend. Thanks to Michael Owen for help communicating with Jiwan and Young Mee, and for translating Duk Koo Kim's journal.

The interviews themselves were translated with great care by Su Hyun Lee, who graciously took time from her day job at the *New York Times* bureau in Seoul.

ICM's Nick Khan, my friend and *consigliere*, looks out for clients with a unique combination of ferocity and brilliance. He suggested a companion documentary to this book as a way to defray my mounting travel costs. What he put together, however—along with Jesse James Miller, Jimmy Lynn, and the ever-generous Chris Tavlarides—became a way to grant Jiwan's wish.

During our interview in Seoul Jiwan said he wanted to come to America and meet Ray. Travel and accomodations for him and his mother would come out of the documentary's budget. Their encounter would be filmed, but only if Ray agreed.

It was an emotionally fraught proposition. Then again, how could Ray really turn it down?

All these years later, to see Young Mee is to know why Duk Koo fought so hard.

To see his son is to know he's redeemed.

Turns out Jiwan did for his father what Ray did for Boom.

Finally, all my love and gratitude to my daughter. Holiday Kriegel, I hope one day you'll be as proud of me as I am of you.

Notes

The interviews with Ray Mancini took place from August 14 to 20, August 25, and September 8, 2009, in Santa Monica. In addition, through the reporting and writing stages, I spoke with him most days, traveled with him to Youngstown, and had him answer and clarify innumerable questions and queries. Apart from the dated interviews, I also had regular follow-up conversations with Ed O'Neill, Carmen Vazquez, Chuck Fagan, Gina Andriolo, Paul Percifield, Sam Henry Kass, and Michael Owen.

Prologue: Dementia

Interviews: Ray Mancini; David Mamet, October 10, 2010; Bill Clark, July 12, 2011; Carmen Vazquez, May 12, 2010; Michael Giudice, September 22, 2010; Ed O'Neill, September 1, 2010; Bobby Chacon, September 25, 2010.

1. Lenny Mancino

Interviews: Ray Mancini; Benedict D'Amato, October 15, 2009; Pat Zill, October 30, 2010; Vincent Mancino, January 8, 2010; John Congemi, December 28, 2009; George DeLost, January 2, 2010; Bill Gallo, October 10, 2009.

1 SS Palermo: Ellisisland.org http://www.ellisisland.org/search/shipManifest
  .asp?order_num=2118498131&MID=088470187600016658144&order_
  num=2118498131&ORDER_ID=1600191807&pID=100734100517&s
  how=100734100517&origFN=100734100517&fromEI=1.
1 *second only to Pittsburgh: A Citizen's Guide to Youngstown.* The League of
  Women Voters of Greater Youngstown, OH: Youngstown State University,
  2010, 8.

2 *Pilots landing in Youngstown:* Howard C. Aley, *A Heritage to Share: The Bicentennial History of Youngstown and Mahoning County* (Youngstown, OH: The Bicentennial Commission of Youngstown and Mahoning County, Ohio, 1975), 290.

2 *"sheer anarchy":* Ibid, 205–7.

2 *December 12, 1917:* Marriage License Application, volume 38, p. 221. Probate Court, Mahoning County, Ohio.

2 *had 324 grocery stores:* Aley, *A Heritage to Share,* 215.

2 *ten thousand gallons of:* Ibid., 297.

2 *twelve-hour shifts:* Ibid.

4 *"baseball mitts":* Benedict R. D'Amato, "Memories: A History of the D'Amato Family," 8.

5 *"We were about to lose":* Joseph L. Heffernan, "The Hungry City: A Mayor's Experience with Unemployment," *Atlantic Monthly,* May 1932.

5 *a third of Youngstown's work force: A Citizen's Guide,* 11.

6 *a scathing report:* Aley, *A Heritage to Share,* 306.

6 *"My mother would hand make":* Lester Bromberg, "Top New York Writer Recalls Boxing Feats of 'Boom Boom' Mancini," *New York Post,* November 25, 1967.

7 *hiring armed guards:* Sherry Lee Linkon and John Russo, *Steeltown U.S.A.: Work and Memory in Youngstown* (Lawrence, KS: University Press of Kansas, 2002), 39.

7 *Casualties included:* Ibid. 40.

7 *Red Delquadri:* Robert Bruno, *Steelworker Alley: How Class Works in Youngstown* (Ithaca, NY: Cornell University Press, 1999), 103.

7 *thirty dollars a month:* http://www.u-s-history.com/pages/h1586.html.

7 *a cook:* Fred Eisenstadt, "Making the Grade," *The Ring,* Sept. 1941; also "Mancini, Foley Head Broadway Arena Show," Lenny Mancini Scrapbook (hereafter, LMS), March 1940.

8 *July 26, 1938:* Letter from Charles J. Worden, acting superintendent, Indian Springs Camp, to Lt. John J. Prokop, C.O. Company 2532, C.C.C., July 26, 1938. Mancini Family Papers (hereafter MFP).

9 *"writhing on the canvas":* Frank B. Ward, "2,500 Fans See Henry Armstrong . . . ," Youngstown, OH, *Vindicator,* September 22, 1937.

10 *crowd estimated at two thousand five hundred:* Ibid.

10 *141 pounder:* http://boxrec.com/list_bouts.php?human_id=024441&cat=boxer.

10 *"Promoter Bill took":* Frank B. Ward, "Small Crowd Sees 'Wild Bill,'" Youngstown, OH, *Vindicator,* November 1, 1938.

10 *"The Lenny Mancini–J. D. Williams:* "1,400 See Billy Soose . . . ," Youngstown, OH, *Vindicator,* February 21, 1939.

11 *"I was pretty fair":* James E. Doyle, "Mancini Gained Top Hard Way," Cleveland *Plain Dealer,* April 29, 1941.

11 *"I'll be back"*: Ibid.

11 *As one old hand*: Lester Bromberg, "Mancini Lightweight Hope," *New York World-Telegram*, January 25, 1941.

2. The Business

Interviews: Ray Mancini, Gallo, October 12, 2009; DeLost; Mancino.

13 *the spring of 1939*: D'Amato, "Memories," 4.

13 *"Just had to"*: Bromberg, "Mancini Lightweight Hope."

14 *Jesus Christ himself*: Ronald K. Fried, *Corner Men: Great Boxing Trainers* (New York: Four Walls Eight Windows, 1991), 33.

14 *"The golden age"*: Lawrence Ritter, *East Side, West Side: Tales of New York Sporting Life, 1910–1960* (New York: Total Sports, 1998), 182. *See* section on Stillman's Gym, 180–83.

14 *"The capital of the world"*: Fried, 31.

14 *"The joint was so thick"*: Stillman quoted in Fried, 34.

14 *five busy pay phones*: Ibid., 36.

15 *The combined records*: Combined records at the time they fought Lenny Mancini calculated from Boxrec.com.

15 DEAR MOTHER: Telegrams from MFP.

15 *"one of the hits"*: "Foran Offers Severe Test for Allie Stoltz," unidentified newspaper clipping, October 24, 1939, LMS.

16 *"severe and decisive"*: A. J. Liebling, *The Sweet Science* (New York: The Penguin Sports Library, 1982, originally published 1956), 121.

16 *"The trainers of that day"*: In the Corner, Dave Anderson (New York: William Morrow and Company, 1991), 122.

16 *"But Boom Boom came back"*: Harold Conrad, "Friedkin Best of Boro 135-Pound Contenders," *Brooklyn Eagle*, December 6, 1939.

16 *"All fall Broadway Arena"*: "Defeat Shows Gameness of Young Mancini," unidentified newspaper clipping, December 6, 1939, LMS.

17 *his boxing license*: New York State Athletic Commission License No. 42, expired September 30, 1941, MFP.

17 *"Joss gave the offer"*: "Mancini, Foley Head Broadway Arena Show," unidentified newspaper clipping, c. March 1940, LMS.

17 *Foley went off as*: "Mancini's Stock Goes Boom-Boom!" unidentified newspaper clipping, March 6, 1940, LMS.

17 *knocked down Foley*: Ibid.

18 *"The nearest thing to Henry Armstrong"*: Unidentified newspaper clipping, c. April 1940, LMS.

18 *"A crowd pleaser"*: "Mancini at Crossroads of His Youthful Career," unidentified newspaper clipping, c. November 1940.

18 *Mancini staggered Vaughn:* "Mancini, Vaughn Draw," *New York Times,*
    May 8, 1940; "Vaughn Again Gets Break in Draw Decision," unidentified
    newspaper clipping, May 8, 1940, LMS.

18 *"a clean-cut eight round":* "Mancini Wins On Points," *New York Times,*
    January 15, 1941.

19 *"Neither of the two":* "Mancini and Marquart Should Provide Thrills,"
    Cleveland *Plain Dealer,* April 28, 1941.

19 *"a fierce eight-round battle":* "Mancini Prevails in 8-Round Fight," *New
    York Times,* April 2, 1941.

19 *"a deep laceration":* "Mancini Defeats Marquart in Eight," April 2, 1941,
    LMS.

19 *"crammed with furious":* "Mancini Displays Punch," unidentified newspa-
    per clipping, April 2, 1941, LMS.

20 *"But the mad Mancini":* James E. Doyle, "Mancini and Berger . . . Lenny
    Dropped for Eight Count," Cleveland *Plain Dealer,* April 30, 1941.

20 *"moved a step closer":* Angott Agrees to Meet Victor of Arena Fight," Cleve-
    land *Plain Dealer,* April 26, 1941.

20 *"poor, ridiculous family":* W. C. Heinz, *Once They Heard Cheers* (New
    York: Doubleday, 1979), 338.

20 *"Famous up and down Broadway":* Red Smith, "Sgt. Lew Jenkins," *New
    York Times,* November 4, 1981.

21 *"I hope the champeen":* James E. Doyle, "Mancini Sure He Will Top
    Angott," Cleveland *Plain Dealer,* May 19, 1941.

21 *"In the sixth":* Associated Press, "Local Boxer Loses Fight," in Youngstown,
    OH, *Vindicator,* May 20, 1941.

21 *"The verdict":* Billy Fogerty, "Referee Calls Len Mancini Winner," *New
    York Enquirer,* May 26, 1941.

21 The Ring: Fred Eisenstadt, "Making the Grade," *The Ring,* September 1941.

21 *"I'll kayo Angott":* Fogerty, "Referee Calls Len Mancini Winner."

21 *Lenny was ranked sixth:* "Youngstown to See Mancini in Action Tonight,"
    unidentified newspaper clipping, August 7, 1941, LMS.

22 *Young had vowed:* "Rivals Square Off for Tonight's Test," *Coney Island
    Daily Press,* July 14, 1941.

22 *"Mancini lived up to":* "Mancini Beats Young in Eight-Round Bout," *New
    York Times,* September 30, 1941.

22 *two and a half years at Sing Sing:* "Terry Young Arrested," *New York Times,*
    July 13, 1952.

22 *like a bear cub:* Dink Carroll, "New York Fighter Crowds In Closely All the
    Way to Win," *Montreal Gazette,* November 12, 1941.

22 *three fractured vertebrae in:* Heinz, 345.

23 *"If he can't fight better:* Al Buck, "Jenkins Dethroned Amid Boos," *New
    York Post,* December 20, 1941.

23 The Ring's *reigning number-two:* http://boxrec.com/media/index.php/ The_Ring_Magazine%27s_Annual_Ratings:_1941.

23 *already registered in Youngstown:* Associated Press in *New York Times,* December 19, 1941.

23 *photographed for the* Journal American: "He's Punchin' for Uncle Sam," *New York Journal American,* January 22, 1942.

23 *number-one contender:* "'The Ring's' Ratings for the Month," *The Ring,* April 1942.

23 *serial number 35 272 387:* Army Separation Qualification Record, June 28, 1945, MFP.

23 *skill as a marksman:* Honorable Discharge, Leonard Mancino, 35272387, Private, Company K, 320th Infantry, 35th Division, received July 3, 1945, MFP.

23 *fifty wounded veterans attended:* "Mancini Stops Nelson," *New York Times,* April 12, 1944.

23 *the "White Armstrong":* Eddie Merrill, "Servicemen Are Hailed in Return to Fistic Warfare," *The Ring,* February 1946.

25 *felt like even money:* Tommy Holmes, "The Comeback of Leonard Mancini," *Brooklyn Eagle,* November 26, 1945.

25 *Three minutes later:* "'Boom Boom' Mancini Bids For Welterweight Honors," United Press, November 2, 1945.

25 *REGRET TO INFORM YOU:* Telegram, MFP.

25 *"totally disabled":* Letter from the Veterans Administration (VA) to Leonard Mancino (LM), March 2, 1949, MFP.

25 *"I wasn't knocked out":* Holmes, "The Comeback of Leonard Mancini."

25 *what most worried the doctors:* "'Boom Boom' Mancini Bids For Welterweight Honors."

26 *"Don't tell Ray":* Fried, 91.

26 *70 percent disabled:* Letter from the VA to LM, July 3, 1945, MFP.

26 *five foot one and a half:* Honorable Discharge, MFP.

26 *DiCarlo's men in Youngstown:* http://members.fortunecity.com/sosdie/ mob/family/buffalo/bufyoungs.htm.

27 *asked Max Joss:* Holmes, "The Comeback of Leonard Mancini."

27 *a match with Rocky Graziano:* Eddie Merrill, "Servicemen Are Hailed in Return to Fistic Warfare," *The Ring,* February 1946.

27 *He might have become the lightweight champion:* Frank Graham, "Graham's Corner: From Hudkins to Mancini to Janiro," *New York Journal American,* September 19, 1945.

27 *"never took a backward step":* Bill Goodrich, "Mancini's Return Postwar Success," *Brooklyn Eagle,* July 10, 1946.

27 *a 3½ to 1 favorite:* Bill Goodrich, "Mancini Upsets Gallie in 1 Heat at B'Way Arena," *Brooklyn Eagle,* October 8, 1946.

27 *"a bit on the fat side"*: Frank B. Ward, "Along the Sports Rialto," Youngstown, OH, *Vindicator*, c. June 1946, MFP.

27 *"A little chunkier"*: Fred Roberts, "Early In-Fighting Draws Crowd's Ire," *Montreal Gazette*, September 18, 1946.

28 *fans raised his arm in victory*: "Hurst Gets Judges (But Not Crowd)," *Montreal Gazette*, October 19, 1946.

28 *walking home from a bar*: Dave Anderson, "Legacy Of a Father," *New York Times*, July 12, 1982.

28 *a loan of $5,599.95*: Mortgage Deed for 807 Cambridge Avenue, Youngstown, Ohio, June 23, 1948, Mahoning County Courthouse.

29 *"A careful review has been made"*: Letter from VA to LM, November 14, 1949, MFP.

29 *"Milton Berle"*: Leonard Cohen, "The Sports Parade," *New York Post*, April 6, 1949.

3. Youngstown Tune-up

Interviews: Mike Cefalde, January 1, 2010; Ellen Kosa, December 29, 2009; Tank Dicioccio, January 2, 2010; Ray Mancini; Bill Blanchard, January 12, 2010; Dave Shaffer, January 2, 2010; Tony Congemi, December 27, 2009; Father Tim O'Neill, October 15 and 18, 2009.

31 *$136.30*: Letter from VA to LM, January 17, 1957, MFP.

32 *twenty thousand unemployed*: Aley, *A Heritage to Share*, p. 453.

32 *"steel's sick city"*: Ibid.

32 *eighty-two bombings*: Fred J. Cook, "Youngstown: Anatomy of a Murder Town," *Saga*, May 1962.

32 *owned six cars*: Ibid.

32 *"When you're in politics here"*: John Kobler, "Crimetown USA," *The Saturday Evening Post*, March 9, 1963.

33 *Police found a twelve-gauge*: Cook, "Youngstown: Anatomy of a Murder Town."

33 *more showed up for Naples's wake*: Aley, 449, estimates the crowd at Senator Kennedy's campaign stop at 1,500. The death "brought thousands to a local funeral home while 1,500 attended their funeral services."

39 *a record twenty-nine times*: Frank Litsky, "Bell Tolls 10 Times for Madison Square Garden's Ring," *New York Times*, September 20, 2007.

39 *The State Liquor Authority*: "Canzoneri Bar Gets Stay on Shutdown," *New York Times*, April 8, 1965.

42 *the headlines would flash*: LMS.

43 *Raymond's first mention in*: "Butch McCrae Is Mound Ace," Youngstown, OH, *Vindicator*, June 21, 1971.

44 *1940 Youngstown Gloves:* http://rossifunerals.com/obits/sullivan.html.

46 *consecutive state titles:* "Youngstown Babe Ruth Stars Win 2nd State Title," Youngstown, OH, *Vindicator,* August 1, 1974.

48 *knocked out his first opponent:* "Ray Mancini, Hamilton Win," Youngstown, OH, *Vindicator,* April 25, 1976.

48 *thirty-two:* "Warren AC boxers advance," Youngstown, OH, *Vindicator,* April 26, 1976.

48 *eleven hundred at the Campbell Memorial:* Youngstown, OH, *Vindicator,* April 29, 1976. Ray Mancini's Scrapbook (RMS).

48 *"a bruising affair":* "Mancini Bows in Mitt Finals," Youngstown, OH, *Vindicator,* June 14, 1976.

48 *"I Walk in His Shadow":* In Dave Anderson, "Legacy Of a Father," *New York Times,* July 12, 1982.

50 *"Mancini continued to":* Dave Burcham, "18 Local Boxers Advance to Regionals," Youngstown, OH, *Vindicator,* February 3, 1977.

50 *winning the regional gloves:* "Five Area Boxers Win District 'Gloves' Titles," Youngstown, OH, *Vindicator,* March 12, 1977.

51 *fifty-five seconds:* "Mancini, McPherson Win Quick," Youngstown, OH, *Vindicator,* April 16, 1977.

51 *Ray (Boom Boom):* Ibid.

51 *Ray dropped a split decision:* O'Neill's memory jibes exactly with "3 Boxers Win at Canton," Youngstown, OH, *Vindicator,* April 27, 1977.

4. Black Monday

Interviews: Cefalde; Fagan; Rick Rufh, January 7, 2010; Ray Mancini; Toby Falk, October 12, 2009; Duane Bobick, October 11, 2009; Gina Andriolo, October 9, 2009; Ed Jones, December 5, 2009; Don Cronson, October 12, 2009.

53 *released a statement:* Bruno, 9.

53 *"seemed content to run":* Linkon and Russo, 48.

53 *the Brier Hill Works:* "A Citizen's Guide to Youngstown," 13.

53 *U.S. Steel announced:* http://www4.vindy.com/content/local_regional/325599506558106.php.

54 *"There's more money floating":* Matthew Kennedy, "Mob Rule: Despite Economic Woes, Organized Crime Remains Thriving Racket in Tri-State Area," *Pittsburgh Press,* February 27, 1983.

54 *"Gambling permeates everything":* Edward P. Whelan, "Getting Away with Murder," *Cleveland Magazine,* March 1982.

55 *Mary Francis Panno:* Certified Abstract of Marriage, Volume 197, Page 243, November 15, 1977, Mahoning County Probate Court, Youngstown, OH.

56 *The Struthers Field House:* http://www.struthers.k12.oh.us/schools/shs/sports_shs/bball/basketball/FieldHouse.htm.

57 *Phifer somehow managed to hold:* Dene Spalvieri, "Mancini outslugs foe; TRA has two finalists," Portsmouth, OH, *Daily Times,* February 2, 1978.

57 *"A tremendous bout":* Pete Mollica, "Ray 'Boom Boom' Mancini Victor in GG Semis," Youngstown, OH, *Vindicator,* February 2, 1978.

57 *"If you don't have a ticket":* Dave Burcham, "Tickets Gone for GG Finals," Youngstown, OH, *Vindicator,* February 5, 1978.

57 *"Mancini continued to fire":* Dave Burcham, "Ray Mancini, Edwards named Best in GG Finals," Youngstown, OH, *Vindicator,* February 9, 1978.

58 *"put out more lights":* Dave Burcham, "Eight City Boxers Await National Golden Gloves," Youngstown, OH, *Vindicator,* March 19, 1978.

58 *invariably smiling: Eminence,* 1978–79, Yearbook from Cardinal Mooney High School, Youngstown, OH, Volume 19.

59 *"A little Rocky":* Chuck Perazich, "Mancini Joins 'Too Tall' Jones in Wolf's Boxing Stable," Youngstown, OH, *Vindicator,* September 16, 1979.

59 *Paul had considerable international experience:* http://boxrec.com/media/index.php?title=Human:2522.

59 *"Even some of Paul's people":* Larry Ringler, "Boxer On the Way Up," Warren, OH, *Sunday Tribune Magazine,* December 7, 1980.

59 *Paul's mouthpiece fly:* Ibid.

60 *winning three bronze stars:* Mark Kriegel, "Murphy Griffith dies at 88; trained 'Boom Boom' Mancini," *FOXSports.com,* January 22, 2010.

60 *At the University of Wisconsin:* Peter Alfano, "From Sportswriter to Fight Manager," *New York Times,* November 30, 1982.

61 *On a prefight tour of:* John Schulian, "Lights Out—a Lesson Learned," *Chicago Sun-Times,* January 23, 1980, from Schulian, *Writers' Fighters & Other Sweet Scientists* (Kansas City: Andrews and McMeel, 1983).

62 *Eddie Futch lost interest:* Robert Mladinich, "Duane Bobick: 'Sadness Prepared Me,'" http://www.thesweetscience.com/boxing-article/5651/duane-bobick-sadness-prepared/

62 *"I didn't know it then":* Alfano, "From Sportswriter to Fight Manager."

62 *ranked fourth:* Pepe, "Mancini's Manager Could Write Book On Boxing," New York *Daily News,* September 15, 1983.

63 *journalistic differences:* Alfano, "From Sportswriter to Fight Manager,"

64 *Blue Cross–Blue Shield:* Pepe, "Mancini's Manager Could Write Book On Boxing."

5. The Family Name

Interviews: Ray Mancini; Randy Stephens, November 27, 2009; Andriolo; Jones; Sal Marchiano, December 12, 2009; Bruce Trampler, March 12, 2010; Mort Sharnik, September 15 and 16, 2009; Royce Feour, October 12, 2009; Chuck Fagan; Paul Percifield, October 11, 2009, December 18, 2009, and November 27, 2009; Cefalde; Shaffer.

67 *"I'm going to win the title"*: Dave Burcham, "Mancini Vows He'll Get Title," Youngstown, OH, *Vindicator*, September 18, 1979.

69 *founded in 1976 by Jimmy Glenn*: John Goodman (photographs) and Pete Hamill (text), *The Times Square Gym* (New York: EVAN Publishing, 1996).

69 *"school and clubhouse"*: Ibid.

69 *Rocky II*: Theater listings from *New York Times*, September 19, 1979.

69 *"New SEXtacular"*: William Plummer, "Boom Boom Mancini: The Son Also Rises," *The Ring*, July 1982.

71 *big-name fighters*: Goodman and Hamill.

72 *hyped as 5–2*: Larry Ringler, " 'Boom' Sees Tough Fight," *Warren Tribune Chronicle*, October 17, 1979.

72 *2–6*: http://boxrec.com/list_bouts.php?human_id=1639&cat=boxer.

72 *ten minutes would elapse*: Youngstown, OH, *Vindicator*, January 27, 1980.

72 *"A truly honest fighter"*: Ralph Wiley, *Serenity: A Boxing Memoir* (Lincoln and London: University of Nebraska Press, 2000), 129. Originally published, Holt: New York, 1989.

74 *"A tough, energetic"*: Bill Gallo, "Mancini to Defend vs. Chacon," New York *Daily News*, September 24, 1983.

75 *"destroyed"*: Tommy Lopez, "Finch in Fast Strip victory," *Las Vegas Review-Journal*, July 24, 1980.

75 *Jaime Nava*: Tommy Lopez, " 'Boom Boom' No Strip Bomb," *Las Vegas Review-Journal*, July 31, 1980.

75 *an injured knuckle*: "Mancini Gets 12th Triumph," Youngstown, OH, *Vindicator*, August 29, 1980.

76 *"I got knocked out"*: John Bassetti, "Mancini Lowers 'Boom' on Evelyn in Round Two," Youngstown, OH, *Vindicator*, June 19, 1980.

76 *"earned a reputation"*: Larry Ringler, "Mancini Is Unanimous Choice in 10," *Warren Tribune Chronicle*, September 10, 1980.

76 *"I didn't know"*: Ibid.

6. Valentine's Day

Interviews: Blanchard; Father Tim O'Neill; Shaffer; Stephens; Ray Mancini; Kosa; DiCioccio; Fagan.

79 *case no. 81-648:* Kirkland/Mancini case file hereafter identified as CF.

79 *told a hospital administrator:* Patient admission form, Trumbull Memorial Hospital, December 9, 1980, CF.

79 *"sort of walked out":* Diana Louise Kirkland, aka Karen Sue Donovan, interviewed by Det. Frank Mowrey, February 16, 1981, CF.

79 *316 Manhattan Boulevard:* Supplementary Report, Det. Mowery, February 17, 1981, CF.

79 *fictitious birth dates:* Teletype from Toledo P.D. to Youngstown P.D., February 18, 1981, CF.

79 *the Outlaws:* Letter from Captain Harold Patterson, Records Section, Toledo P.D., to Det. Mowery, Youngstown P.D., February 20, 1981, CF.

79 *"He said he loved me":* Diana Louise Kirkland, interviewed as Karen Sue Donovan, by Mowrey, February 14, 1981, CF.

80 *"I loved him":* Kirkwood interview, February 16, 1981, CF.

80 *.22-caliber pistol:* Supplementary Report, Mancini Investigation, Detective Division, February 16, 1981, CF.

80 *owed them fifteen hundred dollars:* Kirkwood interviews, February 14 and 16, 1981, CF.

80 *"Next thing I know":* Voluntary Statement of Patricia Bartolivich, February 19, 1981, CF.

80 *sharing half a joint:* Kirkwood, February 16, CF.

81 *"We had sex":* Kirkwood/Donovan, February 14, CF.

81 *The crime scene:* Supplementary Report, February 14, 1981, CF.

81 *an inch and a half:* The Inquest Over The Dead Body of Leonard Mancini, Inquest No. 13686, Paul W. Weiss, Deputy Coroner, February 27, 1981, CF.

82 *her birth mother was hospitalized:* "Mancini's Girl Pleads Innocent," Youngstown, OH, *Vindicator*, March 4, 1981.

82 *Diana pleaded guilty:* "Mancini Slayer Committed to OYC," Youngstown, OH, *Vindicator*, March 19, 1981.

85 *"The consensus":* Jim Benagh, "Boom Boom II," *New York Times*, March 9, 1981.

85 *two left hooks:* Leonard Lewin, "Mancini wins by KO," *New York Post*, March 13, 1981.

85 *"Just like his father":* "Boom Boom II Stops Goins in 2d Round," *New York Times*, March 13, 1981.

7. The Kiss

Interviews: Marchiano; Ray Mancini; Bob Arum, March 4, 2010; Trampler; Morton Sharnik; Tim Ryan, April 15, 2010; David Dinkins, December 9, 2009; Andriolo; Fagan; DiCioccio.

87 *It's almost like a scenario: Top Rank Boxing*, originally broadcast from Chicago, IL, April 2, 1981. DVD courtesy of ESPN.

88 *"must be unconscious"*: Ibid.

90 *cracked in the head*: Fried, 96–97.

90 *"boxing's silent kingmaker"*: William Taaffe, "A Gulliver Big On Lilliputians," *Sports Illustrated*, June 18, 1984.

91 *"Death of a Champion"*: Morton Sharnik, "Death of a Champion," *Sports Illustrated*, April 1, 1963.

91 *"A boxing match is like a cowboy movie"*: Gilbert Rogin, Morton Sharnik, "Can't A Fellow Make a Mistake?" *Sports Illustrated*, July 17, 1961.

92 *"promised a title shot"*: http://il.youtube.com/watch?v=NRsVWblz32U&feature=related.

92 *"I'm going to keep this"*: http://il.youtube.com/watch?v=1eJJ247kLes&feature=related.

94 *"His showing convixes"*: Michael Strauss, "Mancini Winner In Boxing," *New York Times*, May 17, 1981.

94 *71–3*: http://boxrec.com/list_bouts.php?human_id=1639&cat=boxer.

96 *a Nicaraguan Omar Sharif*: John Schulian, *Writers' Fighters and Other Sweet Scientists*, 98.

97 *"one of the old fight clubs"*: CBS Sports Saturday, originally broadcast July 19, 1981. DVD courtesy of CBS Sports.

99 *"a game kid from Mexico"*: Plummer, "Boom Boom Mancini: The Son Also Rises."

100 *"We have a contract"*: UPI, "Mancini Manager Threatens to Pull Out of Arguello Bout," *New York Post*, October 3, 1981.

101 *tears streaming down her face*: Michael Katz, "Arguello Stops Mancini in 14," *New York Times*, October 4, 1981.

102 *a rating of 9.7*: Ratings for CBS weekend broadcasts featuring Mancini provided by CBS Sports.

8. Title Shots

Interviews: Sharnik; Arum; Trampler; Ray Mancini; Fagan; DiCioccio; Kosa; Cefalde; Andriolo.

103 *the Mahoning County Nursing Home:* Associated Press, "Boxer's Death Revealed," *New York Times*, April 17, 1982.

104 *Rodrigo Sanchez and Venezuela's Gilberto Mendoza:* Ben Sharav, "Arum Tells of $100,000 Payments to WBA 'Bagman,'" *The Ring*, May 1983.

104 *$300,000:* Kevin Mitchell, "The Motor City Legend; Emanuel Steward, the Detroit Corner Man, Hones Champions," London *Observer*, March 5, 2000. Harry Mullan, "The Champs' Champion; Lennox Lewis Is the Latest Top Boxer to Benefit from Emanuel Steward's Gifts," London *Independent*, February 16, 1997.

104 *"There's one bagman":* Sharav, "Arum Tells of $100,000 Payments."

105 *below Frias's left eye:* United Press International, February 1, 1982.

105 *Salinas Productions:* Sharav, "Arum Tells of $100,000 Payments."

105 *"Cordero took me to the cleaners":* Steve Springer, "Arum Paints a Dark Picture," *Los Angeles Times*, August 16, 2000.

108 *"These are two":* CBS *Sports Saturday*, broadcast May 8, 1982. DVD courtesy of CBS Sports.

109 *"Possibly the single most concussive":* Richard Hoffer, "It Was Furious, Bloody and Brief," *Los Angeles Times*, May 9, 1982.

109 *thirty-six unanswered blows:* CBS *Sports Saturday*, May 8, 1982.

109 *"I don't care":* Hoffer, "It Was Furious, Bloody and Brief."

110 *"I have finally served":* "Boom Boom the Champ," *New York Post*, May 10, 1982, from wire services.

110 *a key to the city:* "Sports People," *New York Times*, May 12, 1982.

110 *"Mancini has the ebullient":* Michael Katz, "A Champion Inspired by Family Ties," *New York Times*, May 19, 1982.

111 *Top tickets:* Michael Katz, "Mancini Goes Home to Fight," *New York Times*, July 24, 1982.

112 *"This is the biggest":* John Goodall, "Tapping Mancini Bout's Potential To Promote Area Proves Problem," Youngstown, OH, *Vindicator*, June 13, 1982.

112 *Unemployment would reach:* UPI, "Youngstown Remains at Top in Unemployment Rate, 18.7%," *New York Times*, November 17, 1982.

112 *chairman of the county Democratic Party:* Edward P. Whelan, "Getting Away With Murder," *Cleveland Magazine*, March 1982.

112 *Traficant would admit:* http://www.moldea.com/Traficant.html, originally published as Dan Moldea, "The Mafia and the Congressman," *Washington Weekly*, April 19, 1985.

113 *DeRose had been the tenth:* Whelan, "Getting Away with Murder."

113 *Assault numbers:* Annual Reports, Record Room, Youngstown Police Department.

113 *almost doubled:* Ibid.

113 *"The office"*: Jerry Izenberg, "Mancini Puts Boom Back into Hometown," *New York Post*, July 23, 1982.

114 *"as if he were preparing"*: Ralph Wiley, "A Shining Ray Of Hope," *Sports Illustrated*, August 2, 1982.

114 *He had him bash:* Ibid.

114 *eighteen square feet:* Neil Amdur, Lawrie Mifflin, "100-Ring Circus," *New York Times*, July 24, 1982.

114 *a crowd of 2,500:* "Espana: 'I'll Drop Mancini within Seven,'" *New York Post*, July 24, 1982, wire services.

114 *"The All-American boy"*: Irving Rudd and Stan Fischler, *The Sporting Life*, (New York: St. Martin's Press, 1990), 265.

114 *His first press release:* Dave Anderson, "One Gladiator Left," *New York Times*, May 22, 1984.

114 *"If half the horses"*: Donn Esmonde, "Hype Getting High in Tahoe Playground," *The Buffalo News*, May 5, 1984.

114 *"A pep rally"*: Katz, "Mancini Goes Home to Fight."

115 *nearly twenty thousand:* CBS's Tim Ryan called it "nearly 20,000," *Sports Illustrated* had "20,000," and the *Vindicator* estimated 17,500.

115 *"Like a giraffe"*: CBS Sports Saturday, broadcast July 24, 1982. DVD provided courtesy of CBS Sports.

116 *"I started ripping"*: Michael Katz, "Mancini Knocks Out Espana," *New York Times*, July 25, 1982.

116 *"Maybe he should have retired"*: Ibid.

116 *"If we do a* Rocky IV": John Goodall, "Mancini Upstages 'Rocky' In TKO Before Multitude," Youngstown, OH, *Vindicator*, July 25, 1982.

118 *"De Niro?"*: Michael Katz, "Boom Boom Blitz," *New York Times*, August 23, 1982.

118 *lizard, ostrich, and python:* Ted Green, "Ray Mancini Is Actually Boom Boom Mancini II; Lenny Mancini, Ray's Father, Was the First," *Los Angeles Times*, December 2, 1981.

119 *Leonard had now pulled out:* Dave Anderson, Sports of The Times, "Will Pryor Tempt Sugar Ray?" *New York Times*, November 14, 1982.

119 *Mancini drew twenty thousand:* Ibid.

119 *"That's what I want"*: Curt W. Nix, "Boom Boom Is Eyeing Another Shot at Arguello," *New York Post*, August 18, 1982.

120 *former Olympian Howard Davis:* Curt Nix, "Davis Eyeing Boom-Boom," *New York Post*, July 21, 1982; Curt Nix, "Davis Sets Aug. 26 Bout," *New York Post*, August 10, 1982.

120 *a 2–1 favorite:* Anderson, "Will Pryor Tempt Sugar Ray?"

9. The Desire for a Harmonious Family

Interviews: Kun Sik Kim, June 26, 2010; Kun Yeung Kim, June 29, 2010; Hyun-Chi Kim, June 28, 2010; Yoon Gu Kim, June 24, 2010; Sang-Bong Lee, June 30, 2010; Seo In Seong, June 25, 2010; Young Mee Lee, July 1, 2010.

123 *July 29, 1955*: Duk Koo Kim's Journal, translated by Michael Owen.
123 *"a woman of great misfortune"*: Michael Shapiro, "Remembering Duk Koo Kim," *Sports Illustrated*, April 27, 1987.
123 *"That first day"*: Kim's Journal
124 *swim out under a blazing sun*: Shapiro, "Remembering Duk Koo Kim."
124 *"I would ask my mother"*: Kim's Journal.
125 *"One new brother used to drag me"*: Shapiro.
125 *"I never had a happy home"*: Ibid.

10. Heaven

Interviews: Ray Mancini; Trampler; Hyun-Chi Kim; Feour; Sharnik; Seo In Seong; Yoon Gu Kim; DiCioccio; Arum; Kosa; Fagan; Father Tim O'Neill; Dr. Lonnie Hammargren, February 26, 2010.

133 *Duk-Koo's newfound status*: UPI, "Ray Mancini Plans Title Defense," *Los Angeles Times*, September 13, 1982.
133 *Korean and Japanese boxing establishments*: See Pat Putnam, "Fighting the Rulers of the WBA," *Sports Illustrated*, March 23, 1981.
136 *"Kim's expression changed"*: Wiley, *Serenity*, 126–27.
136 *the son of a rich man*: Royce Feour, "Kim Doesn't Have to Fight, but Tests Mancini Saturday," *Las Vegas Review-Journal*, November 11, 1982.
136 *"Live or die"*: Royce Feour, "Boxer Kim's Slogan Tragically Prophetic," *Las Vegas Review-Journal*, November 21, 1982.
137 *"We're going to have a war"*: Royce Feour, "Mancini Defends Title Today," *Las Vegas Review-Journal*, November 13, 1982.
137 *crowd of nine thousand*: Associated Press, "Sugar Ray Says He's Had Enough," *Las Vegas Review-Journal*, November 10, 1982.
138 *Wolf had already received*: Royce Feour, "Mancini's Future: Arguello or Pryor?" *Las Vegas Review-Journal*, November 12, 1982.
138 *"The one I mixed"*: http://www.youtube.com/watch?v=7kmY44hJbV0.
138 *"remained motionless in the ring"*: Associated Press, "Pryor Ends Arguello's Dream in 14," *Las Vegas Review-Journal*, November 13, 1982.
138 *"I always wanted to be the one"*: Wiley, *Serenity*, 126.
140 *"That'll take your heart"*: Mark Kriegel, "Ray Mancini, Duk Koo Kim . . .

'something that happened in boxing,'" New York *Daily News*, November 15, 1999.

140 *spouting blood*: Ralph Wiley, "Then All the Joy Turned to Sorrow," *Sports Illustrated*, November 22, 1982.

141 *"Something's going to happen"*: CBS *Sports Saturday*, November 13, 1982, courtesy of CBS Sports.

143 *"One of the greatest physical feats"*: Wiley, *Serenity*, 127.

143 *Duk Koo kept slipping*: Royce Feour, "Arum Calls for Halt to Boxing," *Las Vegas Review-Journal*, November 14, 1982.

143 *four breaths per minute*: Wiley, "Then All the Joy."

143 *100 ccs*: Hammargren's eleven-page account of Kim's death. Part of an unpublished memoir.

144 *his notes of that day*: Ibid.

144 *"Look at me"*: Leonard Lewin, "Priest: Boom Boom Faces Toughest Battle," November 17, 1982.

145 *The opening act*: Deborah Munch, vice president of public relations for Harrah's Entertainment, checked the Caesars Palace records to see who had performed that night.

146 *"There are no signs"*: Associated Press, "Fighter Is Close To Death," *New York Times*, November 14, 1982.

146 *"The hemorrhage was quite"*: Wiley, "Then All the Joy."

147 *"just about dead"*: AP, "Fighter Is Close . . . ," *New York Times*, November 14, 1982.

147 *"It was a terrific fight"*: Peter Alfano, "Fighter Lingers Near Death," *New York Times*, November 15, 1982.

147 *his left hand bandaged, bowed his head*: Royce Feour, "Korean Fighter Kim Remains Very Critical," *Las Vegas Review-Journal*, November 15, 1982.

11. Ghosts

Interviews: Ray Mancini; Kun Yeung Kim; Sang-Bong Lee; Hyun-Chi Kim; Sharnik; Arum; Chuck Tanner, October 14, 2009; Kae Bae Chun, January 16, 2010; Kun Sik Kim; Fagan; DiCioccio.

149 *"my heart"*: UPI, " 'My Heart Has Been Broken Apart,'" *New York Post*, November 16, 1982.

150 *"It's not your fault"*: UPI, "Kim's mom begs boxer: 'Open eyes'," *New York Post*, November 17, 1982.

150 *"What will happen"*: Ibid.

150 *"I am not optimistic"*: Royce Feour, "Korean Boxer Kim Still Very Critical as Family Arrives," *Las Vegas Review-Journal*, November 17, 1982.

150 *Surgeons from Stanford*: Richard Cornett and Gary Ebbels, "Service Planned for Kim," *Las Vegas Review-Journal*, November 18, 1982.

150 *declined to take his heart*: Wire Services, "Kidneys Taken, Kim's Body Sent Home," *New York Post*, November 19, 1982.

150 *"The American doctors"*: UPI, "Judge Calls Kim 'Legally Dead,'" *New York Post*, November 18, 1982.

150 *Those who paid their respects*: Jeanne M. Hall, "Boxer Eulogized in Service," *Las Vegas Review-Journal*, November 20, 1982.

151 *"If it's a boy"*: Marsha Kranes (wire services), "Pregnant Fiancée's Plan for Funeral," *New York Post*, November 19, 1982.

152 *"He goes from periods"*: Peter Alfano, "Kim's Mother to Be Consulted," *New York Times*, November 17, 1982.

152 *"I don't think Emile"*: Larry Fox, "Life on Street Riskier than Contact Sport," New York *Daily News*, November 16, 1982.

153 *"You don't forget"*: Wiley, "Then All The Joy . . ."

153 *"I'd like him to quit"*: Associated Press, "Mancini Dream a Nightmare After Kim KO," New York *Daily News*, November 16, 1982.

153 *"If he broods"*: Joe O'Day, "Fearful Fighters: They Still Want to Be Contenders," New York *Daily News*, November 17, 1982.

153 *"I have realized"*: Skip Watcher, United Press International, November 17, 1982.

153 *"The old excuses"*: Royce Feour, "Arum Calls for Halt to Boxing," *Las Vegas Review-Journal*, November 14, 1982.

154 *"The beast"*: George Vecsey, "The Beastliness in Boxing," *New York Times*, November 15, 1982.

154 *"Doesn't he know"*: Dave Kindred, *Sound and Fury* (New York: Free Press, 2006), 249.

155 *"Either that or abolish"*: Dave Kindred, "Fighting Mad, Cosell Walks Away From Sport Turned Spectacle," *Washington Post*, December 2, 1982.

155 *"Boxing is an obscenity"*: George D. Lundberg, "Boxing Should Be Banned in Civilized Countries," *Journal of the American Medical Association*, January 14, 1983; http://jama.ama-assn.org/content/249/2/250.1.full.pdf+html.

155 *337 pro fighters*: UPI, "'My heart has been broken apart.'"

155 *eight young men have died*: Jerry Izenberg, "Let's Clean up Boxing or Get Rid of It Forever," *New York Post*, November 16, 1982.

155 *an 8.7 Nielsen rating*: Ratings, provided by CBS Sports.

156 *"Paret died on his feet"*: Norman Mailer, "The Death of Benny Paret," in *The Time of Our Time* (New York: Random House, 1998), 466.

156 *"There is something about his pale face"*: Hugh McIlvanney, "Johnny Owen's Last Fight," originally published in the London *Observer*, September 19, 1980, in *The Hardest Game* (New York: Contemporary Books, 2001), 109–10.

158 *Expressions of condolence:* Joseph Durso, "Help for Mancini," *New York Times,* November 27, 1982.

158 *"The kid":* Phil Gailey, Warren Weaver Jr., "To Cheer a Boxer," *New York Times,* December 8, 1982.

159 *"I knew the fire":* UPI, "Boom-Boom Plans to Keep Fighting," *New York Post,* November 30, 1982.

160 *I have no mental:* Bill Gallo, "Mancini: I'll Throw Punch Hard as Ever," New York *Daily News,* January 14, 1983.

160 *"Emile came up to me":* Leonard Lewin, "Mancini Puts Tragedy Behind Him," *New York Post,* January 13, 1983.

160 *"It was an especially good time":* Jane Gross, "Mancini Shows His Desire," *New York Times,* February 6, 1983.

161 *"My title's not at risk":* Katz, "Mancini Looking Beyond Kim Tragedy," *New York Times,* January 14, 1983.

161 *begun to well up:* Ibid.

161 *Turin Football Club:* Milton Richman, "Today's Sport Parade," United Press International, February 1, 1983.

161 *An elderly contessa:* Dave Anderson, "Mancini Reacts to More Tragedy," *New York Times,* February 3, 1983.

162 *playing accordions:* Jane Gross, "Mancini Wins in Return," *New York Times,* February 7, 1983.

162 *Wolf had won $359,000:* Richman, "Today's Sport Parade," United Press International, February 1, 1983.

163 *$158,108:* United Press International, December 3, 1982.

163 *regular Sunday night dinner:* Richman, "Today's Sport Parade."

163 *They said he cloistered himself:* United Press International, February 1, 1983.

164 *"God forbid":* Anderson, "Mancini Reacts To More Tragedy."

164 *take a nap:* Gross, "Mancini Wins in Return."

165 *If it had been an easy fight:* Ibid.

165 *contemplating "a sensational upset":* AP, "Close, Unanimous Decision for Mancini," New York *Daily News,* February 7, 1983.

165 *"a place only about four people":* Jim Murray, "Last Place on Earth for a Fight," *Los Angeles Times,* March 3, 1983.

166 *"I found none":* Ibid.

166 *gross revenues:* Roger Bennett, "Strangers In The Night?" United Press International, March 1, 1983.

166 *"It felt like something":* Associated Press, "Mancini's Collarbone Broken; Fight Cancelled," New York *Daily News,* April 29, 1983.

167 *"In twenty years":* UPI, "Shoulder Injury Kayoes Mancini Fight, Sinatra Concert," April 28, 1983.

167 *"I apologize":* Associated Press, "Mancini's Collarbone Broken."

167 *talk of Maureen Stapleton:* "Stallone to Bang Away at Boom Boom's Life," New York *Daily News,* March 10, 1983.

167 *"We think an 'up'"*: David Remnick, "Now, Even Hollywood Feels the Boom Boom Boom," *Washington Post*, September 15, 1983.

167 *Sambuca-sponsored bocci*: "Boom Boom Ready for Bocci Ball," New York *Daily News*, July 24, 1983.

167 *Teamsters Local 966*: "Boom Boom's a Dock Walloper Now," New York *Daily News*, September 4, 1983.

168 *"How many more"*: "Boxing's Great Hope Down for the Count," *New York Post*, July 27, 1983.

168 *Perez made two thousand dollars*: Sam Goldaper, "Boxer Injured in Bout Dies," *New York Times*, October 7, 1983.

169 *"Friends said he"*: "Funeral Services Scheduled for Green," *Las Vegas Review-Journal*, July 5, 1983.

169 *"Police said Green"*: George Staresinic, "Boxing Referee Green Dead at 46," *Las Vegas Sun*, July 6, 1983.

169 *"a professional hit"*: Wiley, *Serenity*, 145.

169 *"Your daddy"*: Ibid.

169 *always been his dream*: Joe O'Day, "Mancini hopes Romero bout proves a Boom to his career," New York *Daily News*, July 19, 1983.

169 *black shorts with red trim*: Sam Goldaper, "Garden Party for Mancini," *New York Times*, September 15, 1985

170 *"There was no decision"*: Malcolm Moran, "Business Booming For Ray Mancini," *New York Times*, July 19, 1983.

12. The Ballad of Bobby Chacon

Interviews: Ray Mancini; Arum; DiCioccio; Fagan; Ross Greenburg, April 23, 2010; Chacon.

171 *"middle-class sissy"*: Bill Gallo, "Mancini–Camacho Big-$ Possibility," New York *Daily News*, August 7, 1983.

171 *"That's the one I want"*: Bill Gallo, "Chacon Challenged Mancini," New York *Daily News*, June 22, 1983.

171 *"I can make all"*: Leonard Lewin, "Boom Boom Lining 'em Up," *New York Post*, July 19, 1983.

171 *"Pryor–Mancini would be"*: Dick Young, "Please, Boom Boom, Call It Quits in '84," *New York Post*, September 15, 1983.

171 *"Megabucks"*: Vic Carucci, "Boom Boom Makes His Dad Squirm," *Buffalo News*, April 5, 1983.

172 *"Romero is the lightweight"*: Young, "Please, Boom Boom, Call It Quits in '84."

172 *he sparred 125 rounds*: Ray DeGraw, "Boom Boom Can't Break Bank Until After He Breaks Romero," New York *Daily News*, September 15, 1983.

173 *"the happiest person"*: Carucci, "Boom Boom Makes His Dad Squirm."

173 *"I'm twenty-two"*: Bob Drury, "Boom Boom hits 135 for Romero (134¾)," *New York Post*, September 15, 1983.

173 *"Bobby Chacon, walking"*: Young, "Please, Boom Boom, Call It Quits in '84."

174 *the fight was reported to be even*: Dick Young, "Sum Discrepancy Found on Judges' Scorecards," *New York Post*, September 16, 1983.

174 *"exploded"*: Michael Katz, "Mancini a Winner By Knockout in 9th," *New York Times*, September 16, 1983.

174 *"There goes the mortgage"*: Ralph Wiley, "A Tough Way to Save Face," *Sports Illustrated*, September 26, 1983.

174 *"Perhaps he was rusty"*: Ibid.

174 *"Sketchy"*: Bob Drury, "Mancini Mulls Rich Future," *New York Post*, September 17, 1983.

174 *"Listless, dull and immobile"*: Michael Katz, "Title Bout Hurts Mancini's Prestige," *New York Times*, September 17, 1983.

174 *"A perfect punch"*: Phil Pepe, "One Perfect Punch," New York *Daily News*, September 16, 1983.

174 *"Oh, God"*: Wiley, "A Tough Way to Save Face," *Sports Illustrated*, September 26, 1983.

175 *"You can do that"*: Wiley, *Serenity*, 136.

176 *"She said that"*: Ibid., 140.

176 $6,000: "A Fighter's Creed," *New York Times*, March 18, 1982.

176 *"I tried to kill"*: Wiley, *Serenity*, 140.

176 *"Fight of the Year"*: http://en.wikipedia.org/wiki/Ring_Magazine_fights_of_the_year#1980s.

176 *"He still smiled"*: Wiley, *Serenity*, 130.

176 *"my idol"*: Dick Young, "Mancini Signs for Chacon," *New York Post*, September 20, 1983.

177 *real estate and costume jewelry*: Milton Richman, United Press International, September 19, 1983.

177 *So were Madison Square Garden*: Steve Barenfeld, "Mancini to Fight Chacon," *New York Post*, September 3, 1983.

177 *butted open a small cut*: Hal Madsen, "Torres Outlives Frazier by Full Second," *Las Vegas Review-Journal*, November 26, 1983.

178 *had no memory*: Bill Verigan, "Mancini KOs Torres in 1," New York *Daily News*, November 26, 1983.

178 *"Mancini–Torres never should"*: Jerry Lisker, *New York Post*, December 2, 1983.

178 *Marv Albert*: Phil Mushnick, "NBC to Boom Boom: Marv Albert Stays," *New York Post*, November 25, 1983.

178 *"I can understand"*: Bob Raissman, Sports View, "Was Albert a No-No for Boom-Boom?" New York *Daily News*, January 14, 1984.

178 *"bleeding by the pint"*: Bob Drury, "Mancini, Chacon Ready for Bloody Battle," *New York Post*, January 13, 1984.

178 *"not one for the squeamish"*: Michael Katz, "Mancini Tops a Big Weekend," *New York Times*, January 12, 1984.

179 *"He was constantly nailed"*: Michael Katz, "Mancini Can Answer Critics," *New York Times*, January 14, 1984.

179 *"mute many of his critics"*: Michael Katz, "Mancini Stops Chacon in 3d," *New York Times*, January 15, 1984.

179 *"a mask of blood"*: AP, "Mancini stops Chacon in 3d to retain WBA title," New York *Daily News*, January 15, 1984.

179 *beer cans and ice cubes*: Michael Katz, "Things Booming for Mancini," *New York Times*, January 16, 1984.

179 *finish their broadcast*: Phil Mushnick, "HBO's Coverage Simply Superb," *New York Post*, January 17, 1984.

179 *"Sure, there's been deaths"*: David Remnick, "Chacon Unhappy Fight Was Halted, But Bruises Told Different Story," *Washington Post*, January 16, 1984.

180 *"Boza-Edwards doesn't have"*: Ibid.

180 *"Thank you"*: Katz, "Things Booming."

13. Cutman

Interviews: Ray Mancini; Don Elbaum, January 11, 2011; Livingstone Bramble, February 24, 2010; Lou Duva, February 17, 2010; DiCioccio; Cefalde; Fagan; Percifield.

181 *"Six million for Mancini"*: Leonard Lewin, "Boom Boom, Camacho Map Bout," *New York Post*, February 29, 1984.

182 *Greater Buffalo Chamber*: "Mancini Bout Near Certain," *Buffalo News*, April 4, 1984.

182 *"Cooley's anemia is to"*: Phil Pepe, "Mancini a Fighter with a Cause," New York *Daily News*, April 13, 1984.

183 *"You should come from Cincinnati"*: Milton Richman, Sports News, United Press International, April 23, 1984.

183 *"Watch your language"*: Ibid.

183 *cursed Ray's sister*: Leonard Lewin, "Boom Boom Blows up at Challenger Bramble," *New York Post*, April 13, 1984.

183 *"Like waving a cape"*: Donn Esmonde, "Holmes 'Pushes' Bout Here," *Buffalo News*, April 17, 1984.

183 *"I will get you"*: Bill Gallo, "The Bramble Ambush," New York *Daily News*, April 13, 1984.

184 *"I'll tell you after"*: Donn Esmonde, "Bramble: Just a Bit Peculiar," *Buffalo News*, April 13, 1984.

185 *"You run one mile"*: Donn Esmonde, "Mancini Hype Getting High in Tahoe Playground," *Buffalo News*, May 5, 1984.

186 *a "murderer"*: Donn Esmonde, "Mancini's Camp Reacts to 'Slurs,'" *Buffalo News*, May 21, 1984.

186 *"His ethnic slurs"*: Ibid.

186 *"a subhuman wart hog"*: Vic Carucci, "Can We Cheer At the Fight?" *Buffalo News*, May 23, 1984.

186 *"He says Bramble is anti-white"*: Donn Esmonde, "Verbal Battle Between Boxers Turns Into War," *Buffalo News*, May 23, 1984.

187 *"It lets me see right through"*: Ibid.

187 *"It hurts me"*: Vic Carucci, "Mancini Just Here to Do Job," *Buffalo News*, May 25, 1984.

187 *115 stations*: Alan Pergament, "Network Television and the Mancini Fight," *Buffalo News*, June 1, 1984.

188 *"I can't recall"*: Dick Young, "Bramble-Mancini: This One's for Real," *New York Post*, May 31, 1984.

188 *"But the evil that men do"*: Ibid.

188 *"The line that used to stand"*: Dick Young, "Boom Boom Ranks as Boxing's Biggest Draw," *New York Post*, May 23, 1984.

189 *"practicing"*: Bob Drury, "Mancini 135; Bramble 134½," *New York Post*, June 1, 1984.

189 *"a terrible cut"*: Bramble vs. Mancini, as broadcast June 1, 1984. http://www.youtube.com/watch?v=Mhm4b9e0GhA&feature=related.

190 *"a war"*: Ibid.

190 *in the seventh*: Bramble vs. Mancini, June 1, 1984. http://www.youtube.com/watch?v=SP81r_uNv5o&NR=1.

191 *"Psychologically, what Bramble did"*: Bramble vs. Mancini, June 1, 1984. http://www.youtube.com/watch?v=4biqG6PCHdM&NR=1.

191 *"He can't hurt Bramble"*: Ibid.

191 *1,408 punches*: HBO Sports broadcast of Mancini–Bramble II, February 16, 1985. DVD courtesy of HBO Sports.

191 *throw in the towel*: Milt Northrop, "Beaten Boom Boom Wants a Rematch," *Buffalo News*, June 2, 1984. Donn Esmonde, "Champ Rocked, Lost Title on a Flurry of Punches," *Buffalo News*, June 2, 1984.

191 *"Somebody beat me"*: Michael Katz, "Bramble Takes Mancini's Title," *New York Times*, June 2, 1984.

192 *"I'm sorry for Ray"*: Ray Swanson, "Many Local Fans Mourn Ray's Loss," Youngstown, OH, *Vindicator*, June 2, 1984.

192 *"You could see something"*: Larry Felser, "Has Mancini Fought His Last Fight?" *Buffalo News*, June 3, 1984.

192 *"If Dave Wolf"*: Michael Katz, "A Rematch Lingers on Mancini's Mind," *New York Times*, June 3, 1984.

192 *He was given a sedative*: Ray Swanson, "Bramble Claims TKO Win in 14th," Youngstown, OH, *Vindicator*, June 2, 1984.

192 *"It's there"*: Katz, "A Rematch Lingers On Mancini's Mind."

192 *"The story's already been written"*: Steve Barenfeld, "Boom-Boom Wants Rematch," *New York Post*, June 27, 1984.

193 *team of five physicians*: "Mancini OK, Eyes Title Shot," New York *Daily News*, June 29, 1984.

193 *CAT Scan, an EKG and an EEG*: "Mancini Gets Go-Ahead," *New York Times*, July 29, 1984.

193 *"a good, hard fight"*: "Mancini OK, Eyes Title Shot," New York *Daily News*, June 29, 1984.

193 *second highest-paid athlete of 1984, grossing $3.2 million*: Bruce Lowitt, Associated Press, "A Rookie in '70s, The Green Monster Dominates in '80s," *Los Angeles Times*, August 29, 1985.

193 *"I thought one time he was a real good fighter"*: Bill Gallo, "Boom Boom Plotting Return to Throne," New York *Daily News*, July 29, 1984.

194 *"Not worried at all"*: "Mancini Unfazed by Cut," *New York Times*, September 6, 1984.

194 *"Any light hit"*: "Mancini Fight Called Off," *New York Times*, September 7, 1984.

194 *"It's like revoking my Romanian citizenship"*: "Suspension Protested," *New York Times*, September 9, 1984.

195 *Bramble's promoter*: Richard Hoffer, "Mancini Has Fame and Fortune . . . Why Fight It?" *Los Angeles Times*, February 25, 1985.

195 *production for his CBS movie*: Dave Anderson, "The Double Life of Ray Mancini," *New York Times*, February 5, 1985.

196 *predict his demise*: "Bramble Predicts He'll KO Mancini," *New York Post*, December 29, 1984.

196 *The fighters refused*: Bill Gallo, "Boom Boom Gets Shot for Revenge," New York *Daily News*, January 4, 1985.

196 *picked up Dog's scent*: Bill Barich, "Never Say Never," *Missouri Review*, Summer 1986.

196 *"First I beat him dead"*: John Ed Bradley, "Mancini: All Work, No Play: Recovery of Championship a Serious Business," *Washington Post*, February 15, 1985.

196 *skull and crossbones*: Michael Katz, "A Bruised Mancini Mulls Retirement," *New York Times*, February 18, 1985.

197 *"The press-kit photos"*: Barich, "Never Say Never."

197 *"There are thick humps"*: John Ed Bradley, "Mancini: All Work, No Play: Recovery of Championship a Serious Business," *Washington Post*, February 15, 1985.

197 *"That doll's you"*: Ibid.

198 *had to drop his drawers*: Norm Miller, "Hard Weigh," New York *Daily News*, February 17, 1985.

198 *gold lamé suit*: Barich.

198 *"I tried to work that left eye"*: John Ed Bradley, "Bramble Retains His Title," *Washington Post*, February 17, 1985.

199 *"I'm ready to give the Nobel Prize"*: HBO Sports, Mancini–Bramble II, broadcast February 16, 1985. DVD courtesy of HBO Sports.

199 *"My eye is closing"*: Ibid.

199 *"leaned over the ropes"*: Barich.

199 *"I want to destroy him"*: John Ed Bradley, "For Bramble, Light Touch Has Serious Edge" *Washington Post*, February 16, 1985.

200 *The HBO crew was*: HBO Sports, Mancini–Bramble II.

200 *"I see good"*: Ibid.

201 *"I love you, Ray"*: John Ed Bradley, "Bramble Retains His Title," *Washington Post*, February 17, 1985.

201 *"It's his decision"*: Norm Miller, "Mancini Mulls Retirement," New York *Daily News*, February 18, 1985.

201 *"I wish I had a wife"*: Michael Katz, "Bramble Keeps His Title by Outpointing Mancini," *New York Times*, February 17, 1985.

201 *"As if he had red slugs"*: Bradley, "Bramble Retains His Title."

201 *seventy-five stitches*: "Mancini: 75 stitches," *New York Post*, February 18, 1985.

14. Show Biz

Interviews: Ray Mancini; Tim Dahlberg, March 30, 2010; Robert Knapp, November 27, 2009; Janet Fryman, November 27, 2009; Fagan; Ed O'Neill; Vazquez; Fagan.

203 *"I had it even"*: Dick Young, "Young Ideas," *New York Post*, February 26, 1985.

203 *fined Bramble $15,000*: Dick Young, "Bramble, Manager Fined over Drug Use in Title Fight," *New York Post*, April 17, 1985.

203 *"The program's press release"*: *Frontline* press release from Raymond Mancini file in *New York Post* library.

203 *"For a film to be"*: Stephen Farber, "TV Movie on Ray Mancini Sparks Controversy," *New York Times*, April 25, 1985.

204 *"I went to my first fight"*: Ibid.

204 *"There's no need"*: Tim Dahlberg, "CBS's 'Heart of a Champion: The Ray Mancini Story' Tonight," Associated Press, May 1, 1985.

204 *in a hallway at Sharpsville*: Lawrence Sanata, "Horseplay Leads to Fight for Life," Sharon, PA, *Herald*, October 15, 1985.

205 *due to food particles:* "Rites Planned for Sharpsville Student," Sharon, PA, *Herald,* October 22, 1985.

206 *"looks like an associate professor":* John Corry, " 'Champion,' Story of Ray Mancini," *New York Times,* May 1, 1985.

206 *"heedlessly deceitful":* Tom Shales, "Fistful of Deceit; CBS's 'Mancini Story': the Boxer as Saint," *Washington Post,* May 1, 1985.

206 *Steadfastly refused to meet with:* Tim Boxer, " 'Boom Boom' Boos Blake," *New York Post,* April 30, 1985.

209 *the prospect of another training camp:* Mike Bires, "Crossroads: Mancini May Have Fought His Last Fight," *Beaver County Times,* June 2, 1985.

209 *a $3 million offer:* Lenny Lewin, "Mancini Decides to Hang Up Gloves," *New York Post,* August 22, 1985.

209 *"time to move on":* Robert McG. Thomas Jr., "Mancini Trades in Gloves for Acting," *New York Times,* August 23, 1985.

210 *"A sort of TV Rambo":* Ibid.

211 *"I was in a bad state":* John Pine, "Ex-Boxer Ray Mancini is Looking for New, Exciting Worlds to Conquer," Reuters in *Los Angeles Times,* April 20, 1986.

211 *called Father O'Neill:* Ibid.

217 *"I was in the light":* Ron Borges, "Mancini Chases the Light," *Boston Globe,* March 6, 1989.

218 *fifteen-round nontitle:* Craig Modderno, "Boxing," *USA Today,* May 14, 1987.

219 *give the All-American boy:* Borges, "Mancini Chases the Light."

219 *"He runs like a dog":* " 'Boom Boom' Gets in Jab," *USA Today,* October 2, 1987.

219 *By February 1988:* Jon Saraceno, "Mancini, Camacho to Square Off in May," *USA Today,* February 8, 1988.

219 *"It's sick":* Mike Katz, New York *Daily News,* February 4, 1988.

219 *"A horrid mismatch":* Michael Marley, "May Date for Macho, Mancini," *New York Post,* February 8, 1988.

219 *"If this becomes":* Michael Marley, "Camacho Eager to Get Boom Boom," *New York Post,* October 22, 1988.

219 *"What do I need":* Commentator Sean O'Grady quoting Mancini Showtime broadcast, March 6, 1989.

219 *When the Mancini entourage:* Michael Katz, "Macho's Barbs Weigh on Ray," New York *Daily News,* March 7, 1989.

220 *"I feed off":* Borges, "Mancini Chases the Light."

221 *"a crybaby":* Michael Marley, "Camacho Hands Mancini Split-Decision Setback," *New York Post,* March 7, 1989.

221 *listed his occupation:* Certified Abstract of Marriage, Vol. 263, Page 12, May 9, 1989, Mahoning County Probate Court, Youngstown, OH.

15. Body and Soul

Interviews: Ray Mancini; Vazquez; Sam Henry Kass, March 31, 2010; DiCioccio; Fagan; Carmenina Mancini, August 27, 2010; Kosa.

223 *"Who is gonna hire"*: Dave Friedman, "Changing Titles," *Newsday*, November 7, 1991.
223 *"This wasn't school"*: Ibid.
223 *"Like he was"*: Ibid.
223 *"I love Raymond"*: Jerry Stahl, "Mickey Rourke; Interview," *Playboy*, February 1987.
224 *Peter Kass was a protégé*: Bruce Weber, "Peter Kass, 85, Bold Teacher of Acting," *New York Times*, August 8, 2008.
225 *"an engaging comedy"*: Mel Gussow, "Stage: 'Snapshots,' Father and Son," *New York Times*, May 20, 1984.
225 *"sharp and witty"*: Wilborn Hampton, "Review/Theater; Generals and Troops In the War of Love," *New York Times*, September 30, 1990.
227 *"You act the way"*: Robert Lipsyte, "Somebody Out There Likes Mancini," *New York Times*, November 8, 1991.
228 *"I have a wife"*: Rich Tosches, "Haugen: Mancini Is No Laughing Matter," *Los Angeles Times*, February 9, 1992.
229 *"I want to punish him"*: Ibid.
230 *"positively demonic"*: Mancini–Haugen, broadcast on Showtime Sports, April 4, 1992. DVD courtesy of Showtime Sports.
231 *"No, son"*: Associated Press, "Mancini Calls It Quits After Loss to Haugen," *Los Angeles Times*, April 5, 1992.
237 *"better than his mother"*: Mark Kriegel, "Heartbreaking Seventeen Years Later, Ray (Boom Boom) Mancini Is Still Haunted by His Fight with Duk Koo Kim," New York *Daily News*, November 14, 1999.
237 *Baskin-Robbins–type*: Mike Downey, "An Ex-Champion Goes at It With Body and Soul," *Los Angeles Times*, April 26, 1998.
237 *a producer of Hollywood*: Mace Neufeld, whose many hits included *The Hunt for Red October* and *Patriot Games*.
243 *There was a rave*: Marilyn Moss, "Body and Soul," *The Hollywood Reporter*, September 10–12, 1999.

16. Modern Family

Interviews: Ray Mancini; Giudice; Clark; Ed O'Neill; Vazquez; Ray Mancini Jr., September 18, 2010; Carmenina Mancini; Leonardo Mancini, September 7, 2011; Chacon; Rose Legaspi, September 25, 2010; Tina Rozzi, August 9, 2011.

246 *"a best-selling author"*: Lou Eppolito and Bob Drury, *Mafia Cop* (New York: Simon & Schuster, 1992).

246 *an aging British director:* Ronald Bergan, "Obituary: Charles Jarrott: British-born Director Known for *Anne of the Thousand Days* and *Mary, Queen of Scots,*" London *Guardian*, March 7, 2011.

250 *"One doesn't play"*: Joyce Carol Oates, *On Boxing* (New York: Harper Perennial, 2006), 19.

254 *survived five gunshots*: Julie Shaw, "Another shot for 'Two Guns'?" *Philadelphia Daily News*, March 15, 2007.

261 *several rows of folding chairs*: DVD of the January 17, 2009, three-rounder between David "Junebug" Mijares and Ray "Little Boom" Mancini Jr., courtesy of Ray-Ray.

Epilogue: The Gift

Interviews: Young Mee Lee; Jiwan Kim, July 2, 2010; Michael Owen, July 24, 2011.

As explained in the acknowledgments, the scenes taking place June 23, 2011, are from my own observation and from footage gathered while filming *The Good Son*, a documentary based on this book.

Index

About the Author

Mark Kriegel is the author of two critically acclaimed bestsellers, *Namath: A Biography* and *Pistol: The Life of Pete Maravich*. He's a veteran columnist and a commentator for the NFL Network. He lives in Santa Monica, California, with his daughter, Holiday.